A   LIFE   IN   BALANCE

A Life in Balance
Nourishing the Four Roots
of True Happiness

DR. KATHLEEN HALL

AMACOM AMERICAN MANAGEMENT ASSOCIATION
New York ▸ Atlanta ▸ Brussels ▸ Chicago ▸ Mexico City
San Francisco ▸ Shanghai ▸ Tokyo ▸ Toronto ▸ Washington, D.C.

Special discounts on bulk quantities of AMACOM books are available to corporations, professional associations, and other organizations. For details, contact Special Sales Department, AMACOM, a division of American Management Association, 1601 Broadway, New York, NY 10019.
Tel.: 212-903-8316. Fax: 212-903-8083.
Website: www.amacombooks.org

This publication is designed to provide accurate and authoritative information in regard to the subject matter covered. It is sold with the understanding that the publisher is not engaged in rendering legal, accounting, or other professional service. If legal advice or other expert assistance is required, the services of a competent professional person should be sought.

Library of Congress Cataloging-in-Publication Data

Hall, Kathleen, 1951-
  A life in balance : nourishing the four roots of true happiness / Kathleen Hall.
    p. cm.
  Includes bibliographical references and index.
  ISBN 0-8144-7334-2 (hardcover)
  1. Self-actualization (Psychology) 2. Life skills. 3. Conduct of life. 4. Spirituality.
  I. Title.

BF637.S4H335 2006
158.1—dc22

                                                             2005028534

Printing number
10 9 8 7 6 5 4 3 2 1

To my beloved husband
Jim
and our daughters
Brittany Anne
and
Mary Elizabeth

CONTENTS

Part III Celebrate Your New Growth

Part IV Appendixes

ACKNOWLEDGMENTS

I am grateful for the many people who made this book possible.

Thank you, Amanda Brown-Olmstead, for pushing me out of the nest. You are a friend and mentor.

I am most grateful to the Dupree-Miller Group who helped me birth this baby. To my agent Jan Miller, your seasoned skill challenged me to become a better author, and I will always be grateful to you. Annabelle, you are an angel who guided me so many times and were my anchor during this magnificent journey, and I will always hold you in my heart with love. Shannon, you nailed down the nuts and bolts and I am thankful. Wes, you were my cheerleader and voice of wisdom in my moments of disorientation, and I shall always be grateful.

My AMACOM editor Jacquie Flynn has been an inspiration and support.

My editor Niels Buessem is a true gift who has guided me through this process with great wisdom, kindness, and grounded this work in true excellence.

Thank you Willy Spizman, Robyn Spizman, and Jenny Corsey for your passion and integrity at all times. I really love you guys.

Thank you, my friends, for your encouragement, inspiration, and love throughout this project: Pamela, Helen, Joyce, Jean, Donna, Carol, and Amy.

I am indebted to the patients and clients who have given me the privilege of sharing their times of crisis and healing and became my teachers and mentors.

Thank you to Oak Haven—my farm, my sanctuary, my Avalon, my Camelot, and my Walden Pond, all in one. This incredible place has been a source of healing, hope, and renewal to thousands of individuals seeking an intentional life of balance through the years.

I am grateful to the animals at Oak Haven who have truly been my most profound teachers. You have taught me powerful lessons about love, power, loyalty, fear, and death.

I am most grateful to my daughters Brittany and Elizabeth. Brittany, you are such a gift to our world. You are a true healer, my darling, an incredibly brilliant and compassionate physician whose wisdom and passion aided in the writing of my book. Elizabeth, thank you for the lessons you taught me during the writing of this book. They have been invaluable.

Jim, my husband, you have been my cheerleader, advisor, and partner in this great odyssey called life. I loved you from the first moment I looked into those big brown eyes. Your invaluable skills as a critical editor and an esteemed physician helped me write this book. You have inspired me with your integrity, vision, and passion in the fields of medicine and wellness.

This book is an act of co-creation. I am grateful Holy One, Divine Presence, Light, God for the unfolding of *A Life in Balance*. Every moment is pregnant with the unfolding of balance and happiness. Our job is to wake up and experience this gift!

Why Can't We Find Happiness?

THE SINGLE GREATEST *threat to our lives is not the terrorists putting poison in the water, or the pollution in the air: The greatest threat to our lives is our lifestyle.*

Ask people how they are doing these days, and the first word you will hear is "busy." Probe deeper, and soon you may see frustration as they say, "exhausted." We do more, go more, and buy more. Our gas tanks are full, our bank accounts are full, and our closets are full, but we are running on empty. Surveys say we don't get enough sleep, we eat more meals on the run than at home, we take too many pills, and, worst of all, we don't spend enough time with our children and the people we love.

Clearly, our lives are out of balance. It is time to stop being the victim of our lives and make choices that will create an intentional life of happiness.

A Life in Balance: Nourishing the Four Roots of True Happiness is a handbook for people seeking to reclaim balance and order in their chaotic lives. Based on the overwhelming response to my speeches and articles about stress reduction, work-life balance, happiness, self-care, and wellness, I've come to understand that millions of intelligent, energetic, and ambitious individuals are looking for approaches to bring balance to their lives and work so they may discover daily sources of energy, fulfillment, and intimacy.

Over the many years thousands of individuals have asked the same questions again and again:

How can I keep from losing myself in my busy life?

When I give so much to my job, my children, my partner, and my community, what's left for me?

The answers to these questions can only come when we decide to create balance in our lives by examining and challenging society's boilerplate definition of happiness. It is time to create new systems that nourish and sustain, rather than diminish and deplete, our families, businesses, and communities. We have enormous power to make the choices in our lives that create health, balance, and energy—lives that reflect our own individual and unique definitions of happiness and success.

If you have picked up this book, you have already begun your journey to happiness and balance. Remember the old saying, "Home is where the heart is?" Nothing could be more true. But most of us have lived in a culture that has driven us from our Self, from our heart, from our true home. We have been lured out of our natural state of happiness into a fast-paced existence in which we find little meaning. This book is about discovering different ways to live that create true and lasting happiness in our lives.

Let's stop for a moment and ask ourselves some serious questions about our own lives and this world in which we all share a common destiny:

▶ Why are depression, anxiety, and fear rising to epidemic proportions?

▶ Why has obesity become our #1 health crisis despite our cutting-edge understanding of health and nutrition?

▶ Why is insomnia one of the most pressing problems in medical practices and in our corporations?

▶ Why is heart disease rising while there are now more drugs to prevent and treat the disease?

▶ Why is our health-care system on the brink of collapse?

▶ Why is the fiber of the family being torn apart at its very core?

- ❯ Why have we allowed ourselves to become prisoners of our own fear in the light of increased terrorism?

- ❯ How does the stress and fear of job loss, globalization, and economic instability of the world affect our mind and body?

We can no longer keep running faster than our bodies and souls were created to travel. The mind, body, and soul have a rhythm, a cadence, which cannot be ignored or disrespected. We violate natural, scientific, and spiritual laws when we do not live our lives with great reverence, awe, and gratitude.

What Is Happiness?

Happiness, many of us believe, is inextricably linked to wealth and status. We have traditionally measured happiness through our accumulation of possessions: trendy clothes and cars, fine jewelry, homes in the best neighborhoods. These are the things we work for, and there's nothing wrong with that.

In the modern culture, we tend to think we can find happiness "out there," at the mall, in the gym, or in a bottle in our medicine cabinet. All we need is a thinner body, a better job, a new spouse, or more successful children. We think if we throw enough money at the problem, one morning we will wake up in a state of bliss. But if money could buy happiness, the rich and famous would not be a constant source of material for the tabloids, with their sagas of addiction, betrayal, bankruptcy, and shame.

Still, we continue to work harder and consume more. Over the past several decades the average work week has gotten longer and longer. And, as we spend more and more time in the workplace, many of us struggle to raise a family at the same time.

Most of us live in a constant state of exhaustion and duress: Our jobs need us, our children need us, and, increasingly, our aging parents need us. But it seems there is not enough of us to go around. (No wonder cloning has a certain appeal!)

We feel unhappy, frantic, and out of balance. We push ourselves to the brink of exhaustion on a daily basis. We have overstretched our personal boundaries and forgotten that true happiness comes from living an authentic life fueled with a sense of purpose and balance. We mistakenly think happiness is the absence of stress, but we cannot find happiness by running away from our fears, away from our worries, away from our daily challenges.

It is time to carefully examine the lifestyle we have accepted in the past, but are now questioning. It is time to ask why most of our population lives in a constant state of exhaustion. Is this "balance"? Where has the vital energy in our bodies and souls gone?

If we seek true happiness, we must first explore how our world has become victimized by fear. On some level, most people live in a constant state of anxiety and fear, in the shadow of the events of 9/11 and the increase in bombings in other countries around the world. Living in a constant state of fear or anxiety has far-reaching, disastrous effects on our mental, physical, and spiritual health. What can we do to develop confidence and peace of mind?

Individuals cannot experience true happiness without a sense of personal power in their lives. How can we restore our own sense of authentic power within ourselves? Our challenge is to explore the concept of power as force (power over) and power as strength (power with). It is important we make the distinction between the self-serving, destructive power of domination and greed we have witnessed in the stories of Enron and Tyco, and the life-affirming, creative power of compassion and charity we have witnessed in the works of Gandhi, Mother Teresa, and many others.

This book offers proven practices for creating a life of true happiness that don't compromise, but actually enhance, your personal life and relationships, as well as career performance.

Opportunities for balance, true happiness, and strength, exist in every minute of the day, but most us have lost the ability to recognize the happiness waiting to be discovered in the simple moments of our lives.

We have lost sight of our guiding star on a sea of distractions; we have lost our connection to our true source of happiness.

Happiness is your natural gift. I will help you recognize this gift of happiness, develop it, and increase your capacity to live joyfully in the day-to-day activities of your life.

This book will not ask you to add anything more to your overwhelming "to do" list. You will learn that it is small shifts in awareness and simple practices that will guide you to a level of happiness and balance that will dramatically change your life. You will find yourself in touch with a deeper, more contented, and relaxed self that comes not from some mystical temple but from within the familiar and the commonplace experiences of your daily life.

A Life in Balance will guide you to find your own source of true happiness and balance in your everyday life. You will discover how you can generate a life that genuinely supports you and those you love. Step by step, you will learn how to transform fear and anxiety into purpose and passion, build and sustain real intimacy, and reenergize your life and your future, restoring mental, physical, and spiritual well-being. Not only that, but unlike most books, *A Life in Balance* won't leave you alone in a room: It seeks to deepen a sense of connection in our fractured society by linking you and other readers to each other, so that you can discover happiness and balance, not only for yourself, but for your family, your community, and the world as a whole.

A Life in Balance points you in the direction of your true and natural Self, where you can generate dynamic and evolving definitions of what it is to experience true happiness. It offers proven practices, based on science, practical experience, and time-honored traditions, for creating balance in your life. You will more easily discern the difference between what is important and what is urgent. You will find new levels of energy and a greater capacity for happiness than you have ever experienced. You will reclaim your ability to take challenges and chaos in stride and will radiate a new sense of confidence and security. People will draw closer to you and your life will unfold in greater balance every day.

This book is for the myriads of people who struggle to hold the fabric of society together in an often ethically and spiritually barren workplace. The individuals I see in my work are creative, dynamic, and committed, but they are also overwhelmed, fearful, lonely, and isolated. When our children feel alone and afraid, we turn on a nightlight for them. This book is my nightlight for people everywhere who think they face this struggle alone.

But *A Life in Balance* is not just for individuals; it is also a wake-up call for corporations and businesses. By focusing continually on the bottom line, our corporations have neglected their ethical and moral responsibility to incorporate work-life balance programs and education in the workplace. We now have an overwhelming amount of scientific, medical, and sociological research on the profound personal, cultural, and financial effects of chronic stress in the workplace. Remedies are available for little or no cost; they take very little time, and yield immediate benefits to individuals and corporations.

The phrase "work-life balance" has emerged in reaction to the unhealthy choices that many of us are making in favor of the workplace, as we opt to neglect family, friends, and leisure activities in the pursuit of corporate goals. The cost to corporations and businesses when workers are unhappy and overstressed is enormous, estimated at over $300 billion annually.[1] The cost of depression, loss of productivity, and missed work days has an annual estimated value of over $600 per full time employee.[2] In some surveys, 30 percent of workers felt their health was suffering because of their work, and over 40 percent of managers believe the quality of their working life has deteriorated over the past three years.[3] Worker turnover and the costs of replacing and or retraining employees have never been higher. The attitude of workers and the morale within companies are at an all-time low.

The costs of chronic stress are harming our families, our corporate institutions, and the government. When a company promotes work-life balance for its employees, it benefits the employees, their families, and that all-important bottom line. A corporation that focuses on work-life balance provides a "benefits package" that does not add to the cost of the payroll, so everyone wins. Encouraging self-care, stress reduction, and wellness gives enormous and lasting benefits to the growth and prosperity of every company. How can a corporation be "successful" if its success comes at the expense of its workers? How can a corporation be successful if it does not root itself in the principles of work-life balance? True work-life balance benefits the employees, their families, the corporation, the community, and our world. We must come together in both our homes and our businesses to discover a higher purpose in our lives. We can now live intentional lives and experience true happiness and balance.

I am a parent, wife, and business owner—just like many of you. Further, I bring a rare mix of education and life experience to my work, which I love. Today my life is rooted in the rich earth of my ranch at Oak Haven. I have also experienced "real world" success in the glass-and-steel canyons of Wall Street. With experience as a professor, counselor, and stress and wellness educator, I have had the privilege of studying with some of the greatest medical and spiritual leaders of our time. I have worked with the critically ill, and I have tirelessly devoted my time, energy, and resources to meeting the needs of people struggling to survive in the margins of our society. These experiences have allowed me to create an interdisciplinary approach, weaving the fields of science and medicine, psychology, and spirituality into a holistic approach to define true happiness and balance.

This book speaks directly to you and the core of your experience. It offers down-to-earth wisdom and solutions that bring balance to your daily struggles and challenging lives. The current solutions for balance are about coping techniques, not about creating change within individuals and institutions. My perspective on work-life balance focuses on you and all aspects of your life, your work, your family, your friends, your community, and your Self. This book provides simple steps that will allow you to change healthily within, thereby precipitating virtually effortless improvements in your personal life, your home, and your work environment.

This book is about providing solutions to these growing problems. Unlike many books that give readers "feel good" insights but leave them with little significant change in their daily lives, *A Life in Balance* is dynamic and interactive in three ways. It provides questions for self-exploration. It grounds insights gained from the book in real-world applications that are easy to employ in daily life. And it connects you to like-minded souls.

A Life in Balance radically reexamines your notion of happiness and balance by inviting you to shift from experiencing your world from the *outside in* to experiencing it from the *inside out*. I convey complex theories and teachings from the world's scientists, medical experts, philosophers, sociologists, and spiritual leaders in a direct, easy-to-understand manner so that you can apply the latest findings in the science of mind-body medicine as well as the wisdom of the ancients without having to study quantum physics, science, or spirituality.

We were created to experience a life of happiness, but how many of us have that experience? The opportunity to live a life in balance and happiness is the promise of all major religious and spiritual texts. We spend our lives spending untold amounts of money and time chasing after this illusive goal. The quest for happiness goes back to the ancient philosophers Plato and Aristotle, and to the great theologians who have sought this prescription for thousands of years.

When you choose to live a life of balance and happiness, you will experience a sense of peace and gratitude you haven't known in years, perhaps not in your lifetime. You will notice the stresses of life become opportunities that you will more easily transcend and learn from. Your life is the result of the choices you have or have not made.

Life Is a Classroom, Not a Prison

This book is a tool, a guide for you in the classroom of your life. Use it as you would use a book in a class. Read it, underline in it, write in the margins, and take notes. Use this book at work, in your place of worship, or in your neighborhood as a study guide. This is your book, so use it as a workbook to learn how to make new choices that will lead you to happiness and balance.

A Life in Balance doesn't offer yet another way to "fix" or "help" you, but rather reassures you that *absolutely nothing is wrong with you.* However, something *is* wrong with the way you are living. It repositions you by *rebalancing* your life. It helps you generate a balanced life that works—for your family, your community, and most of all, for you.

What would it be worth to you if you could take one class, go to one seminar, or read one book that taught you the basic principles of how to live a life of balance rooted in true happiness?

How many of you wish you could go to a doctor and ask for a prescription on how to live a life of happiness? The doctor smiles tenderly, touches your hand, and writes you a prescription for balance and happiness in your life. This book is that prescription.

PART I: COMING HOME

What Is True Happiness?

MY ADULTHOOD, for many years, was spent on the run from my childhood. In corporate offices and meeting rooms, classrooms, hospital chapels, and churches, I pulled down the blinds, drew the curtains, and blocked out the sound of my father's footsteps by aggressively pursuing society's definition of happiness, which meant success.

That meant having an upwardly mobile career, a husband, children, a nice home, elegant clothes and fabulous vacations. I grabbed my piece of the American dream, furiously exercising and dieting to keep a perfect size, and drove the ultimate driving machine. I was chasing true happiness under the guise of success.

It worked—for a while. Everything was moving at a planned, orchestrated pace when one day, in a split second, everything stopped. At that time, my rapid climb to the top of the ladder of success landed me in a corner office high in the tallest buildings in both Atlanta and New York. I lived in Atlanta and flew in and out of Kennedy Airport every weekend. That particular morning, I followed my usual routine: I grabbed a cab to the World Trade Center, got out, entered the building, and headed for the elevator.

We were all packed into the elevator as usual, but this time, as the elevator sped up to my office, I suddenly felt as if my chest was so tight I could hardly breathe. I thought I was having a heart attack. I lurched off the elevator and lay against the wall.

Three hours later, I was still against the same wall and hadn't moved an inch. An attentive security guard had noticed, and—perhaps because he had seen it before—made a diagnosis of a panic attack. Little did I know that would be the first of many to follow. It wasn't too long until insomnia began to accompany the panic attacks, and my well-planned life began to unravel.

A week later, still in New York, I stumbled upon an old copy of Thoreau's journal in the apartment where I was staying. I dusted off the front of the book, and as I opened to the first page, read: "I went to the woods because I wished to live deliberately, to front only the essential facts of life, and see if I could not learn what it had to teach, and not, when I came to die, discover that I had not lived." Little did I know those words would change my life forever.

My initial response to that famous passage was shock and confusion. Was I living an intentional life? How in the heck did I know what the essential facts of life were? Had I really lived at all? And is living in the middle of chaos really living? I thought that when I became successful, happiness was surely waiting there for me. After all, I had spent years working so hard and my family and I had sacrificed for this success. So where was the happiness we expected to appear?

I remembered the oak tree in the backyard of my childhood—how, in a way, it became my best friend as I escaped from the chaos of my afflictive young life. But I had not been in the woods since I was a child, and knew nothing about the realities of living in nature. The mere thought that it held the possibility of teaching me something both intrigued and terrified me. A fundamental shift occurred in that moment and I knew there was no turning back.

After nearly self-destructing, I decided to begin a search for my own definition of happiness. I didn't know where it would lead me or what it would entail, but I knew I couldn't go back to where I had been.

Two days later I quit my job. One week later I purchased a farm with an old log cabin sitting on a small lake. There wasn't even a road to the cabin from the main road. Determined to live up to Thoreau's challenge, I hiked in to the cabin for the first year. With each step, I released the life that I had so masterfully orchestrated and designed, and surrendered to the unfolding of true happiness.

I chose to stop living my life moving only forward and upward and learned how to begin a new life moving inward and downward into my authentic self. I shifted from grasping for safety, conformity, and status to embracing risk, vision, and my own personal truth. I shifted from living a life of imbalance, chaos, fear, and frustration to living a life of balance, intention, confidence, and happiness. I reclaimed the passion, courage, and soul that I had known as a child, sitting high above the world in the wonder of that magnificent oak tree.

After many seasons of sunrises and sunsets living next to the earth, I learned the difficult lessons of surrender and listening deeply to the inner voice that called me to live an authentic life: one where every event, every experience, every season drove me deeper into the purpose of my life, which is to experience true happiness. My life was no easy journey during those days, as I faced the shadows that I had spent my whole life keeping at bay, but the excitement, passion, and energy I was experiencing was truly heaven on earth.

My curiosity was insatiable. I voraciously read books about nature, horses, spirituality, world religions, science, psychology, and I sought real-world experience to deepen my learning. With each new teacher, university, and adventure I was being pulled to my center, my purpose. Each day I experienced the balance of nature in the magic of the wind in the trees before a storm, the swirling of clouds in the early spring, the profound sound of silence after a deep snowfall. I began to trust this magnificent sense of balance and the cycles of life. The power and energy that were growing within me reminded me of the acorn that does not push, does not try, but simply and joyfully knows that it is an oak tree and trusts the effortless unfolding of its life process.

My quest to understand happiness and balance, rooted in living an intentional life, catapulted me into education, training, and clinical practice. I did not understand the role spirituality and religion played in the mental and physical health of individuals, and so I decided to go to Emory University and get a Masters of Divinity degree and learn about it. During those three years, there was much practical training in the program.

I was a facilitator at the Atlanta Battered Women's Shelter, where I sat each week with a group of women listening to their pain. These women lived in fear and suffering every day of their lives. It was almost overwhelming to listen to the tales of their victimization and the difficult and flawed choices some had made.

I also worked with inner city marginalized children at Capitol Homes at an after-school program for at-risk children. I used every creative spark in my soul to invent programs for these children that would keep these fragile lives from falling victim to their violent surroundings. I began a counseling program and worked with the most violent at-risk boys in an attempt to keep them in school and out of jail. I decided to use the four roots of happiness with these precious children and had great success. It gave hopelessly marginalized children hope, laughter, and happiness.

After that I worked with homeless women and children at the Atlanta Women and Children's Shelter, where I bathed homeless babies and mothers and fed their hungry bodies. It was a daily challenge taking care of the disheveled, cold women and children who had been sleeping under bridges on freezing nights in Atlanta, because the day shelter could only afford to stay open during the day and the night shelters filled up on the coldest nights. I will never forget the overwhelming feeling when we had to lock the doors at the shelter at 4 p.m. and turn away the mothers and children into the dangerous streets of the night. Some of the most humbling moments of my life are remembering eating with these women and children and listening to their incredible stories of abuse and isolation. We developed programs and raised money to help provide solutions to these enormous problems. These women had no skills to get to a job interview, so we provided them with showers, clothes, and interview skills. We built a playground for the children, so they would have a place to play after they had spent untold hours and days walking the streets of Atlanta with their mothers.

Then I became a student chaplain at St. Joseph's and Northside Hospital, where I learned about the horrors of AIDS and cancer and their effects upon patients and their families. These are the places where my counseling and listening skills were first honed as I witnessed and absorbed the suffering of so many different people in so many horrible circumstances. This is where I learned about how short and precious life really is and where death became my teacher about life and happiness. Sitting with untold numbers of individuals as they left this world to go into the next was both a privilege and a classroom. Whether it was unplugging a newborn child from a respirator and handing her to her sobbing mother as she took her last tiny breaths, or sitting with distraught parents as they signed the permission slip to harvest their sixteen-year-old daughter's organs after a tragic car accident, or crawling into bed with an abandoned, frail AIDS patient so he wouldn't die alone, I received a Ph.D. in suffering and reverence for life and death.

The common denominator of the people I served in each of these experiences was the role chronic stress played in the life of each individual. All had faced enormous stress in their lives, and I was learning ways to help different types of individuals deal with the sense of hopelessness and suffering.

After those years, I became an ordained Protestant minister, and I was the pastoral counselor for a church of 3,000 people. The psychological, spiritual, and physical demands were incredible as I listened to the most sacred, intimate parts of individual's lives. This was also where I learned that I loved to listen and I loved to teach. Many profound questions were constantly whirling in my mind:

What makes people suffer?

Why are some individuals destroyed by suffering and others are forged into greatness by suffering?

How can so many of the individuals that I work with experience such true happiness in the midst of such suffering?

Why do so many people live an "insufficient" life?

Why are people willing to "settle" for a mundane existence?

Why do some individuals get "sick" when they are in emotional or psychological conflict?

Do stress, anger, fear, or depression lead to cancer, heart disease, arthritis, or obesity?

Can our thoughts make us sick?

What do happy people know that frustrated, overwhelmed people don't?

It was 1995, and I was fascinated with the burgeoning field of mind-body medicine. My passion for this field led me to get a doctorate in spirituality and immerse myself in the exploration of mind-body medicine. During this time I went to California to study with the pioneering Dr. Dean

Ornish at the Preventive Medicine Research Institute. I also studied with Dr. Herbert Benson at the Harvard Mind-Body Institute, and I subsequently participated in several clinical training programs at Harvard, including Mind-Body Medicine, The Science of the Mind, and Alternative Approaches to Health Care.

At this time I entered a training program for two years to become a certified spiritual director. The more I listened to and counseled individuals, the more I discovered that it didn't matter if they had terminal cancer, were depressed, were going through a divorce, or were rich or poor: The root of their problems was indeed a spiritual conflict. Their lives were out of balance, they didn't know how to begin to discover how to live an intentional life of happiness, and they had learned to accept living hollow busy lives. Often it took a catastrophic event—such as an illness, unemployment, divorce, or death—before they realized their lives were spinning out of control.

It was during this period that I learned of the term "work-life balance." What I had been learning was how to teach individuals to live a life of balance, health, and happiness.

I was still working with marginalized children living in public housing with little hope. These children were often called "throw-away kids." Many had been involved in crimes, were failing in school, and had little or no parental support in the home. These kids were struggling to survive. So I decided to use the same approach I had learned at the medical research centers with my inner-city kids. I worked with these kids for many years and I saw miracles happen in their lives.

In the late 1990s I began facilitating a cardio-pulmonary program at a hospital in the Southern Appalachian Mountains and used a variation of the same program with individuals who were coming to me after a critical heart or pulmonary event. At the same time, I was seeing individuals with cancer and chose to use the same method I had been taught in my many training programs. The longer I used these methods I learned from my patients and clients what worked and what didn't, and I created a new plan, which in my experience worked better and had more long-term affects.

Soon, business persons began seeking me out to help them deal with their empty lives fraught with depression, stress, grief, and medical conditions. I used the same approach with these clients and was quite successful for many years, teaching people how to live an intentional life of balance, health, abundance, and happiness.

It is not necessary for you to sell everything and go "back to nature" in a romantic flourish, but it is essential to turn inward to listen to your own true nature, whatever that may be. I invite you to cultivate the roots of happiness that will provide you with a strong foundation to weather—and enjoy—the wind, the rain, the sun, and the snow of your life.

The time to begin is now. The place to begin is where you are. All you need is an authentic desire to discover your real *self*, the purpose for which you were created. The rewards are extraordinary. So let's get started.

Defining Happiness

The 1980s were an interesting time to be a business person in the financial world. For those of you who have seen the movie *Wall Street*, that was my life in a nutshell. Pressure constantly haunted me as I dressed for work every day, especially on the days when I knew we were having big sales meetings in the boardroom. But that pressure paled compared to the constant stress of knowing that to achieve "success" I had to have some edge on the 75 men who were supposedly my colleagues, but who were more accurately my daily competitors in a cut-throat environment.

I felt enormous pressure to succeed because there were so few women in the financial world. I believed success was the mother of happiness; therefore if I achieved success, happiness would surely follow. But the more I focused on success, the more true happiness seemed to elude me.

There were three bibles that hardly ever left my side: Michael Korda's two books, *Success and Power,* and *Dress for Success* by John Malloy. I literally kept these books with me on a daily basis. How I dressed was critical if I wanted to be taken seriously as an attractive, intelligent woman managing the wealth of individuals, investors, and corporations.

John Malloy taught me how to dress in the current "uniform" of a black or navy blue suit with a high-necked blouse and a silly bow on the collar. Michael Korda instructed me on how to climb the ladder of success at the most rapid pace possible and how to glide into the power moves that would insure my upward mobility. Every facet of my life was inundated with my obsession with power and success—which I believed would eventually lead to happiness.

At that time most of us believed "success" bred wealth and happiness. It really isn't much different today. We work to have the trendiest clothes and cars, homes in the nicest neighborhoods, our children in the best schools. We work hard for these things, and there is nothing wrong with that.

But even though we are working harder than ever, we seem to have less and less time to enjoy those hard-won "fruits"—and often those very things we work so hard for fail to make us happy or to create any sense of balance in our lives.

The definition of success must include the essence of happiness and balance. Success can no longer be narrowly defined as wealth, power, and status. This definition comes with too high of a price, not only for the individual who pursues the traditional definition of success, but it is also destroying the integrity of the family and our world.

The fruits of a life committed to happiness are: enthusiasm, inspiration, passion, compassion, courage, honesty, and authenticity. Happiness is choosing a path of certainty. There will be suffering, accidents, grief, and losses along with laughter, pleasure, and joy. Your life stops being a roller coaster of ups and downs. Instead of going through each day with a certain tentative sense, you live with self-confidence, courage, and optimism. Happiness is confidence that no matter what happens, your life's potential is constantly unfolding.

Happiness requires disciplines or practices. I use "practices" instead of discipline. Many of us have a negative connotation with the word "discipline." The word "practices" means exactly what it says. You keep doing a practice over and over, and practice it over and over.

Happiness is achieved by the inner discipline of practicing the four roots of balance. These four roots help you cultivate positive states of mind and eliminate negative states of mind. The most destructive negative state of mind is chronic fear. Fear is the core of anger, pessimism, hate, depression, shame, perfectionism, and anxiety. When seeds of fear infiltrate every aspect of our life we can begin living lives of quiet desperation, learning to accept and tolerate our lives of unhappiness.

The roots of happiness give you a fresh perspective on life. You will experience a new sense of energy, power, and well-being. The more happiness and balance you experience over time, the more you will detach from your fears and stresses. Instead of fears and stresses destroying your life, as you detach you become the observer of them and begin to make profound choices in your life.

Happiness and Pleasure

We think we can find happiness in perfectionism, consumerism, thinner bodies, more money, status, power, control, possessions, success, better jobs, new spouse, and smarter more accomplished children, but the truth is we can't buy happiness.

We confuse happiness with pleasure. We live our lives moving from satisfying one pleasure to satisfying another pleasure. You will not find happiness in the pleasure prison. Pleasure is short-lived and temporary. Happiness is sustainable for your life time. Pleasure is an event—a moment in time. You can't find happiness through seeking only pleasure.

Pleasure can be seductive and addictive. Our pleasure-seeking obsession is destroying our mental, physical, and spiritual well-being. Searching for pleasure in smoking, drinking, sex, video games, or watching television wastes our fragile short lives, not to mention exposing us to the host of diseases that are directly related to our pleasurable lifestyle. Pleasure is an experience; happiness is a chosen path of a lifetime.

Many of us chase furiously after pleasure—unsatisfied, fleeting, climbing the next highest mountain, riding the next great wave—only to experience another high in our pleasure center of the brain as it constantly expands awaiting the next fix. Whatever our pleasure is can be addictive, whether it is alcohol, drugs, eating, working, shopping, gambling, playing video games, or pornography. The code name is pleasure, disguised as "true happiness," but it is just an illusion, just as so many of the ghosts we continue to chase in our life.

Many of us chase one pleasurable experience after another only to have a greater letdown after each attempt. Pleasure is short-lived. Pleasure is never sustainable. Seeking constant pleasure creates a hollow life. Pleasure is killing us literally in our world: eating, technology, consumerism, materialism, seeking success.

Seeking and experiencing pleasure in and of itself is a dead end. But if your goal is to experience a life of true happiness, pleasure becomes a watering hole on your journey. Having said this, pleasure is a gift, a prized thread that is woven into the tapestry of happiness. It is hard to find anyone who loves to eat more than I do. A good meal is definitely a source of great pleasure for me. But I am clear that this source of pleasure is "only" a meal, and food is woven into my life happiness. The meal does not define my happiness. The meal is a source of pleasure but not necessarily happiness.

When I drive my convertible with the top down at night alone with the stars brightly overhead and the powerful air swirling around me, now that is pure pleasure for me. Again, that is pleasure and it has nothing to do with happiness. If I sold my pleasure mobile tomorrow, I can assure you my happiness would not be affected.

It is tragic how many patients and clients I have seen through the years who have sought pleasure under the guise of happiness. They moved from one house to another, one job to another, one diet to another, one wardrobe to another, and, tragically, one relationship to another—only to discover that happiness eluded them. They really didn't understand the difference between pleasure and happiness.

Happiness is living in a proactive way because you have made the decision to live every day of your life as if each experience is a class in the classroom called life. The power you feel when you choose to live a life of happiness destroys any victim mentality. Choosing happiness is about being the hero of your life, not the victim. Happy people have an attitude of gratitude no matter what circumstance they face. Happiness is inextricably linked to gratitude and reverence for life. Happiness is the ability to receive love and to surrender to love.

true happiness is as sustainable as a fine piece of art: Each day you discover some nuance that makes your life even more precious and sacred.

True Happiness Requires Balance and Sustainability

The sustainability of our planet is a formidable topic today. We know that we cannot keep taking the oil, coal, and gas out of our bruised earth in perpetuity. We cannot keep poisoning our fragile atmosphere, our precious air, and our treasured water that gives us life here on earth. Sustainability means to keep in existence, to supply, nourish, and support life.

I believe that our current definition of happiness is not sustainable and cannot create the balance in our lives we all desire. In the section below I compare the traditional meaning of happiness with my meaning of happiness (see also Table 1-1).

BONDAGE VS. FREEDOM
When the benchmarks for happiness are wealth, power, status, or beauty you can live constantly in a state of bondage. Bondage is a state of subjection to

Traditional Meaning of Happiness (Unsustainable Happiness)		My Meaning of Happiness (Sustainable Happiness)
Bondage	→	Freedom
Scarcity	→	Abundance
Fear-Driven	→	Trust-Driven
Rigid	→	Flexible
Competition	→	Cooperation
High Cost	→	Low Cost
Individual	→	Community
Future	→	Present

Table 1-1

an influence or power. Bondage is your life being controlled by some force outside of yourself. You can never be free when you must always worry about maintaining and growing your wealth. You must tirelessly check on how much power you wield in the world to measure your happiness. Maintaining your status is a constant chore to make sure no one else is gaining on you. And finally, exterior beauty ebbs and flows throughout life and aging is an uphill battle in a cruel world of vanity.

True happiness is the ultimate feeling of freedom. You experience the freedom of choice when you live from the inside out, not allowing your happiness to be defined by the traditional benchmarks, but creating your own. Listening to your own inner voice and trusting your choices will lead you to a life of happiness.

SCARCITY VS. ABUNDANCE

Sadly enough, some of us have distorted lessons of happiness that developed in our childhood. Our experiences developed as we grew up in different systems, such as our original family, our religious community, and our neighborhood. Many of us believe that only a few of us experience true happiness. Most believe attaining true happiness is like winning the lottery and only some of us are lucky enough to win it. Or maybe some of us believe in "works righteousness"—a theology that says if you work hard enough at anything, you will receive what you work for. Any one of these theories of happiness is born of the philosophy that happiness is scarce.

Looking around our world right now I would have to agree that true happiness is in short supply. But this is because we have bought into a belief system that teaches us that happiness is as scarce as hen's teeth.

Happiness is scarce because few of us intentionally choose it. We sit and wait for it to happen. Many philosophies and religions believe that happiness is the natural state of human beings and that our choices keep us away from happiness. Abundance is at the foundation of happiness.

FEAR-DRIVEN VS. TRUST-DRIVEN

We cannot experience happiness when our lives are driven by fear. The child of fear is worry, and we have become a world of worriers and fear-driven individuals. It is impossible to experience true happiness when you are infected with fear.

True happiness is a lifestyle where we trust in life. We trust that life is good and there is purpose in each of our lives, and every circumstance in our lives is about learning while we are alive. A happy life is having confidence that everything in your life happens for a purpose and life is a classroom, not a prison.

RIGID VS. FLEXIBLE

When you close your eyes and imagine yourself and your family being happy, I am sure the word rigid doesn't even enter your mind. But, traditionally, many belief systems tell us that if you live in a prescribed way you will find happiness. These philosophies have rigid definitions of what you must do to be happy.

True happiness is living your life in balance, and authentic balance requires flexibility. Think of a person on a balance beam or on a high wire: It requires extreme flexibility. So it is with our lives. The more flexible you are, the more opportunity you have to experience true happiness.

COMPETITION VS. COOPERATION

A common misconception is that as we compete and win, we can experience true happiness. I recently heard the actor Morgan Freeman interviewed, who was asked how much happier he is now since he won the Academy Award. The actor humbly replied, "I was living a life of happiness before I won that award, and I am living the same life now. My Academy Award sits on a shelf as a sign of an accomplishment of an event, but it has no bearing on the happiness in my life." Morgan Freeman knows that real competition is competition with oneself and the goal of always improving your acting skills, your surgical skills, or your teaching skills. If you believe that competing against the other teacher for teacher of the year and winning is going to give you true happiness you are going to continue on a roller-coaster ride. But if you believe that competing with yourself and becoming a more passionate teacher every day of your life will make you happy, you are on the road to happiness.

We live in a world of nations competing for products, weapons, and natural resources. But the world has become suddenly smaller with globalization, and the scarcity of natural resources cannot be resolved by competition. We are one small fragile magnificent planet, and we must begin cooperation at greater levels each day. Competition for natural resources is no longer an option for the sustainability of our planet. The decisions and attitudes of valuable resources located in each country are inextricably woven into the destiny of our entire planet.

The era of cooperation across borders has been born. We are beginning to cooperate and share various technologies, medical research, cloning, genome, and many financial resources, just to name a few. A good example of our new era of cooperation is the space station, where we are uniting resources, instead of competing.

Remember a time at work when you were working on a project and everyone was cooperating to make the project great. Do you remember the wonderful rich feeling of cooperation and camaraderie you experienced when you worked together on a common goal? Now remember a time at work when you put yourself in direct competition for something. Do you remember the vigilant, intense, relentless energy? Remember the isolation you experienced? A lifetime of competition is exhausting and will not create true happiness. Extreme competition can create a lonely, hollow life.

HIGH COST VS. LOW COST

We spend a tremendous amount of money chasing happiness. We believe we can find it in a new house in a new neighborhood, a new car, a new pair of shoes, a bigger TV set, a more exotic vacation, or by changing jobs. We pay a very high cost to keep chasing happiness only to discover the more we seek it the more it eludes us. We cannot experience happiness outside of ourselves no matter how much we buy, where we move, or how often we change jobs. Our credit card debt is at an all-time high as we continue relentlessly to chase happiness.

True happiness has no cost because it is a condition of the mind and soul. There have been many research projects aimed at trying to find out whether individuals who have wealth are happier than those that do not. The facts are that those with no money are as happy as those with money.

INDIVIDUAL VS. COMMUNITY

We continue to believe the myth of rugged individualism. The image of someone making it to the top of a summit or discovering the cure for cancer by themselves continues the myth that happiness can be experienced only when you achieve some goal alone.

The new paradigm of happiness and success rests in the concept that we cooperate and reach our goal synergistically. The community celebrates and many individuals are transformed when the goal is achieved. There are more lives committed to the goal when a community acts together than when a person pursues a solo mission. We are imprinted with images of individual superheroes—e.g., Rambo or characters played by Arnold Schwarzenegger—saving the world; too many of us seek this myth instead of sharing a dream or goal in community and realizing synergy. "Isolation kills; community heals."

FUTURE VS. PRESENT

Most of us keep working harder and waiting for the day when we will wake up happy or when the event will happen and we will be happy. We believe that we will experience true happiness in the future when "we meet the right person, get the right job, lose this weight, make enough money." These are the mantras of our modern culture.

All great spiritualities and religions proclaim that true happiness is available in the present moment of your life. You don't have to wait for anything or anybody. Go within, connect, experience, and believe that true happiness is not only possible in the present; it has been here our entire lives just waiting to be discovered by you.

WOMEN AND HAPPINESS

We women have lost a sense of ourselves. Many women have become enmeshed with their children, their spouses, and their jobs. Subsequently, they have lost their passion, and continually complain of having no energy, having no interest in sex, and experiencing a constant sense of being overwhelmed. We women have to stop feeling guilty and blaming ourselves for the lack of support our culture and our nation provide us. We work harder, earn less, and are continually frustrated.

Women find parenthood more stressful than men, but men also report that the pressure to remain in an upwardly mobile career and "provide" for the family is overwhelming. Both parents are stressed to the breaking point.

We believe that the faster we go, the quicker we'll get there, but where are we going and why are we going there? Do we believe that we will find happiness over the rainbow? Do we believe that we will find happiness with more money, more status, more successful and accomplished children, more accumulation of stuff? We live with a nagging, haunting sadness, where we feel misunderstood, alone, and disoriented.

THE FAMILY AND HAPPINESS

In a world where we champion the power to choose, what are we really choosing?

We live in a culture that believes that the family structure has little or no value. Yes, we pay lip service of how valuable the family is and how it is the basis for any civilized society with great values, but what have we, our corporations, or our government done to show supports for the value of a family and work-life balance.

Single people have their own set of hurdles to overcome. There is the pressure to find the "right" person in a world where there is little leisure time to find a partner. Dating services are growing exponentially because time and location are limited commodities. Young people are busy moving up the career ladder trying to make more money, accumulate wealth, status, and power to achieve happiness, only to discover that if they aren't happy on the journey, they surely won't find it at the destination.

The politicians talk about family values, but keep spending money on their pork projects and other peripheral projects, instead of on what is the backbone and essence of any healthy society. We continually feel isolated, frustrated, overwhelmed with childcare, by both parents working, by lack of flexible hours in the workplace, and by lack of adequate, affordable health care for our families. Until we absolutely choose to stop this assault on the family system and demand support on levels of businesses and government, we must make the choices we can to transform our own lives so we can discover the fulfillment and happiness in a life of balance.

Parents are so overwhelmed with guilt, worry, and exhaustion, they create poor boundaries to keep the family healthy. Parents put children first, and only if they have time later do they squeeze time in for their marriage relationship and their time alone to practice self-care.

The family has become a source of oppression, anxiety, and fear, instead of the bread of life and the foundation of love.

Self-care has become a luxury and a pipe dream allowed only to the rich or the "spoiled" or the "selfish." This is a perverted sequence for mental, physical, and spiritual health.

The Science of Happiness — How It Affects Our Health

Happiness is the elusive desire of every human being on earth. We seek happiness through the doors of religion, philosophy, psychology, medicine, and even government. In the Declaration of Independence, Thomas Jefferson wrote:

> We hold these truths to be self-evident: that all men are created equal; that they are endowed by their Creator with certain unalienable rights; that among these are life, liberty and *the pursuit of happiness.*

What does the pursuit of happiness mean? Are we guaranteed happiness in our lives? Of course not. Isn't it interesting that over 230 years ago, happiness was considered a "right" by our founding fathers. We have a "right" to be happy.

Most Americans in a recent *Time* magazine poll said they are happy 78 percent of the time.[1] We were an optimistic country seeking happiness when the Declaration of Independence was written in 1776, and we seek happiness now more than ever.

Happiness has moved from a guaranteed right of our government to the forefront of scientific research.

One of the new focuses of psychology has been in the field of positive psychology. We have spent many years focusing on research in the areas of depression and anxiety, but recently there has been an interest in the "science of happiness." How much of our propensity for optimism or pessimism is inherited? Do our genes actually dictate how happy or optimistic we are?

We are wired for happiness from the beginning. Researchers believe that about 50 to 70 percent of our happiness and optimism comes from our genes. Genes impact our happy, content personality, our propensity for anxiety and depression, and our ability to handle stress. Maybe you can look at your parents and family members to see why you are laughing. This is a major factor, but there is still around 50 percent of happiness that is determined by our attitude, behaviors, and values.

We have a great opportunity to understand what science is teaching us about the positive health effects of happiness. We can also learn techniques to learn how to be happy.

Abraham Lincoln knew that we could make choices that directly influence our happiness when he said, "Most people are about as happy as they make up their minds up to be." Our new research supports what Abraham Lincoln said over 150 years ago.

Happiness is a physical state of the brain. When we are happy our brain produces neurochemicals that result in us wanting to eat, have sex, or maybe sing a song. Most researchers study the effects of these neurochemicals by using different measurement techniques, such as FMRI (Functional Magnetic Resonance Imaging), which records blood flow that activates parts of the brain; an EEG (electroencephalogram), which monitors the electrical activity of neuronal circuits; or blood tests that measure the amount of hormones or neurotransmitters in the blood, such as dopamine or serotonin.

Here are some results from our recent research on happiness:

- People who score high on psychological tests assessing happiness produce about 50 percent more antibodies than the average person in response to flu vaccines.[2]

- Individuals who test high on scales for happiness, optimism, and contentment have a reduced risk of cardiovascular disease, hypertension, and infections.

- Researchers found that when subjects practiced acts of happiness and gratitude regularly their energy levels were raised, their physical health improved, and they experienced less fatigue and pain.

- A recent study reveals that optimistic individuals reduced their risk of death by 50 percent over the nine years of the study.[3]

Laughter and humor create health and well being because they:

- Reduce stress

▶ Boost our immune systems

▶ Lower our blood pressure

▶ Improve our brain functioning

A study at the University of Maryland Medical Center tells us the ability to laugh in stressful situations helps us to *not* produce harmful neurochemicals. Laughter increases our capacity to fight various diseases by increasing our antibody production. As our bodies relax when we laugh, we reduce the risk of heart disease, hypertension, strokes, arthritis, and other inflammatory diseases. Laughter reduces the levels of stress hormones like cortisol.[4]

Laughter is also a great exercise for the body. When we laugh we work our facial, abdominal, chest, leg, and back muscles. Laughing fills our lungs with oxygen, which nourishes our vital organs: the brain, heart, lungs, and liver.

A recent study tracked two groups of cardiac patients. One group of patients received medical care alone and the other group received medical care plus they watched thirty minutes of comedy a day. After one year, the laughing group reported fewer repeat heart attacks, fewer episodes of arrhythmia, lower blood pressures, and lower levels of stress hormones.[5]

Here are ten tips on how to live a happier life:

1. *Attitude of Gratitude:* It is physiologically impossible to be grateful and experience stress at the same time. Research shows grateful individuals report having more energy and less physical complaints than their nongrateful counterparts. Studies tell us daily gratitude exercises (see Chapter 6) resulted in higher levels of alertness, enthusiasm, determination, optimism, and happiness.

2. *Choice:* Every moment of our lives is a choice, and every choice we make has a huge ripple effect. If we choose to commit to practicing happiness and optimism, we can transform our lives.

3. *Being Proactive:* Stop being the victim of our lives and constantly responding to other people and their lives. If we create a plan with our passion and live in a proactive manner, we will become the heroes of our lives, not the victims.

4. *Smiling:* Begin the practice of intentionally smiling. A scientist studying facial expressions tells us that when people have smiles on their faces, they release more serotonin and endorphins (happiness hormones) than nonsmilers.[6] Thich Nhat Hanh and his Holiness the Dalai Lama are adamant that a smile is the first step to a life of mental, physical, and spiritual health. Begin a practice of smiling to shift any situation into an optimistic opportunity.

5. *Laughter:* Laugh as often as possible to release the healing hormones endorphins, the body's natural pain killers. Instead of buying pills for our stress, we can go rent a funny movie, or go online to a humorous site daily and share it with our coworkers. Laughter lowers blood pressure, reduces stress hormones, and boosts our immune function.

6. *Playfulness:* Reestablish "childlike" qualities. Science tells us that when we play it increases the immune cells in our bodies that combat disease. Playfulness also increases creativity and optimism at home and at work.

7. *Health:* It is essential that we focus on the health of our bodies. When we care for our physical bodies we create greater possibilities for happiness. Our bodies are our greatest asset, so please care for them tenderly.

8. *Spirituality:* The vast number of happy people have developed spiritual practices that nourish their heart and soul. Discover what brings your soul passion, love, and fulfillment. Our spirituality is what roots us in our lives.

9. *Altruism and Philanthropy:* A generous soul lives a rich, abundant life. Altruism neutralizes negative emotions that affect immune, endocrine, and cardiovascular function. Altruism creates a physiological responses or "helpers high" that makes people feel stronger and more energetic and counters harmful effects of stress.

10. *Forgiveness:* Happy people know forgiveness sets the soul free. A famous person said, "Living with resentment is like taking poison and expecting the other person to get sick." Open your heart to the gift of happiness by letting go of pain, judgment, anger, and resentment.

True happiness is found in the simple, mundane, and ordinary moments of your life. Happiness can be discovered only when you stop and begin to listen to what is really important in your life. What brings you passion, what makes you smile, and what makes your heart sing? Happiness is realizing how short your life really is and that every experience in your life is mysteriously designed to lead you deeper into your real self. You know true happiness when you bless others in the world with the gifts of your life.

~ BEGIN TODAY ~

Ask Your Self   What is my definition of true happiness?

What part of my life creates passion and authenticity?

What part of my life makes me sad and empty?

Tell Your Self   My life is constantly evolving into greater happiness.

Give Your Self   Do a fun thing you have been putting off doing.

Read an inspirational book.

Go someplace in nature and experience your connection with the plants and animals.

CHAPTER 2

Weathering the Seasons
of the Soul

LIZ SLIPPED OFF her tight heels and kicked them under the seat of the airplane. She had been walking to meetings all over London for the last days and was finally heading back to New York. Liz was ticked because she couldn't get a direct flight and had to go through Amsterdam. She had decided that no matter what happened she was exhausted and she would not talk to anyone on the plane. She had been doing presentations in meetings for days and she just wanted to sleep.

Liz closed her eyes and slipped off to a light sleep only to hear, "Excuse me, I think you have my seat belt on." She was furious, opened her eyes, undid her seat belt and grabbed the one the passenger beside her handed to her. She quickly closed the seat belt and closed her eyes again. As she began dozing off again, she remembered seeing a strange bold color on the passenger next to her. She slowly opened her eyes and looked over into the eyes of a saffron-robed monk. Liz sat in silence trying to recoup with a slight smile on her face. The small monk greeted her with a wide smile, teeth showing and head nodding with joy. He said, "Hello, my name is Sing Lapso." She stumbled for a moment but blurted out, "Hi, my name is Liz Barnes. I see your saffron robe, are you a Buddhist monk?" "Yes, I live in a Buddhist monastery in Sri Lanka."

"What were you doing in London?" Liz asked. "I was invited by Oxford to attend a meeting on the long-term effects of the tsunami," answered the monk. "Oh my gosh," said Liz, carefully. It must be devastating for your monastery and your people in Sri Lanka. I am so sorry for all that has happened. The people are so devastated, they must need intense counseling and help with their mental health, and they will probably be traumatized for a long time."

The small-framed monk smiled widely, "No, you do not understand our beliefs about life. Our people have little need for psychological counseling. Most of us are Buddhist and we believe that life is impermanent. We are all a part of nature and are therefore part of the cycles of nature. Nature must continually seek balance and that means that humans are a part of that balance of nature. Imbalance in the earth created the earthquake and this event created the tsunami. The tsunami created destruction but then balance was restored to the earth. We human beings are inextricably woven into nature and are part of the process of restoring balance. We see the tsunami and its effects as part of the natural cycle or process of life. All life is born and is subject to nature. In just a little while, after the tsunami, I looked over the ocean and it was so peaceful and nature was in balance again." Liz sat there in silence as the monk finished thoughts that had never occurred to her.

She sat on the entire flight in silence absorbing this simple monk's philosophy on life. The monk's words kept rolling around in Liz's head and they seemed somewhat cruel. She felt helpless and confused. Are humans helpless in the face of nature and natural disasters? Do we live in an illusion of control over nature that results in our shock, anger, and confusion when we experience a tsunami, hurricane, tornado or earthquake? We see these events as "unfair, tragic and to some even "evil." This little monk in his saffron robe experiences natural disasters as the pure Divine intelligence of nature constantly returning itself to balance and finds comfort in the flow of it all. He experiences every event in his life as a season of his soul.

The Seasons of Our Life

We have such an interesting relationship with nature. We live as if we are separate from nature. Sometimes it is as if we are afraid of nature because it is one thing we know we can't control. We have a weather channel on television that many people stay glued to, and the weather is a main component of every newscast. We ominously and anxiously look to the weather forecast waiting for Mother Nature to define our future plans.

Other cultures know that we are one with nature. The Native Americans, the Asians, the Indians, the Africans—all believe our body systems are directly connected to the seasons of the year and the daily weather. These cultures have great respect for nature and the power she exerts within our bodies and around us at every moment. These cultures know that when we destroy our natural environment we destroy our inner bodies. Our planet is the macro system of nature and our bodies reflect the micro system of exactly the same processes, elements, and chemicals. We are wonderfully and intricately woven together. Our bodies occupy a tiny short cycle of life within the greater dynamic cycle of life of the planets and our solar system.

Our diseases—physically, emotionally, and spiritually—come from separating ourselves from the natural rhythms of nature. If we are one with nature, why do we think we can create lives that move faster than the natural cycle of life? When we attempt to orchestrate time according to our needs and desires we disconnect from the natural cycles of life.

After living at Oak Haven for many years, I have acquired great respect for and dread of the sudden shock of a violent thunderstorm as it rips through our ranch on a blistering, sultry summer afternoon. Rooted deep in the earth, the strong trunks of the venerable trees hold steady, while their branches express flexibility, yielding with humility to the wind and the rain. The utter chaos Mother Nature imposes during the storm may appear as destruction and violence on the exterior; however, the experience eventually brings pruning and rebalance into our natural world.

The trees in these storms have taught me much about the human soul. It is not *whether* suffering, loss, disappointment, and disease come into our lives, it is *when* they show up. I have found that, like the trees on our ranch, we all have the capacity to weather the storms of our lives when we are deeply rooted and can emerge transformed. The crucial element for us to remember is not to fear the magnitude of the storm, but to trust that we have cultivated the roots that anchor and sustain us in the face of the events of our lives. The reason to cultivate this essential rootedness is not merely to survive, but to create an incredibly prosperous balanced life rooted of true happiness.

The farmers that live around us in the mountains have taught me quite a bit about the weather. The older farmers have ways of predicting the weather that have been preciously handed down from generation to generation. They have taught me that when you live in nature with great awareness, many times she will tell you what to expect. Many of us have lost our deep awareness and our intimate relationship with nature because of our busy lives or our urban dwelling. I really believe that when we disconnect from nature we loose our reverence and awe for all of life.

The "weather" of our lives helps to define our meaning and purpose. Instead of attempting to change the weather, or to run from the storms, we can choose to turn within and cultivate deep roots, a strong trunk, and flexible branches. When we turn within, we create the opportunity to emerge transformed by the storm, creating a new sense of strength and balance.

In the same way, imagine a tree complaining of the coming of autumn, or whining that its new spring buds aren't the right shade of green. It may sound silly, but we do this when we resist the cycles in our lives. The tree becomes a dynamic part of the stages of this magnificent life, not the victim of it. The tree becomes the regal hero of hundreds of years of surviving and thriving in the direst of circumstances. You can look at a cross section of a tree and know the age of the tree, what years there were droughts, and when there were rainy seasons. Its majestic life is recorded within the tree as a journal.

The natural world does not comprehend the concept of victimization. Why should we? Each season throughout the year, and every season throughout your life, offers opportunities for reflection, choices, and action. As you weather the seasons of life, be courageous and confident that your authentic Self is evolving and creating an intentional life.

The seasons—spring, summer, fall, and winter—can inform or guide the seasons of your life. The interesting fact is your psychological and spiritual issues will rarely disappear but they cycle back to you and give you the opportunity to experience them in a different way. For example: Anger, fear, grief, shame—all change as we age. We have the opportunity to improve the way we experience and express these emotions, or if we continue to ignore or deny our issues, they can eventually make us sick.

Nature in her infinite wisdom continually reminds us that nothing stays stagnant. It is delusional to believe anything in our lives stays stationary. Each dynamic cycle of our life is an opportunity to create a new and different experience and response.

Autumn shows us that there is a time to let go, be bare, vulnerable, and surrender. As the winds and cold strip the covering and protection of the leaves the trees don't experience panic or fear but trust this process. Because it is only in this process of surrender and trust, the tree can continue to grow, prosper, and age. The deciduous trees that do not release their leaves are either dying or dead. *Winter* invites us to turn inward, sit in stillness, and listen deeply. It becomes an opportunity to mirror the natural world, be courageous to stand naked as the trees, and examine this season of your life. *Spring* is a time of infinite potential and fertility. Reflecting spring we realize there are a host of opportunities that begin with planting the seeds to create a life of happiness and balance. Spring reassures us that after every cold dark season of our life there is a warm bright rebirth. *Summer* invites us to enjoy the leisure and fruits of our lives. The leisure of summer reminds us to rest and play. We are beckoned to bask in the warm, long, sunny days of this season and become aware that the summers of our lives are becoming shorter and shorter.

The cycles and seasons of nature are metaphors for the aging process constantly transforming our own lives. Aging is a natural wondrous process that most of us experience as oppressive victimization instead of a Divine process involving dignity, wisdom and spirituality. The quality of our aging is in direct proportion to the depth and strength of our root system. On the journey to true happiness it is crucial to observe and listen to nature. She will teach us her invaluable lessons for our journey: flexibility, surrender, nourishment, healing, patience, rest, perseverance and hope.

Discovering Your Authentic Self

Each season is an invitation to explore the potential within your Self. The seasons and the natural world must correspond to the cycles of nature. A pear tree must blossom and produce pears; a cherry tree must bloom and produce cherries. Unlike these trees who cannot choose, spring holds the opportunity for you to choose to plant the seeds that call you home to your authentic Self.

Your authentic Self is when you feel at one with your Self and your experience. You experience a sense of energy, power, and connection. The ancients used to call this "the place of knowing." You "know" you are aware and fully present. This is an experience of fullness and communion. It feels as if you are living in a state of grace. It is your original Self before you were influenced by the effects of your primary family, society, school, and other experiences that began to define and shape your life.

Many of us have experienced fleeting moments of our authentic Self. For you, it may have been when you were passionately lost while reading a book, having no sense of time or place because the story was so real. Maybe you were playing the piano, while your fingers were playing a score and your body and soul were the music. Or, were you writing an essay with your heart, and noticed your fingers trembling as you became the words? Close your eyes for a moment, take a deep breath, and journey back to your childhood. Remember a time or a place where you felt a communion and connection with your authentic Self. Do you remember experiencing confidence, peace, and power? If you recognize that place of bliss you were at home with your authentic Self.

Seasons of Surrender

The natural world issues an open invitation to one of life's most challenging but essential practices: surrender. Nature makes no conscious choice to surrender: In spring, tulip bulbs sleeping under the cold ground, tiny leaves budding on ancient oaks, cheerful birds seeking the safest place to build their nests—all freely surrender with certainty and confidence to the power of spring to bring life, growth, beauty, and joy.

Nature—our teacher—is always surrendering, unfolding, transforming, becoming new. Surrender brings new life, prosperity, order, fruits, and flowers. The earth surrenders to sun, wind, and rain as she is challenged to bring forth something new and wondrous.

To weather the seasons of your life and experience true happiness, the tool of surrender is essential. Nature teaches us that anything too brittle and nonflexible not only breaks, but often dies. Everything in nature weathers, ebbs and flows, grows and sloughs, experiences times of expansion and contractions. Surrender is an act of courage, trust and power. Surrender is your sure path to balance and living an authentic life of true happiness.

We live in a culture that places a high value on individual accomplishment. We are inundated from the day we are born with the ideal of achievement and success, being taught to compete our entire life in sports, school, and business. We learn early in life that there are winners and losers—and the word "surrender" is traditionally associated with losers. Embracing the concept of surrender as essential to experiencing true happiness is counter-intuitive.

In my competitive sports and business-driven family, "surrender" was a dirty word. My father, brother, and grandfathers were all in the military. "Surrender" meant to lose, fail, or to be conquered. "Surrender" conjured up images of a defeated soldier on a bleak battlefield waving a white flag.

But when we examine the way our ideals of success have constructed our lives, many of us are not happy with what we have orchestrated. Our well-designed lives may be wrought with sadness, depression, apathy, or turmoil. We may feel overwhelmed. The more plans we make, the more complicated our lives become, the more surrender becomes a welcome balm to a life that feels out of control. The idea of giving up control may bring momentary anxiety but as you move into the grace of surrender, grace and healing flows in.

Surrender may sound simple, but it is often not easy. Letting go can be one of the deepest and most challenging of emotional and spiritual practices. If the idea of surrender brings anxiety, take a moment to consider that your ego and will may have constructed the life you are living. Consider that you may not be connected to your true life's purpose, that you may not be living an intentional life with the authentic you in balance with your life.

Surrender is the perfect tool to discover your true life's purpose. Great spiritual and psychological minds throughout history have extolled the amazing power of letting go and trusting the process. When you embrace surrender, you release your ego and your attachment to life the way you have constructed it. When you embrace surrender, you trust a power greater than your own.

There is immense power in this surrendering and letting go. Surrender restores us to our Source. Surrender restores our balance. Surrender is trusting the flow of energy, intelligence, and love that created your life. This omnipotent energy knows what you need and will move you in the direction of your full potential.

We innately know about the cycles, flows, and balance of life. We are fluid, flowing, surrendering, tied to the cycles of nature. Just as the seasons, the moon, and the tides cycle in nature, we are also part of this vast rhythm of life. And we innately know when we are out of this magnificent rhythm and imbalanced. We have detectors inside us that go off like alarms, screaming, "Red alert, red alert, out of balance." But often, to survive in our hectic lives, we have learned to turn a deaf ear to our inner alarms. Sometimes we unplug our inner alarms. Sometimes we even yank the batteries out so we can move faster and faster and faster, like a train running out of control on a track.

Believe me, I know about the power of surrender. My life was moving at a well-planned pace when one day my intermittent panic attacks returned with a vengeance and tried to consume my life. I seemed to have had the "perfect life": the wonderful career, model family, fabulous home, hottest cars, ideal vacations. But there was always something calling me under the surface of my "perfect life." With the wise guidance of a spiritual director and a loving therapist, I decided to do the most terrifying thing I could imagine in my well-orchestrated world: surrender to my authentic Self.

I could never have imagined the rich rewarding life that I experience now. My earlier conception of a "perfect life" doesn't even compare to the intentional life I now live. When you surrender, you begin an adventure of discovering who you are and what the purpose of your life is. A new sense of freedom, power, and energy stirs within you.

Aging Joyfully

The CDC (Centers for Disease Control and Prevention) reports that we now live thirty years longer than we did in 1900.[1] With the advent of genetics and the unraveling of the genome, the science of aging has emerged and new discoveries are expected to dramatically transform the aging process. We have spent many years taking fountain of youth supplements, creams, and tonics. We now know aging goes much deeper, all the way to our genes. Our genes are our blueprints for life, and in the future there will undoubtedly be genetic interventions to enhance the aging process.

There are other ways to enrich our lives as we age: mentally, physically, and spiritually. In this book you will discover the benefits of grounding your life in the four roots. With this new science of aging, I want to give you some specific tips for aging joyfully.

I believe the concept of "anti-aging" is faulty. Aging is a part of the natural cycle of our lives: birth, aging, and death. We begin aging from the moment we are conceived in our mother's womb. The enormous number of people who are trying to outrun aging grieves me. Many of us have actually developed a phobic reaction to aging. I believe that we should stay healthy as long as possible. My hope for you is that you live a healthier life and age joyfully.

Gifts for Every Season

There are certain practices that science has demonstrated create health, longevity, and happiness. Whether you are in your twenties, midlife or celebrating your retirement, there are many gifts for you to include in your life, no matter what season of your life you are enjoying.

SLEEP

I was born and bred in a family that held great reverence for sleep, and especially the holiness of naps. My parents and grandparents would take a nap in a moment. We learned from an early age to go play outside quietly during nap time. I continued the sacred ritual of the nap in my family. We always had nap time and still do. Recent research tells us that there are health benefits in a quick nap. (If you have insomnia please check with your doctor because napping could interfere with your insomnia treatment.)

Sleep has always fascinated me. I loved watching dogs, cats, birds, horses, and baby and adult humans sleep. Sleep must be pretty important when we spend one third of our lives sleeping.

For those of you interested in learning more about sleep there are two great resources on sleep that I recommend and have used for years: Dr. James B. Maas's *Power Sleep* and Dr. Gregg Jacobs's *Say Good Night to Insomnia*. I actually listened to Dr. Jacobs's passionate lectures on sleep and insomnia when I was at Harvard, and he has had impressive results with this sleep program.

Lack of sleep has profound effects on your mind, body, and soul. When you are sleep deprived you have more automobile and other accidents, your thinking is unclear, your memory is inexact, and your health is directly affected. Chronic sleep deprivation affects your immune, cardiovascular, gastrointestinal, and endocrine systems.

Over half of the adult population is not getting enough sleep and are chronically tired. This is a serious problem, and if you are one of these individuals suffering from insomnia or sleep deprivation, please get help. First I suggest you get the two books mentioned above, which are an excellent introduction to understanding sleep and your body. Then, if you are still having problems after reading these books, go to one of the sleep clinics in your area.

EXERCISE

We are a culture of obesity and live a sedentary lifestyle. It is time for all of us, no matter what our age, to get up off the couch and get moving. Mothers, fathers, children, grandparent, and dog need to get involved in some activity. Walk, dance, play or run, just get going. The research is overwhelming on the positive effects of exercise in every season of our lives. With the increase of childhood obesity this has become a very serious issue. A University of Illinois study showed adults who walked 45 minutes three times a week improved performance on cognitive tasks by 15 percent.[2] More information on exercise is in Chapter 7.

LEARNING

From the time we are young until the moment of our last breath, continual learning keeps producing new brain cells in every season of our lives. Princeton University's Elizabeth Gould, Ph.D., revealed continued learning ensures the survival of new brains cells.[3]

ANTIOXIDANTS

Research continues to reveal the incredible power of antioxidants in our diet. Mounting evidence indicates the key to slowing aging is antioxidants. Antioxidants protect the brain from free radicals. Free radicals are unstable molecules produced through the body's use of oxygen; free radicals weaken cell walls and damage the cells of the body including the brain. Antioxidants, which protect cells by disabling the free radicals, are discussed more in Chapter 9, Food.

DIET

There are so many diets on the market it may be almost overwhelming to choose which one is right for you. A study in the Journal of the *American Medical Association* reported that women and men over the age of 70 who adhered to special diets and a healthy lifestyle and were followed over a period of 12 years had a significantly lower death rate (more than 50 percent lower) than other individuals of the same age.[4] The participants who lived longer ate a Mediterranean diet and adhered to a healthy lifestyle (regular exercise, no smoking, and moderate alcohol). The Mediterranean diet is high in fiber and low in fat, with legumes, nuts, whole grains, fish, olive oil and lots of fruits and vegetables.

STRESS MANAGEMENT (SERENITY PRACTICES)

There is a direct link between stress and accelerated aging. A recent study from the University of California, San Francisco, is proving that stress causes premature aging. Telomeres located at the ends of DNA are essential for the replication of DNA and the growth of cells. Under extreme stress, the telomeres are damaged and cell growth is inhibited. This study found that stress can accelerate aging 10 years.[5] The good news is that this same study also found that this damage is reversible with self-care methods.

OPTIMISM

Newly released scientific studies confirm the health benefits of a "Pollyanna attitude." Maintaining a positive outlook on life has direct benefits to aging. This doesn't surprise me after working with a cardiac rehabilitation group for years. In my experience most of the geriatric patients that have survived incredibly painful life events are optimistic and incredibly wise. The patients who were optimistic had a great affect upon the patients who were pessimistic or "sour." These optimistic patients spread their optimism as if it were a viral infection. No matter what life dealt them, they had a proactive, optimistic approach to life. These optimistic patients had no resistance to the concept of how to stay healthy and adapted the four roots of happiness and health into their lives.

We know through research that every thought or emotion you experience has electrical energy and a chemical response attached to it. Therefore when you are optimistic you are just sending those little healing chemicals all over your body and they are boosting your immune system, affecting your blood pressure favorably, and creating health in your mind, body and soul.

I am so fortunate to have come from a gene pool of eternal optimists. My father was a salesman who lived each week whistling as he headed out the door, expecting that to be the week he had the most sales in his career. To earn extra money for our family, my father would drive a dump truck from northern Ohio to the coal mines in the south to pick up coal at night after his sales job during the day. He would let me ride with him some nights. It was a special treat because we would stay up all night despite my having school the next day. There was no heat in the truck and it was the dead of winter and yet it was one of the few times I remember having a good time with my father. If I was really lucky I got to stay home from school the next day and go with him to deliver the coal to his customers. During those long cold nights my father would talk about the difficult sale he made and how exciting it was to be a salesman. He had this incredible optimism that every sale would eventually transpire. He always said you have to believe in yourself, your product, and the public. This incredibly powerful energy would emanate from him as he would talk about how life was all about being positive about the outcome.

My mother was devoutly religious, and she believed that the power of God would overcome anything, anywhere, at anytime. No matter how bad a situation or a particular person was in my mind, she would find a silver lining in any dark cloud. Every cell of her body was the essence of optimism. My optimism was born out of an interesting combination of parents. My father did not grace the door of a church and thought that religion was a bag of wind for the helpless and desperate, and my mother believed salespeople were slick snake oil dealers, not to be trusted and born liars to the bone.

Researchers are verifying what my parents, aunts, uncles and grandparents taught me many years ago. The *Journal of Personality and Psychology* released a study that found people who had positive attitudes toward aging lived an average of 7.5 years longer than those who viewed aging in a negative manner.[6]

Margery Silver, Ed.D., of the Beth Deaconess Medical Center has studied the psychological profiles of 200 healthy centenarians. She has discovered that the common theme that runs through these centenarians is that they remain positive thinkers.[7] A study in the *Archives of General Psychiatry* showed after 10 years of follow-up, people who were very optimistic had a 55 percent lower risk of death from all causes and a 23 percent lower risk of heart-related death, compared with people who reported a high level of pessimism.[8]

The MacArthur Foundation Study of Aging in America showed that lifestyle choices are more important than genetics in determining the quality of an individual aging.[9] The optimal lifestyle for aging is the four roots I explore in this book.

LAUGHTER

Researchers find laughter creates health and well being. Laughing reduces stress, boosts our immune system, lowers our blood pressure, and improves our brain functioning. Laugh as often as possible to release the healing hormones endorphins, the body's natural pain killers. Instead of taking a pill for your stress, go and rent a funny movie.

▶ A study at the University of Maryland Medical Center shows laughter increases our capacity to fight various diseases by increasing our antibody production. Laughter reduces the levels of stress hormones like cortisol. Our bodies relax when we laugh, and we reduce our risk of heart disease, hypertension, strokes, arthritis, and other inflammatory diseases.[10]

▶ Researchers found that laughter has a health effect on blood vessel function. They discovered under ultrasound that artery diameter increased by 22 percent during laughter and decreased by 35 percent during mental stress.[11]

ALTRUISM

A generous soul lives a rich abundant life. Altruism neutralizes negative emotions that affect immune, endocrine, and cardiovascular function. Altruism creates physiological responses or a "helpers high," which makes people feel stronger and more energetic and counters harmful effects of stress.

Altruism was the foundation of my mother's home. There were no shelters in the city where we lived, and homeless people were cared for by a group of churches. It was a radical notion that you don't send homeless people to a shelter, you invite them into your home. Each church had a certain day on the monthly schedule, and when that day came up if there was a homeless person the police found, they would call that church, which then would become responsible for that homeless person. My mother signed us up as the designated family for our church. My mother's spiritual view was that a stranger was our opportunity to practice hospitality and grace. What a gift that was in my life.

When the call would come from the church, my mother acted as if the President of the United States was about to arrive. We immediately stripped the linens from the bed and put fresh linens on, cleaned the house until it sparkled, and I was sent to the kitchen to begin cooking. It was a time of celebration and feasting. My mother felt that every stranger was an angel or God disguised. She believed welcoming this homeless stranger into our home was our gift because our hospitality defined who we were.

What a difference the homeless stranger is in our world today. It is someone feared and rejected, now often understandably so. But what gifts we miss when we miss the opportunity to practice real hospitality and altruism.

Many of the strangers taught me my most valuable lessons about poverty, abuse, violence, and the rejected of our society. It taught me the power of serving another and the glorious emotion that researchers now call the "helper's high." It also gave me the gift of knowing that we are one human family and sitting at a dinner table with someone whose life is so radically different can be life changing.

I had the privilege in my own life to create space in our home where we were able to take in a variety of marginalized individuals until they could get back on their feet. We have been graced with innumerable angels and saints who have visited our home allowing us to practice the gift of hospitality: individuals and families of most races, others with many diseases, some victims of violence, and others who were children neglected on the streets. Each brought an invaluable lesson to me and my family.

Research shows altruism creates health and happiness in your life. When Harvard researchers showed a documentary of Mother Teresa and her work, feelings of altruism were evoked in the group being studied. Researchers measured a component of the subjects' immune system, Immunoglobulin A. They found that Immunoglobulin A increased after the group experienced feelings of altruism.[12]

COMPASSION

Compassion has been the core of all spiritual and religious tenants. Buddha, Jesus, Gandhi, Lao Tsu, and many other leaders throughout history have extolled the virtue of compassion. It is critical to understand the true concept of compassion. Compassion is not having pity on someone else or empathy for someone while watching the evening news. Compassion requires action by the individual who experiences empathy.

The Dalai Lama has shown the significance of compassion as he says, "It is my belief that compassion is more important than religion. Compassion is the true sign of inner strength."[13]

Compassion actually changes your biology. Compassion is dissolving boundaries among people, religions, and countries.

The Hebrew word that is translated often for compassion is *rachamin,* which comes from the word *rechem,* meaning womb, uterus, or "the womb of God." It has to do with the very being of God. Having compassion for another is similar to a mother's feeling for a child in her womb. Compassion is actually feeling the suffering of another and responding to their suffering.

Another Greek word for compassion is *splanchnizomai,* which is the word for guts, viscera, or the bowels. Writers of the Bible used this word for compassion only when they described Jesus' compassion for others. This is a very rare word and it literally means that what Jesus felt for others was so deep he was moved at a gut level.

I believe compassion and love are two aspects of the same thing. We love others as ourselves and the action we bestow on the "other" is compassion. The compassion is born in our decision to love. I keep a sign on my desk to remind me that "love is a decision." I also believe that compassion is a decision. In our lives we may not always feel a natural emotional love for another, but we can choose to love others as a decision, not as a transient emotion. Compassion becomes the filter that continues to remind us that our differences are secondary and our sameness primary. Especially when I do not feel warm and fuzzy in a situation I continue to choose to be loving and compassionate in my personal life, my family life, and my business life as a spiritual practice.

Choosing compassion is living a life from the womb of God and the gut of God, according to ancient texts. When you choose to live a life of compassion you will experience true happiness through every season of you soul.

What a gift it is to realize that we are inextricably connected to the cycles of nature and life as we age. We are constantly evolving and being made new. Every new cycle and every new situation in you life is pregnant with possibilities. Stop, close your eyes, take a deep breath. Listen to the perfect rhythm of your heart. Your life is one note in the great symphony of life. May you surrender to the lessons and to the wonder of every season of your soul as you journey into true happiness.

~ BEGIN TODAY ~

Ask Your Self   Do I feel connected with nature? If not why not?

What are my feelings about aging?

How can I begin to learn the power of surrender?

Tell Your Self   I am safe and secure in every season of my life.

Give Your Self   Set up a birdfeeder to watch the birds through the seasons.

Rent a funny movie and feel the healing power of laughter.

Select a charity and give money to it. How does it feel to be altruistic?

CHAPTER 3

Understanding the Direction of Happiness

AS I BEGAN to wake up I noticed the exquisite texture of the cover that was lying over my sore tired body. I slowly looked around the room and quickly remembered where I was. I couldn't believe that we had spent this much money on a vacation and I was so sick that all I did was sleep.

My fever was finally breaking and I was in such a bad mood. We had waited for two years for this vacation as a couple and I had been sick as a dog. My husband sat beside me on the bed and announced he had booked me a massage for the next day, at 7 A.M. Sunday morning the 4th of July. It was the only time they had available the entire day, and Jim really believed that it would make me feel better. A massage was the last thing in the world I wanted, and getting up at 6 A.M. on Sunday morning on a holiday seemed more like punishment than a gift.

I hesitantly took the elevator down to the wellness center on the first floor and gingerly signed in with the attendant, who patiently walked me to the massage room. She told me to take off my clothes, lie face down, cover myself with the sheet and the massage therapist would be right in. I ached all over there lying in the silence, with my head spinning recalling the last year of my life. I had graduated with my doctorate in May, spent June at Harvard in a clinical training, and came to San Francisco to train with the pioneering cardiologist, Dr. Dean Ornish, right after that. I had been on the run for a long time. I had spent so many years taking classes from one teacher and then another to get a doctorate. I wanted to make sure that I had the latest knowledge in mind-body medicine, and so I spent any extra moment at another clinical training to learn as much as I could.

It seemed no matter how much I learned, I was afraid it was never enough. I had been going so fast for so long that I actually worked myself into getting sick. My racing thoughts were suddenly interrupted by the squeak of the door opening. I heard a gentle male voice say, "And how are you doing today, Ms. Hall? Is there anything special I should know about you before I begin your massage?" I began with the simple line, "I have been busy and traveling for months and it has finally caught up with me. I have been sick." He pulled the sheet off my back and gently began my massage.

A few minutes later he asked, "Well, what brings you out to San Francisco?" I told him that I was in San Francisco to train with Dr. Ornish, and then my husband I were going to take some time off, and I got sick. He asked me where I had been and what I did for a living. It was as if a flood gate had opened.

I told him how I left a financial career and had been on an intense focused quest to learn all I could about stress, mind-body medicine, spirituality, and wellness. There were years of endless degrees, the many trainings with teachers from all over the world, the intense spiritual practices that I practiced with great discipline. As I kept explaining my insatiable curiosity and obsession to learn all I could and the years of going from one class to another and one teacher to another, all at once, I stopped. There was stark silence in the room. Tears were streaming down my face as I found myself softly sobbing, embarrassed that this stranger was experiencing my exhaustion and sadness. After a few moments of silence, he whispered, "May I tell you a story?" I nodded yes as he handed me a tissue to wipe my nose and face.

He began:

"A long time ago in India there was a healer named Sanjay, who lived in a small village and he gave teachings and performed healings. People came from all over the countryside to hear this humble man and ask for him to heal their wounded bodies. He was a happy man who loved his people and his work. Everything was fine for many years and then one day after he gave his afternoon teaching a small old man walked up to him leaned forward and said, 'You are a good man and you have wonderful teachings, but there is a man over the mountain who heals more people than you and he teaches new and different ideas than you do. But that is okay; you are a simple man and you do well in this place.' The old man walked off into the dusk, but the healer was haunted by the words of the old man. Sanjay couldn't sleep, he found himself worried the following days. He kept thinking, 'There is someone who knows more than me and he does better work than I do.' This gnawing in his soul went on for weeks and finally he couldn't stand it anymore.

"Sanjay woke up one morning, packed his bag, and headed over the mountain to visit this superior healer that he had heard about. He wanted to go and learn what greater things this man did than he could do. He arrived in the mountain village and everyone knew this wonderful healer. Sanjay walked to the corner of town and waited under the Bohdi tree to hear the afternoon teachings of this famous healer. He listened with great fascination and admiration to this great healer and watched as the people lined up to be healed. Sanjay decided at that moment he would not leave this teacher until he learned the great secrets of his power. So one week led into one month and one month led into a year. Each day the healer would come to the Bodhi tree, and there sat Sanjay adoring and devoted to every word. Finally one day the healer called Sanjay up in front of the crowd. He asked, 'Sanjay, do you want to know everything I know and do you want to know how to do everything the same way I do?' 'Oh yes, master, that is what I want.'

In a split second, the healer cut off his head and put it on top of Sanjay's head. The head immediately said, 'Now you have my head and you can know all I know.' Sanjay was very happy and he packed his bag and headed back to his village. He was very happy because the word spread of his knowledge and ability and people came from all over the province to hear his teachings and receive his healings. Sanjay was satisfied for many years. One day a young foreigner sat in the garden to listen to Sanjay's teachings. At the end of the session as Sanjay was beginning to leave, the young man approached Sanjay and said, 'You have great knowledge, Master, and you have great power, but there is one who has more knowledge who lives down the river in Leong province. He is such a wise and noble man.' As the young man walked away, Sanjay wondered why he had not heard of this great man before. Again, he could not fall asleep that night and was distracted the next day. This continued for weeks.

Finally, Sanjay packed his bag and left on the morning boat heading down the river to visit this great teacher.

"Sanjay went to this beautiful village by the river and waited by an orchard of pear trees for the healer to give his afternoon lesson. After hearing this Master give his lesson and observing his method of healing the sick, he decided that he must stay and learn what this great person had to teach. One week led into one month, which led into many months until the monsoons came. One afternoon after the teachings, the Master called Sanjay over to his seat. 'Sanjay, you sit here day after day and follow me everywhere. You are my shadow. What do you want of me?' 'Oh Master, I desire to know the secrets of your mind and the great knowledge you possess.' As quick as a strike of lightning, the Master cut off his head and put it on top of the two heads already on Sanjay's shoulder.

"Sanjay was very happy and he quickly took the next boat home to his village. This became the habit of Sanjay's life. He would be happy and do teachings and healing for a while, until he heard of a greater teacher in another place and he would pack up his bag and go find the new teacher. Each teacher would eventually confront Sanjay, and each teacher subsequently cut off his head and placed it on Sanjay's other heads.

"This went on for many years, and Sanjay stayed in a constant state of exhaustion, confusion, and frustration. Every time a person would approach him with a question or need for a healing, all of the heads would talk, give advice, and argue. The constant talking, arguing and balancing of the heads were almost more than Sanjay could bear.

"One afternoon in late fall, as Sanjay was giving his usual afternoon teachings, a very quiet simple monk sat in the back of the gathering. After the teaching, this monk approached Sanjay and said, 'Oh, my poor man. You look as if you are in a horrible state of agitation, confusion, and pain. Can I help you?' Sanjay, almost breaking down in tears, said, 'Yes, holy man, I have traveled all over the world to gain the most knowledge so I would be the wisest teacher on earth. Now I have all these heads on my shoulders and they all have answers and talk and I am so confused and exhausted I do not know what to do. I just wanted all the knowledge and wisdom I could find.'

"At that moment, the monk reached up and removed all the heads that were on top of Sanjay's head and put them on the ground beside him. Sanjay stood in the stark silence in disbelief. The simple monk gently said, 'Sanjay, you did not need to travel the world to collect great wisdom and knowledge. All you have to do is listen to your own mind and it will teach you all you need to know.' Sanjay looked into the gentle eyes of the monk, and, with tears streaming down his face, asked, 'What is your name, kind sir?' 'My name is Siddhartha Gautama, the Buddha.'"

As he ended the story, I lay on the massage bed in the stark silence. Then he said, "Go home to your farm. Do not leave. No more teachers, no more classes. You will find everything you need to know at your farm." He turned around and walked out of the room. As he closed the door behind him, I sat there in a state of shock. I felt as if some angel had guided me in that moment. I dressed slowly and went to the attendant's desk to sign the check to pay for the massage. I leaned forward and asked the attendant, "Who is the man who did my massage this morning? He is a very kind man and he is very wise and gentle." The attendant smiled and said, "His name is Samuel, he is a Buddhist monk and lives at a monastery near San Francisco. He does massages a couple days a week and gives the money to the monastery. You are very lucky that you got him, Ms. Hall. He is really an angel."

I went back to my farm and took the monk's advice. I did not go to any more teachers or "gurus." No more seminars, classes, retreats, or academic destinations. I worked the ranch and made a conscious decision to learn what the land had to teach me. I changed the direction of my life. Instead of continuing on my insatiable fast life upward and forward, the farm taught me how to grow roots and to create a solid foundation. The ranch moved me inward and downward where I discovered my true Self and the direction of true happiness. Many of the most important lessons in life I learned not in a classroom, or from some famous teacher. I learned the most pivotal lessons of my life as my precious simple monk promised, in the simple, ordinary mundane tasks of my life on the land.

The Direction of Imbalance: Living Upward and Forward

For so many of us the image of success was that nice office at the top of a tall building, with windows overlooking the urban surroundings. I remember the wonderful status my ego enjoyed when I worked on an upper floor at the Atlanta Financial Center and on the 104th floor of the World Trade Center. I assumed happiness would be the twin of success and would follow somewhere down the line. The two seemed inextricably connected, but I discovered that to be a great fable. I had spent my life looking upward and forward, like so many others being lured upward and forward to seek success, status, and money. There is nothing wrong with success, status, and money, if you have the roots and foundation to support your upward and forward movement.

Many of us are in such a hurry on the fast track of life to "make it"— whatever that means for each of us. "Making it" for you may be an organization you want to join, a promotion, money, status, or to be the "best" mom in the neighborhood. For whatever you desire in life to be lasting and sustainable, you must have a foundation and roots. Once you are caught up in the whirlwind of success and the upward and forward lifestyle, it is very difficult to sustain that life without a solid foundation.

We focus our lives on the prize, many times to discover when we reach our upward and forward goals that we have created hollow, busy lives. If you haven't developed any practices or disciplines grounding you in health and well-being, when the storms of your personal and business life come you can suffer severe damage.

Success without balance, roots, and happiness creates "golden shackles." Success and happiness based on the upward and forward movement of our lives can only be fed and sustained with experiences that focus on moving upward and forward. This is why people spend so much time and money looking for the thrill. Many individuals pay large amounts of money to spend a weekend proving they can walk over hot coals, and they don't realize they are walking over hot coals in their everyday lives. In the country that champions freedom we wear "golden shackles" of our own making. We have blindly followed a path to seek happiness limiting our lives by focusing upward and forward. As a result we have collectively created a hollowness of our soul; we have put our lives on autopilot. We have chosen this path upward and forward. We now have the ability to make new healthy choices today.

The Direction of Happiness: Inward and Downward

The movement toward living an intentional life of balance and happiness is a movement inward and downward. This movement creates the rootedness we need to be grounded and nourished. If we first focus our lives moving inward and downward, we naturally will move upward and forward to continue our natural growth throughout our lives. Think of the foundation of a home. A solid home is based on a foundation. This foundation for our happiness is cultivated by moving inward to our authentic Self (see Figure 3–1). Living from the inside out creates our anchor, our guidance, the key to living a life of happiness (see Figure 3–2).

Just as a great oak tree sustains its wondrous growth upward and forward, it naturally does this because the oak is rooted deeply inward and downward first. The direction to discover happiness begins inward and downward followed by the movement upward and forward. Just as a tree is dependent upon its deeply grounded roots, we must be grounded in our values, beliefs and self-knowledge. As we begin to really listen to our authentic voice, our growth will naturally move downward to create a strong healthy center.

Figure 3–1

Figure 3–2

Each of us has a computer chip, an inner voice, a spark of light within us seeking fulfillment. Many of us have not had respect for this inner light. We have ignored this light, denied it, or tamed it so we do not experience its power anymore. We have created so many distractions in our lives that we cannot feel its energy and power. But this innate power or light will never be extinguished. It will keep gnawing at us and calling our name until we listen. The longer we ignore what our inner spark is calling us to do, the more elusive true happiness will become.

When we honor this voice or light, if we listen, it will guide us, draw us, lead us to true happiness and fulfillment, and our purpose will naturally unfold. We will be led home to our Self. The oak tree's acorn falls to the earth and does not struggle or apply force to become an oak tree. The tiny acorn naturally unfolds and roots itself into the ground eventually developing deep rich roots that will sustain the oak for the hundreds of years of life as it grows powerfully upward and forward.

Your Global Positioning System

We have our own inner global positioning system (GPS). When we choose to accept responsibility for our own happiness, we become aware of our internal compass.

Our internal GPS will guide us. We can choose to be more aware of our internal GPS, pay attention, and then choose the direction of our life. Just like the GPS in our automobiles, we are given the information, we are guided, but we are not forced to follow or listen to the directions. We don't have to turn where the GPS tells us to turn, we always have free will. It is our guide, our beacon, our light calling us to live an intentional life. We can ignore it, and many of us do. Our internal GPS is programmed in the direction of happiness. The destination is already keyed in, it is certain. We can trust the process with confidence.

You may go down some bumpy roads, travel through uncertain weather, but just listen to the voice on your inner GPS, follow the map. There are certain things that can damage your trust of your inner GPS. These are shame, fear and anger, they create uncertainty and chaos.

Spirituality: The Movement Inward and Downward

True spirituality is to be aware that if we are interdependent with everything and everyone else, even our smallest, least significant thought, work, and action have real consequences throughout the universe.

Sogyal Rinpoche

There is a clear difference between spirituality and religion. The general public many times confuses the two terms; they are very different and have diverse implications. Spirituality is your connection with your soul and God, Creator, Source, Higher Power, Nature, or whatever name you call the Holy. Religion is "a personal or institutionalized system grounded in belief in and reverence for a supernatural power or powers regarded as creator and governor of the universe."[1]

The mind-body medicine movement and the research done in this field have taken us into a new direction in recent years. "Spirituality and Medicine" is a course at the University of Texas Southwestern Medical School that teaches students how to talk with patients about their spirituality and disease. More than half of the medical schools in the country, from Harvard to Stanford, now offer such courses. Illustrious institutions such as Harvard, Duke, Columbia, and the National Institute of Health have researchers attempting to assess the relationship of spirituality and health.

There is a body of research exploring the neurological underpinnings of spiritual experience and health. Brain circuits are affected when we have spiritual experiences. Many researchers believe that spirituality affects your health, happiness, and well-being.

Many medical research centers now study the mind-body connection and call their research, "The Study of Religion/Spirituality and Health." Columbia University's new center is called "Study of Science and Religion." I have a problem when institutions do studies and interchange the words religion with spirituality. Spirituality and religion are very different. Yes, they may at times be relational, but not necessarily. Spirituality and religion can be woven together into the fabric of your life, but may not be. Through my many years of experience I have known many religious individuals in my practice who were devoted to their religion and God, but were not spiritual. I have also known many individuals who are incredibly spiritual but have no use for formal religion.

In this book I focus on the more inclusive term, *spirituality,* because everyone has a spiritual nature, but many individuals are not religious.

A friend of mine, who is a psychiatrist, and I were having coffee the other day and he said that in his practice he believed that 90 percent of his patients had spiritual problems presenting themselves as psychiatric conditions. The fact of the matter is that we are mind, body, and soul. Science and spirituality are confirming that these are all inextricably woven together. We must take seriously the requirement to nourish all three for our mental, physical, and spiritual well-being.

Science is getting very interested in what happens in the brain when we have spiritual experiences. We now have technology—such as FMRIs, EEGs, PET scans, and blood, saliva and urine tests—that actually show us what is happening in real time in our bodies when we perform certain activities.

Dr. Andrew Newberg of the University of Pennsylvania uses brain imaging to identify where the brain's spirituality circuits are located and how the brain reacts to spiritual and religious practices. Dr. Newberg says, "There is no way to determine whether the neurological changes associated with spiritual experience mean that the brain is causing those experiences or is instead perceiving a spiritual reality."[2]

There is a new area of emerging science called neurotheology. Neurotheologians do research on the effects of religious or spiritual practices upon the brain.

This new science is begging the question, "Are we wired for spirituality?" Do we have inner antennas or receptors that respond to "spiritual experiences"? When we choose to open our souls, do specific areas of our brain receive this energy, light, or electrical stimulation? We are seeing research that is saying yes.

Living from the Inside Out

After many years of vast experience, I have come to see that the path to one's true Self comes from living from the inside out. It is the keystone teaching of all the great religious and spiritual teachers throughout time. Whether it is Jesus, Buddha, Lao Tsu, Confucius, Mohammad, Gandhi, Thoreau, Emerson, Dr. Martin Luther King, Jr., Mother Teresa, Father Thomas Keating, or a host of other great holy leaders, their teachings can be distilled down into one basic message: Look within, listen, and live from your center.

The Bible, the Torah, the Koran, the Upanishads, the Vedas, the I Ching, the Discourses of Buddha, the Midrash, and the Bhagavad Gita— all of the seminal religious texts in our world—are grounded in teaching us how to live from the inside out. Each sacred text may have different nuances, diverse methods, and varied perspectives on how to live from the inside out, but the essential message is the same.

Not only is this message found in the minds of great teachers and the sacred texts, we also see it reflected in nature and science. Every tree has heartwood at its center; every organic system evolves from the inside out. All species share in the awe-inspiring design of this magnificent universe.

Why do we think we can redirect the flow of our lives when nature, science, spirituality, and religion all whisper, "Look within...come home"? We are obsessed with seeking happiness, peace of mind, and balance on the exterior, and as a result are at odds with the natural world into which we are inextricably woven. We, as a society, a nation, and as individuals, only need to look at a newspaper, listen to the news, or read a magazine to realize that we continue to move our lives in an outward direction. As we continue the relentless search to accumulate more possessions, money, and power, we continue to sink deeper into apathy, confusion and fear.

Living from the inside out is the only way to find balance and truly experience an authentic sense of happiness in our lives. As we individually, and as a community, define true happiness, it must be grounded in a commitment to organically living from our core—that sacred space of vital energy and unlimited potential. Clearly our world, our families, and our selves cannot be sustained if we do not choose, on every level of our lives, to live from the inside out. We must become intimate with ourselves and be happy and in balance inside ourselves, before we can truly experience happiness with another person, our families, or our communities.

Making a life commitment to live from the inside out will transform your life and the world in which we live. I challenge you, your family, your corporation, and your community to begin living from the inside out, with integrity, love, and balance in every aspect of your life. When you choose to live from the inside out beginning from this very moment, our planet will shift from what it is now an unsustainable and dying system, to a flourishing and sustainable system for every part of our human family and for every forest, river, and bird on Earth.

When you choose to begin your journey inward and downward to your authentic Self I promise you will enjoy the experience of living from the inside out.

~ BEGIN TODAY ~

Ask Your Self   In what direction is my life going?

Do I listen to my own "GPS"?

Do I consider spirituality important in my life?

Tell Your Self   I am living from my inside out.

Give Your Self   Read a journal to reflect your decision-making process.

Visit someplace you consider spiritual.

Create your own small ritual of gratitude to practice daily.

CHAPTER 4

Finding Your Pulse

I SPENT YEARS of my life going to medical doctors, experimenting with a wide array of medications to ease my chronic piercing pain. From a tiny tick that lived in the fields of Oak Haven, I had contracted Lyme disease, a bacterial disease that affects the neurological system on many levels. My nightmare began with horrendous headaches, then progressed to pain in my legs so severe that I could not walk, and was soon followed with delayed thought processes and confusing speech patterns. For someone who had enjoyed a lifelong sense of control over my mind, my body, and my entire life, this was hell on earth. I was eventually diagnosed, and after several courses of drug treatment over many months, the doctors pronounced me cured.

I may have been "cured," but the horrendous haunting pain never stopped, and my body was consistently failing me in many ways. I found it incredibly difficult to run my ranch, lift bags of horse feed, and round up mares and foals. Eventually, I found myself having to talk to my feet, one at a time, and lovingly coax each foot to remember how to walk, step by step by agonizing step. The 50-pound bags of horse feed I was accustomed to picking up and throwing over my hip now felt as if they were full of lead. In my stables that once were a place of great joy, I would collapse on bales of alfalfa, sobbing as the pain piercing through my body threatened to drive me mad. I could feel the seeds of depression sprouting and growing. Life felt hopeless.

One night while I was lying on the couch, heating pads covering my body to ease the pain, I was absent-mindedly channel surfing when I was suddenly riveted by a beautiful woman in a white physician's coat talking about acupuncture. She described the efficacy of acupuncture for a variety of diseases, and that it was especially effective with pain management. I was desperate, and also very curious. My husband and my daughter are both physicians, and we have enjoyed many spirited dinner-table talks about alternative medicine and the future of integrated medicine: The science and the possibilities of acupuncture had been the topic of many of our lively discussions.

The next day I called my physician, got a referral to a Chinese medical doctor, and a new odyssey began. The first time I met Dr. Logan, she skipped the small talk and went from one wrist to the other, feeling tiny pulses in both of my arms. As she felt the delicate drumbeats under my skin, she mumbled softly and once in a while grunted "hmmm" with a wisdom I couldn't fathom. At one point she stopped suddenly and asked me to stick out my tongue, which she examined carefully. As I lay there pensively, watching the examination with great curiosity, I knew deep within that this woman would help me. A healing wave of hope flowed through my pain-riddled body.

Dr. Logan said that even though Western doctors had pronounced me cured, she could tell, from feeling my pulses in my arms that residual Lyme disease still coursed through my cells. The disease may not have been showing up on the Western threshold tests for Lyme disease, but she could tell it was still living deep inside me from my weak and struggling pulses. Dr. Logan performed acupuncture and created a mixture of herbs that she said would work on an elemental level of my cells and finally extract the bacteria from my body.

Dr. Logan explained that Chinese medicine listens to each person's body through the pulses. The pulses serve as information centers that tell us when we are out of rhythm in our bodies, and, subsequently, out of rhythm in our lives. This ancient form of medicine depends on honoring the rhythms of our bodies and our bodies' relationship to nature's cycles of spring, summer, fall, and winter. The body is in a constant fluid, or dynamic, state of transformation as it moves through the seasons of the year and the seasons of our lives: All our bodily organs function differently in the fall than they do in the spring.

It all rang true to me. Here at Oak Haven, the plant and animal kingdom flow with the rhythms of Mother Nature. If my dog Chloe sheds in the spring and puts on coarse heavy hair for the winter, it would make sense that as the seasons change, there are also subtle shifts inside her body. If the cells of our organs are constantly shedding and being recreated, why wouldn't our organs change with the seasons also? And, if all of nature is changing as the seasons cycle throughout the year, why shouldn't we do the same? We are not separate from nature. We come from the earth and are returned to the earth, inextricably woven into the fabric of nature.

The pulses also reveal immediate information on the stress levels in the body. If there is a physical, psychological, or spiritual disease in the body, your pulse tells the story. Disease in any of these areas will produce stress on your body showing up in the pulses. There is no hiding from the truth of the pulse. An individual can tell a physician that they only have a headache, or a stomach pain, and hold back what else is going on in the body, but the pulses are a mirror to what your body is experiencing on every level.

Three weeks later, as I picked up a can of tomato soup in a grocery store, I noticed that for the first time in a year, I was walking without instructing my feet, one at a time, to walk. My head had reconnected with my feet. I held the soup to my chest and began to cry tears of pure joy and gratitude. Over the next year, the pain gradually subsided, until, at last, it was completely gone.

That experience was my ultimate lesson in compassion for the vast number of people in our world living with chronic pain on a daily basis. Chronic pain produces chronic stress. With every hardship comes a gift, and the gift of this horrible experience was a new way of looking at my body and the natural universe. Chinese medicine teaches us that every living cell, every living system's survival, depends upon its ability to not only hold a deep reverence for the pulse, rhythm and cycles of our bodies, our lives and our families, but that if we do not listen deeply, we will lose connection with our life force, get sick, and even perish.

Listening to Your Pulse

Finding our pulse is about living from the inside, about tuning in to the rhythms of our lives. When we find our authentic pulse, our very own rhythm, we will find our true Self. I define the Self as our vital force, the energy of life, our soul, our breath. When we discover and revere the pulse of our lives, our primal rhythm, we can begin to understand what authentic work-life balance can mean and explore the kaleidoscope of new possibilities available in every moment on every level of our lives.

Pulse diagnosis is one of the more important diagnostic tools used in acupuncture. The pulse provides the practitioner with immediate and specific information that can lead to a diagnosis and tell why the body is out of balance. Just listen to some of the pulse descriptions in acupuncture: floating (superficial), sinking (deep), slow, rapid, hesitant, slippery, tight, wiry, big, thin, empty, full, short, long, hurried, intermittent, and knotted. I just love the words they use to describe what is going on inside the patient.

Start with yourself and see if any of these words describe you. Do they describe your spouse, your coworker, your mother, or your neighbor? Maybe our pulses reveal what kind of life we are living and the pulse is a reflection of what is happening in our lives.

It is also interesting that the strength and quality of our pulses declines as we age. Men are generally stronger on the left and women are generally stronger on the right. This is interesting since the right side of the brain is the creative side, and the left is the task-logical side of the brain. There are seasonal influences on the brain; each season of the year affects the pulse differently.[1]

Acupuncture uses the pulses to identify any imbalances in your body. It is an ancient science that today is used as an accepted and legitimate treatment for many conditions. A large body of research is being done by the National Institutes of Health (NIH) on acupuncture, and they have found clear evidence that acupuncture helps relieve some pain. They now state that acupuncture is an acceptable alternative or adjunct to conventional medical therapy for many conditions. The NIH has also revealed there is considerable evidence that acupuncture causes the release of endorphins—natural pain relieving substances—and now acupuncture is offered in many pain clinics.[2]

Research shows acupuncture has been used effectively in the treatment of addictions, depression, nausea due to pregnancy and chemotherapy, asthma, and infertility.

One of the greatest influences upon your body, which is reflected in your pulses, is chronic stress.

Stress: The Good, The Bad, The Ugly

Stress is epidemic in the twenty-first century. In my life and work, I have witnessed firsthand the physiological, psychological, and spiritual effects of stress on our lives.

Stress is a natural and essential part of life. Our stress response is designed to protect and preserve our lives. We need a certain amount of stress in our lives but not too much for too long. Our bodies are constantly responding to positive and negative stress. Positive stress motivates and drives us. We may get excited about working on a new project at work or moving to a new city for a new opportunity. Negative stress affects our physical and mental health and can rob us from experiencing true happiness.

Each of us had tremendous untapped potential, and each of us has passions we have never explored. Reaching our full potential in our lives is stopped by the stress of our fears. If you want to experience living an intentional life of true happiness you can't run from stress or avoid it. Stress is as much a part of life as breathing, eating, and drinking water. Stress is a constant in our lives. There is a reason for stress. Stress discovers our dark places and brings them to our attention. Each stressor that we perceive as an obstacle is actually an opportunity.

You know what the consequences are if you neglect a wound or a sore— it gets worse and can eventually lead to gangrene and amputation, or even worse, cost you your life. Stress will get worse if you ignore it and don't respect the gift it is offering you. Denying stress, like denying a wound, can make you rot on spiritual, psychological, and physical levels. Situational or acute stress can shift into chronic, continual, unabated stress.

Stress is your guide and can be quite a gift. Observe what stresses you. Try to embrace your stress and be compassionate with yourself. Most of the clients I have worked with are so hard on themselves. A common complain on their first visit is, "I just don't know what is wrong with me. I am just so stressed out. Other people can handle this kind of stress. I just can't." These individuals feel victimized and overwhelmed by the stress in their lives. The faster we try to override our stress with alcohol, sleep aids, drugs, eating, or the massive variety of other harmful behaviors, the more we create lives running from it. The more we live in denial or running from our stress, the more insidious ways our stress will discover to get our attention.

Stress is your teacher; you can run for a while, but it will find a way to get your attention. It will surface in your psychological or spiritual well-being at first and eventually reek havoc in your physical body. Your wondrous potential wants to be expressed in your life and anything that is holding your gift back will create the stress to let you know about it. Stress invites you to make new choices in your life and these choices require action. As you learn to deal with the stresses of your life, your incredible potential will unfold, leading you deeper on the path to true happiness.

We have an ancient brain that was created to protect our survival. This brain is called the *reptilian brain*. This reptilian brain is our fear system. The "fight or flight" response, residing in this primitive brain stem, is a pattern of physiological responses that prepares you to respond to an emergency.

When we are stressed, we release excitatory neurotransmitters. Your body responds to these hormones by increasing your heart rate, blood pressure, and respiration. More blood is pumped into your muscles, sending more oxygen to your muscles, brain, heart and lungs. Blood flow may increase 300 percent to 400 percent, preparing your lungs, muscles, and brain for added demands. The amount of sugar or glucose increases in your blood, which accelerates your metabolism so you can take immediate action in an emergency. Your blood thickens as platelets prepare to stop bleeding quickly. As the blood thickens, oxygen increases in red cells and promotes better function of the white cells that prevent infections. The spleen discharges red and white blood cells, allowing the blood to transport more oxygen.

Your "fight or flight" response is similar to the most advanced computer system in the world. Your body instantly prioritizes what it needs: it increases the blood supply to the brain, heart, and peripheral muscles, at the same time decreasing the blood supply to your digestive system and any other regions that are irrelevant. Whatever you do, you have to have the greatest respect and awe for your incredible body. It is obvious that your body is perfectly created to deal with immediate or acute stress.

Stress has an immediate effect on your mind and body in many ways:

‣ Memory: Becomes vague and inexact.

‣ Learning: Difficult learning and problem solving.

‣ Perception: Is limited and narrow.

❱ Attitude: Defensive and aggressive.

❱ Mood: Negative, wants to flee.

❱ Body: Jaws clench, muscles tense because you are ready for action.

❱ Physiological responses: There are immediate increases of heart rate, breathing rate, blood pressure, blood sugar, and adrenaline. Blood vessels constrict in face and hands and your digestive tract shuts down so your muscles get the needed blood.

THE FIGHT AND FLIGHT TEAM

The two survival hormones our body emits in our state of extreme stress are adrenaline and cortisol.

Adrenaline is produced and secreted by the adrenal glands. The adrenal glands are located adjacent to the kidneys and are responsible for the synthesis and secretion of different hormones that are essential for your body to function. Several stress hormones are produced in the adrenal glands, including epinephrine and cortisol. Adrenaline or epinephrine is involved in neural and hormonal processes in the body and is the important hormone in the fight or flight reaction to acute or sudden stress.

Cortisol has many functions. It is critical for the regulation of our metabolism and the body's use of proteins, carbohydrates, and fats, regulation of blood pressure, and cardiovascular function, and it helps our bodies manage stress. Cortisol is produced by the adrenal glands in response to signals from the pituitary gland and hypothalamus of the brain. The secretion of cortisol increases in response to psychological or physical stress of any kind. Following a stressful event, adrenaline levels return to normal while cortisol levels can remain elevated over a much longer period of time.

ACUTE VS. CHRONIC STRESS

Acute stress is anything you perceive as an immediate threat. Acute stress is your normal mental and physical response to an emergency or traumatic event. This may be an automobile accident, an argument with another person, or you losing a tennis match. Acute stress can be caused by any sense of danger, noise, crowding, hunger, or infection in your body. Acute stress occurs as a natural short term response and is healthy and normal. You release stress related chemicals into the body and they quickly dissipate from your body after the trauma or emergency.

Chronic stress is very different from acute stress. Chronic stress is ongoing stress that continues over a long period of time that does not diminish or go away. Chronic stress is unabated and continues to dwell in your mind and body, producing stress chemicals. Chronic stress is a poison to the rooting of your life. Chronic stress, just like many poisons, takes time to get into the system but does harm that can cause illness or death.

Recent scientific research is revealing that the effects of chronic stress are far-reaching. Continual high levels of cortisol destroy bone and muscle. This slows healing and normal cell replacement, disturbs metabolism and mental abilities, and weakens the immune system. Persistently high levels of chronic stress may lead to high levels of cortisol that stimulate your appetite resulting in weight gain and difficulty in losing unwanted weight.

Chronic stress produces chronic release of adrenaline and cortisol which damages the immune system and reduces one's ability to fight infection and inflammation in the body. Long-term elevated levels of adrenaline and cortisol affect many organs and systems in the body.

As your body continues to experience chronic stress, it starts to break down in many ways leading to a variety of conditions and diseases including heart disease, cancer, obesity, arthritis, insomnia, infertility, hypertension, migraine headaches, and digestive disorders, while also accelerating the aging process.

Everyone responds to stress differently because of past experiences and because we are each a product of our gene pool and how our ancestors handled stress. I believe that we must have great flexibility with individuals to discover what their particular stressors are and how they react to them. Rachel Yehuda, Ph.D., of Mt. Sinai Medical Center in New York says, "Stress management is no one-size-fits-all way to reduce stress. Study upon study has shown that simple relaxation does not work in many people. Telling someone who has been sensitized to stress to just relax is like telling an insomniac to just fall asleep."[3]

With emerging technology and science we are beginning to understand how chronic stress affects each individual in various degrees, and the catastrophic effects chronic stress has on our bodies. Neurological science is using scanning techniques that are giving us a deeper understanding of the miraculous physical processes of the body. Typical procedures may include an FMRI, a PET scan, or an EEG. We use FMRI

(Functional Magnetic Resonance Imaging) as a technique for determining which parts of the brain are activated by different types of situations, stressors, sensations, or activities. "Brain mapping" is achieved when the FMRI maps the increased blood flow to activated areas of the brain. With PET (Positron Emission Tomography) scans, a small dose of a chemical called a radionuclide combined with sugar is injected into the patient. The radionuclide emits positrons and the PET scanner rotates around the patient's head to detect the positron emissions given off by the radionuclide. Malignant tumors grow at such a fast pace that they will use more sugar, and the radionuclide attaches to the sugar. The computer then measures the amount of glucose in the picture and they can locate the concentration and make a diagnosis. An EEG (electroencephalogram) records electrical activity at a number of sites in the brain. Neurons produce electrical fields inside the brain, which are measured by the EEG. This test requires leads to be attached to the scalp and the brain's electrical activity is measured.

Researchers also use blood, saliva, and urine tests to evaluate the chemicals your body releases during stress and relaxation. A test for epinephrine and dopamine is most often done on a sample of urine, but it can also be done on a sample of blood taken from a vein. The most common test for measurement of the cortisol level uses the blood, but many times cortisol is measured through a saliva sample.

THE EFFECTS OF STRESS ON YOUR HEALTH
Here are just a few of the many studies available to show how stress has wide ranging effects on your body:

▶ *The Heart:* Research from Thomas Pickering, M.D., cardiologist at Cornell Medical Center, shows that stress causes the release of epinephrine from the adrenal glands into the blood. Epinephrine triggers blood platelets, the cells responsible for repairing blood vessels, to secrete large quantities of ATP, a high-energy phosphate molecule required to provide energy for the body. ATP causes the blood vessels to rapidly narrow, cutting off blood flow, triggering a heart attack or stroke.[4]

▶ *Stroke:* Lawrence Brass, M.D., associate professor of neurology at Yale Medical School, found that severe stress is one of the most potent risk factors for stroke, more than high blood pressure, even 50 years after the trauma. The rate of stroke among prisoners of World War II was eight times higher than among other veterans. Dr. Brass discovered stress can cause disease years after the initial event. The stress of being a POW was so severe it changed the way the individuals responded to stress, it sensitized them.[5]

▶ *Immune System:* Sheldon Cohen, Ph.D., professor of psychology at Carnegie Mellon University, gave 400 people a questionnaire designed to quantify the amount of stress they were under. He then exposed them to nose drops containing cold viruses. Ninety percent of the stressed subjects caught a cold. They had elevated levels of corticotrophin releasing factor, which interferes with the immune system.[6]

▶ *The Brain:* Dr. Amy F.T. Arnsten of Yale Medical School reported research showing that when individuals experience uncontrolled stress, an enzyme in the brain called protein kinase C activates, thus causing impairment in the short term memory and other functions in the executive decision part of the brain, the prefrontal cortex.[7]

▶ *Rheumatoid Arthritis:* The hormone prolactin is released by the pituitary gland in response to stress, which triggers cells that cause swelling in joints. In a study of 100 people with rheumatoid arthritis, Kathleen S. Matt, Ph.D., and colleagues at Arizona State University, found that levels of prolactin were twice as high among those reporting high degrees of interpersonal stress than among those not stressed.[8] Other studies have shown that prolactin migrates to joints, where it initiates a cascade of events leading to swelling, pain and tenderness.

▶ *Child Abuse Survivors:* Lawrence Brass, M.D., of Yale reported in a study of child abuse victims that the psychological stress children suffer from child abuse actually made the hippocampus—a structure in the middle of the brain—smaller than that of normal adults. The hippocampus is partially responsible for storing short-term memory. Dr. Brass states that this is evidence that psychological stress changes the brain's makeup.[9]

Chronic stress must be dealt with wherever it lives, such as your workplace (coworkers, boss, corporate environment, travel), your home (spouse, children, partner, or neighbor), and within yourself.

The Body's Stress Busters: Endorphins, Serotonin, Dopamine

Your body produces incredible "stress busters" in the form of healing chemicals and hormones. I will name just a few so you can get an idea of how every thought, emotion, and attitude has the ability to create powerful healing and happiness in your life.

ENDORPHINS: HELP IS ON THE WAY

The human body produces at least 20 different endorphins. Endorphins are produced by the body and can create a natural high. Endorphins are able to bind to neuroreceptors in the brain and give relief from pain by naturally blocking pain signals produced by the nervous system. Endorphins also interact with the opiate receptors in the brain to reduce your perception of pain, thus producing a similar action to drugs like codeine and morphine. Endorphins are naturally produced by a wide range of activities like deep breathing, meditation, eating spicy food, having sex, laughter, exercise, and many other means.

Endorphins affect the body and the mind in several ways: They relieve pain, they reduce stress, they enhance the immune system, they activate natural killer cells that boost the immune system against cancer cells and other diseases, and they delay the aging process.

Exercise creates endorphins. We label the experiences with terms like "runner's high" or "second wind." Making love increases endorphins 200 percent. Candice Pert of Johns Hopkins has documented the connection between orgasm and endorphins. Dr. David Weeks, a neuropsychologist at the Royal Edinburgh Hospital, found that women and men who have sex four to five times a week look more than 10 years younger than the average person who had sex twice a week.[10]

Certain foods increase your body's production of endorphins. Chocolate is a popular endorphin-producing food. Chili peppers increase the body's production of endorphins. The hotter the pepper, the greater the ability of your body to produce more endorphins.

Acupuncture, massages, hot baths, and showers stimulate the production of endorphins. Laughter triggers the release of endorphins, which not only relieve pain but enhance the healing process.

Meditation and guided imagery help the body produce endorphins, reduce blood pressure, and create a feeling of well-being. Music produces physical and psychological healing in the body as the music enhances endorphin production.

SEROTONIN

Scientific research has led us to the discovery of opiate-like chemicals in our bodies that connect with opiate-specific receptors in the brain and spinal cord. Serotonin is one of these incredible chemicals that creates feelings of well-being. Serotonin is a neurotransmitter involved in the transmission of nerve impulses, and neurotransmitters are exceptionally important because they carry impulses between nerve cells. Serotonin is the key to cellular communication as it keeps all of our cells communicating with each other. Serotonin is a chemical that helps you have a happy feeling, keeps your moods balanced by promoting sleep, calming anxiety and alleviating depression. Tension is eased when serotonin is released.

Low serotonin levels may lead to depression, many sleep disorders including insomnia, obesity, headaches, fibromyalgia, and many other conditions. The number one mental health problem is depression. It affects 15 million Americans who spend $3 billion a year on trying to deal with it.

DOPAMINE

The brain produces another neurotransmitter called dopamine. Dopamine affects your brain processes that control movement of your body, emotional response, and your ability to experience pain and pleasure. Dopamine also plays an essential role in your mental and physical health. Dopamine works by attaching itself to specific proteins called receptors, and the binding of the dopamine molecule with a receptor initiates a cascade of biochemical events inside the cell.

Dopamine is a very important chemical produced by the brain. It helps in the effective transmission of messages from one nerve cell to the next. It helps one cell talk to the next. Individuals with Parkinson's disease have decreased amounts of dopamine in two structures deep in the brain, the basal ganglia and substantia nigra. This becomes important as dopamine coordinates our movements, both balance and walking.

Poisons That Disturb Your Pulse and Kill the Root

There are poisons that can kill your pulse. These poisons may not destroy your healthy pulse immediately but over time they will eat away at your precious life. These poisons are toxic emotions that will continually circulate through your system, distorting your mind, body, and soul. They can destroy and prevent you from being healthy and prospering. Fear, anger, hate, shame, guilt, envy or jealousy, worry, victimization, pessimism, apathy, and greed can rob you of the nourishment you desperately need to live the life of true happiness you desire.

Each of these emotions may affect your mental health first, but it is only a matter of time before they actually grow and actually infect your body and soul. I take these poisons very seriously because I have seen my share of lives shattered from the ravages of these emotions. So please take the following conditions seriously.

FEAR

Fear is the most powerful emotion we experience next to love. Fear is at the root of greed, anger, hate, shame, envy, worry, and victimization. All of the great spiritual and religious leaders and their texts tell us fear will impede your full potential in your mind, body and soul. Fear is a poison if you desire to live a life of true happiness. Fear cannot be avoided as long as we are human, but the four roots teach us healthy ways to deal with our everyday fears. Fear creates stress chemicals that when released into the body can create illness.

ANGER

Anger separates us not only from those we love, but from ourselves. Anger is a poison that will rob you of real intimacy and community. Anger is a voice that will continue to grow like a wild fire destroying your life. Anger must be respected and listened to because anger is telling you something in your life is broken and needs healing. Never deny or dismiss your anger. The stress of living with chronic anger can affect your health. Embrace your anger by journaling it out of you or sharing your feelings with a friend or counselor. Anger is a gift that will lead you to living an intentional life.

HATE

Hate paralyzes your life. Hate is separation from all of life. Hate is violence within you that will inevitably seep into every facet of your life. No seeds of happiness can grow in hate. If you are experiencing hate I suggest you get help from a counselor or clergy person. Hate is lethal to the mind, body, and soul. When you choose to hate someone, that person controls your life. You have surrendered your power to that individual or group. Hate stops you from producing the loving hormones you need to heal.

SHAME

Shame is when we feel flawed. Shame is toxic and is like living with an invisible cloud over our hearts. Shame usually has its genesis in our childhood with issues concerning our original families. Shame is difficult to sort out alone, and I continue to find it sad that so many of us have spent our life plagued with shame. Shame is a stumbling block to experiencing true happiness. Toxic shame can lead to depression, and your body may literally shut down.

GUILT

Guilt is feeling not worthy. Guilt feels like an albatross has taken up residence on our backs. Guilt is toxic, and I have worked with many individuals whose lives have been lost to guilt. Guilt is living your life looking in the rearview mirror. This is no way to live. The past is over and done. Guilt is like a cancer that eats away at your mental, physical and spiritual health.

ENVY OR JEALOUSY

I believe that the reason this is one of the Ten Commandments (thou shall not covet) is that envy plants the seeds of self-destruction and the destruction of others. Envy is the root of murder, stealing, infidelity, violence, and so much more. When you live a life desiring what others have you can never be at peace or be happy. Envy is a very serious spiritual situation. You are given your life to live with your own purpose. It is illogical to envy what others have because if it was destined to be yours it would be. Most individuals with envy are living in a kind of hell, with the delusion that if they only had what another person had—beautiful spouse, great job, new car, children, or a big house—they would be happy. True happiness is never found in what someone else has. True happiness is acquired when you live from the inside out, not from the outside in.

WORRY

Worry is negative guided imagery. When we allow our minds to imagine what "could" happen, it is nothing more than negative guided imagery. Our worries are not real, but worrying will rob you of your life. The fact is most of your worries will never happen, and worrying will only keep you living in a state of fear and uncertainty. Worry creates incredible stress chemicals and will make you sick. Wouldn't you rather live in a state of confidence and happiness? Every time you worry, stop immediately and say a one-to-five word affirmation to stop this nasty habit. Worry is nothing but a bad habit that does nothing good for your life. When I begin to worry, I smile and say, "I am so grateful for my life." Gratitude is an antidote to worry.

VICTIMIZATION

We live in a world where individuals feel entitled and expect certain things. If these expectations are not met the person may feel like a victim. How many times do you hear, "Why did this happen to me? I don't deserve this? I did everything I was supposed to, this just shouldn't happen to me?" Victimization is truly living an insufficient life. A victim mentality can not only ruin your life but the life of those who love you. Take responsibility for your life. You are the product of all of the decisions you made and the ones you chose not to make. Why are you exempt from bad things happening to you? Again, life is a classroom, not a prison. Individuals who live a life as a victim are in prison, yet the key to freedom is already in the door. I have discovered that most victims don't want to open that door because they don't want to take responsibility for their own lives. Be the hero of your life, not the victim.

PESSIMISM

This is definitely a poison to the roots of true happiness. Pessimism is always living as if the cup is half empty, not half full. Most events in your life are neutral, like driving your car or getting the mail from your mail box, but it is your attitude that will define your experience. It is important to realize we now have research on the healthy effects of optimism. Optimists are healthier, have more fun, and live longer than negative individuals. It's your life. You choose.

APATHY

Apathy is a real death sentence to your life. When you just don't have curiosity, don't care, and don't get involved in life, you are dead. Apathy is seductive because you just sit on the sidelines of life, criticize others, and do nothing. Whatever philosophy, spirituality, or religion you espouse, none of them honor apathy. Apathy is living as a zombie in a dynamic, exciting world. The most horrible events and injustices in the world can occur under the guise of apathy. Remember apathy is the opposite of love.

GREED

Greed is a fear-driven emotion. Greed is when you believe that you never have enough. Individuals who are greedy live in a philosophy of scarcity. They believe that there is not enough money, food, or love. When you are greedy there can never be enough of anything. You can really never live in trust because you have to live a life of vigilance. I choose to live in the philosophy of abundance. Trusting that there is enough for all of us, we are just flawed in our allocation of resources.

*   *   *

When you rid yourself of the poisons that are stopping you from experiencing true happiness, your virtues will emerge and flourish. A kaleidoscope of virtues will emerge, such as: energy, forgiveness, gratitude, love, compassion, patience, perseverance, vision, curiosity, optimism, passion, and happiness.

Every Obstacle Is an Opportunity

The moment you choose to live an intentional life of true happiness you will begin to experience obstacles as opportunities for your growth. You will choose to have a new awareness of your pulse of life. The pain of the loss of a job, a failed relationship, or a serious illness can be extremely difficult and decimating, but when you have embedded your life in the four roots of happiness and balance you can flourish after such devastating events occur. Let's face it, none of us go through life without loss and suffering. It is not *if* we suffer and experience losses, it is *when* we do. This is why it is so critical to have a strong healthy pulse. No matter what decimating events occur, you are rooted deeply within your Self.

As you learn to live an intentional life of happiness you will learn to find your own pulse as you listen deeply to the rhythms of your Self, family, and your community. Anytime your pulse begins floating—or gets tight, sinking, empty, hurried, or knotted—just stop. Listen to what your stress is telling you. Your body is trying to give you information about your life. Finding your own pulse, and reverently listening, will lead you to a life of happiness and balance.

∼ Begin Today ∼

Ask Your Self   When I check my pulse, is it rapid, empty, hurried, or what?

What are three things that stress me most?

What are the poisons (fear, anger, shame, etc.) that are affecting my pulse?

Tell Your Self   My life is healthy and constantly being replenished.

Give Your Self   Listen to a guided imagery tape on stress reduction.

Write a list of poisons you want to rid your life of.

Enjoy a relaxing massage and experience your body's calm.

PART II: Y O U R   R O O T S

CHAPTER 5

S.E.L.F.
The Four Roots

AS I LOOKED at the menu and drank my coffee, I was feeling satisfied with my life. Our ranch and the horse operation were the products of many years of hard work, and my education was finally over with the completion of my doctorate and with one daughter in college and the other in medical school. Here I was eating breakfast at my favorite restaurant, The Flying Biscuit, waiting to meet a new friend of just a couple of months. Susan walked in late after seeing her last patient in the clinic and we started the usual chit-chat about kids, husbands, our careers, and politics.

After a great lunch, including those famous hot biscuits covered with cranberry apple butter, we headed to our cars. As I fastened my seat-belt I thought it was one of those moments that you just feel great to have a good friend and your life is in a quiet flow, when all of a sudden Susan stopped outside of her car, turned around, and came back to my car. I rolled down my window and smiled, "What's going on?" Susan looked troubled and leaned against my car. She said, "I don't know how to tell you this. I tried to talk to you about this at lunch but I just didn't know how to say it. So here it is. You may never speak to me again after I say this but I have to say this. Kathleen, you are living an insufficient life." She patted me on the shoulder and walked away to her car and drove off.

I sat there in a state of shock. I couldn't move. Did I hear her right? How could anyone tell someone else they were living an insufficient life? What kind of real friend would do that? I raced from rage to panic then to confusion then back to rage again. I decided to put it out of my mind. After all she had only known me a few months and she didn't know how far I had come from that afflictive family of my childhood to now. She didn't know the insurmountable odds I had overcome. Who was she to tell me I was living an insufficient life? I chose to block her words out of my mind and return to my well-designed life.

There was only one problem. Those words began to haunt me. I repeated the question as I brushed my teeth. The question ruminated in my mind as I showered, drove my car, sat in meetings, as I ate dinner. "Am I living an insufficient life?"

I will forever be grateful for the courage of my friend Susan that day. Susan had a fresh look at her new friend's life and she saw so much more potential in my life than I could. My life could not go on the same way. The panic attacks many years ago at the top of the World Trade Center may have begun my journey, but this charge by Susan catapulted me into a more profound challenge.

I chose to spend time in self-examination and ferret out how my life could be insufficient. It took a few months, but many things eventually surfaced. What I discovered was my need for security and my fears of success and failure had paralyzed me. Again I realized that stress and fear are partners. I was trying to create my life to avoid or side-step my fears. After all my years of hard work, I had created a prison of my own making and told myself not to ask for anything more, because life was stable and I was afraid to risk the dream that was smoldering in my heart. But now there was no turning back. Susan had thrown down the gauntlet. I would not die living a safe, insufficient life.

I had achieved the benchmarks of success that were on my to do list: a five-star education, a great career in the financial world, a successful husband, two "perfect" children, a great home, grand cars, a housekeeper, a second home, and status. After a lifetime of hard work and sacrifices I had finally arrived at the destination of my desires when the hollow aching feeling seeped into my soul. I was lonely, tired, and overwhelmed. Stress and fear shadowed my life. I had done such a good job at keeping this haunting stress at bay, but I was finally tired of my life. I was both motivated and paralyzed by my own stresses and fears.

I wanted to live an intentional life discovering true happiness. I had to begin by being honest about myself, who I was, and where I wanted to go. I explored my restlessness and chose to begin a process of learning, like taking another class. Stress ceased to be terrifying and something to be avoided, risked, and feared. Stress became something to be embraced, and stresses and fears became my teachers.

Are you living an insufficient life? There are millions of individuals around the globe who would be stopped in their tracks if they were asked this question. Be grateful you are hearing this question right now. What if it was near the end of your life when even more of your life had passed you by and you were asked this question? This profound question stressed me out but it was one of the greatest gifts I have ever received. It drew me inward and downward to a great exploration and adventure to discover what my purpose was in my life, and now I know what true happiness and balance is.

What Are the Four Roots of True Happiness?

My journey of learning about the four roots of true happiness began in 1993. It was at this intersection of my life when I saw the PBS television series created by Bill Moyers, called *Healing and the Mind*. Mr. Moyers had traveled the world to seek out the most noted people and institutions working in the area of mind-body medicine. Mind-body medicine was the burgeoning field where science was beginning to research how certain practices of the mind directly affect the body. These research centers focused on various conditions such as cardiac disease, cancer, stress-related conditions, hypertension, pain, and depression.

These cutting-edge research centers developed practices that were creating the emerging fields of alternative, complementary, and blended medicine. I left the financial world and entered this new world of mind-body medicine. Spirituality had fascinated me since my childhood, so I decided to enter this field and explore the relationship between mind, body, and soul. I spent many years in post-graduate work learning the tenants of classic spirituality.

After those three years studying for a Master's of Divinity and the four years spent to complete my doctorate in Spirituality, I decided that I needed practical training and experience in various spiritualities and spiritual practices to better understand the mind-body connection from the spiritual aspect. I studied with Christian monks, priests and nuns, Jewish rabbis, Buddhist monks, Hindu priests, Taoist monks, a Sufi leader, and Native American shamans from various tribes. Over many years I studied with renowned spiritual and religious leaders, such as Dr. Thomas Keating, a Christian Trappist monk who wrote the seminal work on "Centering Prayer," which is the art of Christian meditation; His Holiness the Dalai Lama, a Tibetan Buddhist; Thich Nhat Hanh, a Vietnamese Buddhist monk; Bishop Desmond Tutu; Arun Gandhi, the grandson of Mahatma Gandhi; and President Jimmy Carter.

During that time I chose to enter clinical trainings with the medical doctors doing the pioneering research in this emerging field. I learned from cardiologist Dr. Dean Ornish at the Preventive Medicine Institute the approach he used effectively with his cardiac patients. His program involved diet, exercise, stress reduction, and group support. His results drew great interest in the medical field, and the most prestigious research institutions in the world began asking whether and how Dr. Dean Ornish's cardiac rehabilitation and wellness program was actually reversing heart disease. They were intrigued that if this method was actually reversing heart disease, what promise it could hold for healing other diseases, such as cancer, hypertension, insomnia, obesity, and diabetes.

I had studied with Dr. Herbert Benson at Harvard's Mind Body Institute, where he was using a similar method with his patients and was experiencing impressive results with his research. Dr. Rachel Naomi Remen at the Institute for the Study of Illness and Health in Bolinas, California, was using a comparable approach with cancer patients and experiencing great outcomes. I headed to Bolinas to learn more about how Dr. Remen was using these methods with cancer. I learned mindfulness meditation from Dr. Jon Kabat-Zinn who has done groundbreaking work in the area of mind-body medicine at the Stress Reduction Clinic at the University of Massachusetts.

It intrigued me how the similar approaches to disease, wellness, and healing were being used by different physicians for various diseases all over the world. All of these research centers were advocating the relaxation response or meditation. I was fascinated by the research studies on the healing effects of meditation on the mind and the body. I decided to study meditation and experience firsthand what effect it had upon me.

The great medical research centers of the world were mirroring what the great spiritual and religious leaders had been practicing for mental, physical, and spiritual well-being. Now I was really on fire. The two disciplines of medicine and spirituality had merged into the field of mind-body medicine. What I discovered about these newly integrated disciplines of medicine and spirituality was when individuals practiced the mind-body model, they became healthy and happy. My one foot was in the mind-body model and my other foot was firmly planted in the spiritual model.

There are practices that can keep us holding onto the promise and experience of our own happiness, balance, and well-being. These practices are a culmination of the merging of good science, basic psychology, and classic spirituality. The four roots are about you staying in the center of your life during the most difficult of circumstances. As you learn about the four roots, you will learn how to nourish and strengthen "your" center, listen to "your" self, and be connected to your Source. These practices have brought me a life of happiness and balance and have literally saved my life and the lives of countless others I have had the privilege of working with in my career.

I began working this four-part plan with myself, and then used these methods with groups of patients with various medical maladies—patients with cancer, heart and pulmonary diseases, obesity, anxiety and depression disorders, stress and sleep disorders, hypertension, depression, menopause, and more. The individuals and groups I worked with experienced impressive results almost immediately. It was thrilling.

Research is beginning to show us these four roots create true happiness and health at a very key level of our existence. The four roots— Serenity, Exercise, Love, and Food (or S.E.L.F.)—have an essential effect on our chemical processes of the body. For an example, something as simple as taking a warm shower or going for a walk for a few minutes increases the production of serotonin in the body. This is also true for participating in a group of some kind, such as playing cards, joining a book club, or meeting with a friend. Similar serotonin increases occur when you eat carbohydrates during your busy day. The key to living a life of balance and experiencing true happiness is for you to begin to make informed choices about your lifestyle. When you choose to live an intentional life of true happiness, you will enjoy learning how nourishing these four roots can bring you a dynamic life of balance.

I worked with children who were at risk in the inner city who had lost hope and any sense of purpose in their lives. I used these four practices with amazing results to disadvantaged youth in the inner city. I have taught these resources to high school and college students, teachers, professors, clients, and business executives, only to experience that their lives have been transformed by having real tools to work with.

These four practices became roots for the people in my work. I learned to augment these four practices and expand their meaning in my programs. These four essential healing elements in life rooted each individual's life through cancer treatments, heart disease, the death of a child, the loss of a job, depression, the stress of raising a family, or living through the hell of insomnia. As I observed the abundant miraculous changes in people's lives I felt as if each person was a tree with four basic roots and it was my responsibility to teach them about what their roots are and how to nourish them. It seemed like these folks were growing like a healthy tree, developing new lives with rich fruit, stronger branches, and lots of new growth.

*   *   *

Bill was referred into our cardiac rehab program after he suffered a major heart attack. He had been a senior-level executive at a major Fortune 500 company and had retired after 30 years of work, but he had never been out a day of work in 20 years. Bill loved his work, his coworkers, and his company. He came into the rehab group quite depressed and made it clear he did not want to be in this group of "sick people." His attitude was not unusual for many patients who enter cardiac rehab. There is great resistance when a successful individual develops a serious illness and is forced to stop his busy life and learn self care.

It was such an adventure for Bill entering the group as he began to learn and eventually enjoy learning the four roots of self-care. As he learned about how to eat, exercise, love, and manage his stress, he became more passionate about the possibility of reversing his heart disease. He began to look forward to our weekly meetings and eventually became the resource person for our group. Searching the Internet, reading voraciously, and opening his curious mind, he treated his experience with the four roots as if he were acquiring a new company and needed to learn everything about this new venture. I am very happy to say it has been five years since Bill entered our lives and he is not only happier and healthier than ever before, he has not had another cardiac event.

*   *   *

Discovering and nourishing the four roots is about living a life of true happiness, balance, and freedom by creating choices in your life that will nourish and sustain the roots of happiness. Health is living a lifestyle of freedom, happiness, and balance. Discovering the four roots of true happiness is about learning practices that connect us to your Source, to your Self, and to each other. These practices have been tried and tested for 30 years by others and I have worked with them for more than 15 years on a variety of individuals and groups.

*   *   *

Just after returning from M.D. Anderson Hospital, Elizabeth walked into my office, sat down in silence and stared at the floor. Elizabeth was a 37-year-old woman, with a husband and two children. She told me that she had a very aggressive cancer and her prognosis was not good. They told her even with her chemotherapy and radiation, the odds were very small that she would survive.

I gave her literature and studies on the four roots of self-care and told her that I would work with her in any way I could. She learned about foods that boosted her immune system, how exercise increased her immune function and how stress reduction practices and participation in a support group elevate the healing chemicals of your body that helped her immune function. Elizabeth has been faithful in practicing the four roots, and she is now five years past her initial diagnosis. No matter what happens in the future, her children and husband have had five more years with this wonderful woman. The four roots have given Elizabeth hope.

*   *   *

At the annual meeting of the American Society of Clinical Oncology in May of 2005, one of the major headlines of the conference was about simple lifestyle interventions in cancer, not only to ward off disease, but to help those who already have cancer. Simple steps in your lifestyle, such as cutting the fat in your diet and exercising, were shown to reduce the risk of cancer's recurrence.[1] Your diet and exercise are two of the essential roots to balance and happiness.

I invite you to learn about the four roots of health and happiness. The wonderful thing is that you don't have to have a critical condition to learn about this lifestyle. It is the optimal wellness program for health, longevity, and happiness. By exploring how to live a lifestyle grounded in these four roots, by developing your Self, you will be more complete, more balanced, and more mindful in every aspect of your life. More fulfilled and more capable of giving and receiving love—*really* experiencing happiness.

Defining the Self

I define *Self* as the life force that is our soul, our passion, and our purpose. The Self is your light and primal energy. The life force or Self is identified by different names in various cultures: *prana* in Hindu, *chi* in Chinese, and *ruah* in Hebrew. Ancient cultures define the Self with images such as energy of life, vital force, air, breath, and spirit. *Self* is at the core of human existence. It is the foundation for our mental, physical, and spiritual well-being. From these traditions, I draw the definition of Self I use in my work.

In spirituality we use the image of a spiraling circle when we talk about the Self on its journey to fulfillment. The line begins on the outside of the circle and rotates inward over and over again until the line stops in the middle of the circle. Imagine the image of a hurricane swirling powerfully on the outside but as a hurricane spirals and as you reach the eye of the hurricane, it is calm, powerful, and awing. You, your Self, begin the spiritual journey on the outside of the hurricane where wind and objects move fast and frantically. There are your anger, fears, grief, and attachments. You learn in each rotation how your cravings and attachments are keeping you on the outside of the hurricane and on periphery of true happiness. You realize the more you become aware of what is keeping you on the outside the more you know what is hindering you on your spiritual journey to the center. As you release anger your soul becomes lighter and happier and will naturally move inward. As you surrender your fears you are less weighted and naturally continue to migrate toward the center. This is a very simple metaphor for the spiritual life. The Holy, the Divine, is in the center, the eye, like a magnet calling us home to live our authentic life. The more we heal our Self the more we will naturally be drawn to the center to the place of serenity, peace, and healing.

The four roots of true happiness nourish your life and support your Self throughout the journey to the center of your life where you continually discover happiness and purpose. Whether you are dealing with emptiness, stress, disease, medical conditions, greed, anger, or loss, these four roots can help lead you home. These roots have been the source of happiness in my life for many years and these anchors have never failed me, especially at difficult times when I perceived that the world and others had failed me.

After traveling around the world giving speeches and listening to thousands of individuals, a common concern emerged: "How, in my busy life of work, family, and community responsibilities, do I find my Self?" This perennial question posed by so many people challenged me to find an answer. My own experience, training, and education led me to create my life's work in the fields of stress, happiness, balance, spirituality, and work-life balance.

Work-Life Balance

Work-life balance is becoming a common term in corporations and in public life. When I talk about work-life balance this does not only mean individuals and parents who work outside the home. I have never known a parent who stayed at home with the children who wasn't working harder than many others I know. I define work-life balance as an awareness of your life force, and a discovery of intimacy, serenity, purpose, fulfillment and happiness in every aspect of your life: work, family, community, and Self. I have subsequently developed a system to help individuals create, explore, and sustain balance and true happiness on a daily basis. The four roots S.E.L.F.—Serenity, Exercise, Love, and Food—are part of this (see Figure 5–1).

The challenge we face today is not only to maintain and fuel the Self, but also to discover daily sources of inspiration, energy and strength that allow us to find renewal, fulfillment, and balance in new and dynamic ways. With so many responsibilities at work, at home, and in the community, it is extremely challenging for modern individuals to maintain and nourish a sense of self in their daily lives.

There are four simple methods, or roots, that can be effortlessly woven into the fabric of life: You won't have to add anything to your "to do" lists, and your life will become infused with a new sense of balance, order and, most of all, with time for the things that truly nourish you and create happiness in your life. These four roots were derived from the diverse medical models that I have studied and practiced through the years. The four roots integrate a tried and true medical model, good psychology and classic spirituality.

Serenity   Food

Exercise   Love

Figure 5–1

Why Four Roots?

We have research that shows making these four roots the foundation of your self-care practice prevents, slows, or reverses a multitude of diseases and conditions. I will discuss a few of the diseases and conditions that the four roots have had a significant effect on.

▶ *Heart Disease:* Heart disease is the number one killer in America, affecting more than 12 million people. Sadly, 250,000 people with heart attacks will die each year before they get to the hospital. Heart disease is the leading cause of death in women over 40 years old, especially after menopause. More women die of heart disease than all other cancers combined. Once a woman reaches the age of 50, her risk for heart disease increases dramatically. The pioneering cardiologist, Dr. Dean Ornish, was one of the first in medicine to begin researching how diet, exercise, group support, and stress management not only reduces the risk of heart disease, but can actually reverse heart disease.

▶ *Cancer:* Over 1 million people every year are diagnosed with cancer in the United States. Lung cancer is the leading cause of cancer-related death in both women and men. Breast cancer is the most common cancer among American women. Approximately one in eight women will develop breast cancer in her lifetime. Breast cancer is the leading cause of cancer death among women ages 35 to 54. Colon cancer will be diagnosed in 140,000 people each year. More than 180,000 men will be diagnosed with prostate cancer this year and more than 30,000 men will die of the disease. All of these cancers are positively affected by practicing the four roots and these four roots provide a method to reduce the recurrence of cancers.

▶ *Obesity:* Today 16 percent of all children and teens in this country are overweight, and 65 percent of all people age 20 and older are overweight or obese. Excess weight and obesity are serious health threats because they are major risk factors for cardiovascular disease, hypertension, diabetes, and other serious health problems. The current generation of children may become the first in American history to live shorter lives than their parents. Medical expenditures attributed to both overweight and obesity have reached over $75 billion.[2] A study published in the *New England Journal of Medicine* followed 900,000 adults for 16 years. They found a high body mass index was associated with up to 20 percent of cancer deaths in women and 14 percent in men.[3] The four roots provide the foundation for a healthy lifestyle for each individual and the entire family.

▶ *Hypertension:* Over 50 million people in the United States have hypertension, or high blood pressure. One in four adults has hypertension, which is defined as systolic blood pressure over 140 and diastolic blood pressure over 90. Research shows that practicing the four roots lowers blood pressure. In many studies patients have not only lowered their blood pressure, but many have been able to stop their medication all together.

▶ *Chronic Pain:* A new survey done by *USA Today*/ABC/Stanford University indicates that four in ten adults say they suffer from chronic pain. Dr. Doris K. Cope, director of the Pain Medicine Division at the University of Pittsburgh Medical Center, recently said, "Ancient people saw pain more accurately, pain not only as a physical condition but as an emotional and a spiritual condition. They would work with the entire patient."[4] Chronic pain costs an estimated $100 billion a year in medical costs, lost working days, and workers compensation. The four roots have had positive results in reducing pain when they are used to augment mainstream medical regimens.

▶ *Insomnia:* Many studies show almost two thirds of adults (62 percent) experienced insomnia in the last year. One third of adults say they get fewer than 6.5 hours of sleep each night.[5] Eighty-five percent of insomniacs never seek medical treatment. Millions of insomniacs have turned to over-the-counter night time sleep aids, creating a $100 million-a-year business. They have spent an additional $200 million on melatonin, a sleep-enhancing herb. Dr. Gregg Jacobs at Harvard has used these practices with his patients and 100 percent of his patients said their sleep improved.[6]

▶ *Arthritis:* One in three adults or nearly 70 million people in the United States have arthritis and other chronic joint pain. Arthritis is a general term for a group of more than 100 diseases. The word "arthritis" means joint inflammation. Two of the most common types of arthritis are osteoarthritis and rheumatoid arthritis. *Osteoarthritis* is the most common type and is sometimes called degenerative joint disease because the cartilage in the body breaks down, or degenerates, with age. *Rheumatoid arthritis* is a long lasting disease that affects joints in any part of the body. The immune system causes the joint lining to swell and inflammation spreads to surrounding tissue in rheumatoid arthritis. These can be very painful conditions that are relentless and disabling. Most health-care professionals recommend many of these practices as steps to reduce risk of developing the disease and to slow or prevent permanent joint damage.

▶ *Diabetes:* An estimated 18.2 million individuals are affected by diabetes each year, and that number is on the rise. The four roots are an essential element in managing diabetes.

▶ *Fatigue:* Chronic fatigue is difficult to diagnose. The stress and depression that accompany fatigue disrupt the immune, neurological, and hormone functions. This is why mind-body interventions are essential in fatigue. The four roots are the essence of mind-body medicine and therefore are exactly what fatigue patients need.

▶ *Headaches:* Approximately 45 million Americans suffer from chronic headaches, and 28 million of these suffer from migraines. The four roots are a major aid to support your medical treatment for headaches.

▶ *Depression:* According to a report from the National Institute of Mental Health (NIMH), nearly 18.8 million Americans over the age of 18 suffer from major depression. Depression is a dangerous precursor to many diseases and conditions. Suicide, linked to depression, is the third leading cause of death in 10- to 24-year olds. A recent study by Dr. Shamsah Sonawalla of Massachusetts General Hospital surveyed college students and showed that half of the students surveyed qualified as having major depression.[7] Depression and psychological diseases are increasing enormously on college campuses as well as in the general public. The four roots practices have shown in studies to aid in depression.

▶ *Anxiety:* Over 20 million Americans are afflicted by anxiety disorders, ranging from panic attacks to general anxiety and phobias. UCLA researchers believe that less than 25 percent of adults with anxiety disorders receive any treatment.[8] The four roots are important in the treatment of anxiety disorders.

The vast number of individuals with these common diseases and conditions is hard to comprehend. It is difficult to fathom the economic costs and the pressure these spiraling diseases and conditions have on our health care system, individuals, families, and corporations.

We can no longer wait for our failed health-care system and flawed health education to help us out of this massive dilemma. It is time for each of us to take responsibility for our self-care. There is a vast amount of information today on self-care, much of it confusing and incorrect.

These four roots provide you with a simple, comprehensive, and easy to remember format that easily assimilates into your busy life.

I have spent many years working with patients and clients with these diseases and conditions. The roots of S.E.L.F. have been tremendously beneficial in every case. These practices help decrease metabolism, lower blood pressure, improve breathing and brain waves, and give your immune system a boost. Each of the four roots of S.E.L.F.—Serenity, Exercise, Love, and Food—will guide you to a personal discovery of balance and happiness informed by daily practices that deepen and nourish your physical, mental, and spiritual well-being.

As you learn to nourish your roots you will notice a new sense of confidence and certainty. You will have fewer ups and downs as you begin to experience living a balanced life.

Begin this process of the four roots by taking baby steps, enjoying some deep breaths, and practicing compassion every step of the way.

～ BEGIN TODAY ～

Ask Your Self   What is keeping me from living a healthy lifestyle?

Why do I not make my health a priority in my life?

What parts of my lifestyle do I know needs changing now?

Tell Your Self   I choose to live with physical, mental and spiritual well being.

Give Your Self   Put motivational and inspirational sayings in your home and office.

Soak in a hot lavender bath and drink your favorite tea.

Enjoy a great healthy dinner with a friend or loved one.

CHAPTER 6

Serenity
Reclaim Your Source

I JUMPED OUT of the car, threw my bag over my shoulder, and rushed into the cardiopulmonary wellness group I facilitated every week, late as usual. I smiled as I pushed the door of the room open, and wheelchairs, walkers, oxygen tanks, and canes came into full view. No matter how many times I have walked through that door, the amount of pain and suffering my patients experience in their tormented lives has never ceased to amaze me, yet as the door squeaked open week after week, I was enthusiastically greeted with a flood of smiles, hugs, kisses, and laughter from deep souls who have weathered many painful cycles in their lives. Still, they wake early on these meeting days to bathe their tired sore bodies, take their pills, then get into their wheelchairs and wait for the county disability bus to pick them up and bring them to the hospital for my class. They never complain, never demand, and accept their lot in life with amazing grace, dignity and perseverance. They have been my teachers in many ways far beyond the Ph.D.s I studied under in ivory towers.

I put down my bag and started the session with my group when I noticed a beautiful young woman who stood out in a room of silver hair and stooping postures. I assumed she was the daughter of one of my patients, but when I began the group with my usual question, "Is anyone or anything new today?" she immediately stood up and smiled brightly, "My name is Jennifer. I was referred by my cardiologist."

The young working mother with a husband and two children then shared how, without warning, she'd suffered a massive heart attack at the age of 34. The sole cause of her heart attack? Stress.

She told of a life flooded with exhaustive worries trying to balance carpools, school plays, client meetings, ball practices, meals, finances, and the evening news. What struck me most was that her life was not all that unusual for a woman of her generation, or mine. Rather, it sounded like the life of a typical American woman. In addition, she didn't have the sort of poor diet or bad health habits that normally invite a heart attack at such a young age. Jennifer didn't drink, she didn't smoke, she exercised, and she ate a well-balanced diet. But the stress in her life was literally killing her.

Jennifer might have thought I was her teacher, but *she* taught *me* an important lesson. In her aggressive pursuit of success as a wife, mother, and working woman, she very nearly failed the ultimate measure of success in any species: *Life.* Jennifer's heart attack was a wake-up call for her to redefine success on her own terms and find true work-life balance.

Jennifer's experience brought home the truth that serenity is not a luxury. It is not something that we should look forward to finding only on vacations, in quiet moments, or when we finally retire. Jennifer's heart attack serves as a reminder to all of us that our lives may well depend upon our learning to cultivate the practice of serenity each and every day.

The Power of Thoughts and Emotions

There are more than 100,000 chemical reactions going on every second in your brain. It is so hard to even comprehend. That is why I compare the brain to a magnificent computer. The brain is your personal pharmacy as it produces more than 50 active drugs. Every thought, every second of your life, is connected to a chemical released by your brain at the moment you have that thought. This has incredible implications. Every single thought you have has immediate physical and psychological consequences. Worry is not just something that you do with no effect. Every thought changes your body immediately. Just imagine your body as a chemical soup that is constantly changing with every thought you think, word you say, and every food you eat. We are constantly morphing into something new. What an incredible notion. Just as everything in nature is never the same from one moment to the next, neither are we.

Proactive vs. Reactive Life

You have learned some facts about how stress affects your body, mind, and soul. You may have historically been living a life where you are always surprised by the stressors that pop up in your life. You might even react with somewhat of a victim mentality of "why does this happen to me?" If this is the way you react to the stresses of your life—your job, your family, your friends, or your health—then you are constantly using the reactive approach. Have you ever had the horrible experience of watching a dog futilely chase a car on the road? When you are continually stressed and try to control the stress *after* you are stressed each time, it is like a dog chasing a car going 60 miles an hour. You hear the car coming, your heart races, the car races by, your pulse is pounding; then the car is moving out of sight, you stop, exhausted and depleted, and say, "You know, that car drives by here everyday and stresses me out, someday I will catch it and my stress will go away." Well, that is never going to happen. It's too late. The fact of the matter is every time the dog continues to chase that car the internal stress reactions are being reinforced, just like your stresses reinforce the same neuropathways in your brain. The car going by everyday can symbolize whatever stresses you: your commute, your job, the kids, money, or your marriage.

The most effective long-range method to deal with the stress you will experience as long as you live is embarking upon a proactive approach. You need a tool box of tools to live a proactive approach in the stressful situations of your life. I live on a ranch with livestock, pastures, fences, stables, and barns. I couldn't live without the appropriate tools to run this ranch. It's not *whether* I need tools to repair a fence, it is *when* I need the tools in my tool box. The world in which we all live is only going to get more stressful as new technology develops and life constantly changes beyond our comprehension.

It's time for you to take stress seriously in your life and begin to assemble your own tool box with your own set of special tools just for you. As you learn to use stress reduction tools over time, your stress threshold will change. You will be like the dog who used to chase the cars, but now when you hear the car coming, your take a deep breath, drink some cool water from the water bowl and watch the car go by, tail wagging, and smiling. Instead of falling hopelessly into the trap of stress, you are able to be aware of what is happening and make choices. You will develop a new sense of energy and power which will lead you on to experience true happiness. The psychologist Dr. Robert Epstein, at Cambridge Center for Behavioral Studies and a researcher at San Diego State University, says, "It's more important than ever to learn as many anti-stress techniques as possible, as young as possible."[1]

Stress Management and Stress Reduction

As I worked with individuals for many years in cardiac rehab and other areas, I struggled with what term to use in talking about dealing with an individual's stress in my classes. I would use the medical and psychological terms "stress management and stress reduction" as I was taught in my clinical training. My educational training is also in spirituality. I asked myself, what term does classic spirituality use for stress and what is the term used for the opposite condition of chronic stress? What is it that all individuals desire that is the opposite of stress? Peace of mind, body, and soul is what we all want to experience. Serenity is the opposite of stress. I believe this is a more spiritual word than stress management and it is really what our heart and mind desire. If serenity is our goal, my job was to discover how to change our behavior to deal with the stresses of being human.

Serenity is an antidote to the chronic stress that affects millions of individuals. Scientific evidence in the field of medicine demonstrates how crucial serenity is to our health and longevity. There are enormous sociological, psychological, and physical costs associated with the fallout from chronic stress including divorce, depression and anxiety disorders, unhappiness, alcoholism, obesity, child and spousal abuse, job related problems, and relational issues.

Serenity practices provide many health benefits that directly affect medical conditions such as cancer, heart disease, obesity, insomnia, diabetes, hypertension, infertility, and migraine headaches.

Serenity is about coming home to your real Self and your true purpose. Just say the word serenity over and over a few times and notice what feelings arise within you: sadness, exhaustion, frustration, or grief? I lived a life where my primary family and society held little value and reverence for serenity. Serenity was something monks, nuns, and hermits entertained. Serenity wasn't something a busy successful person with kids, a spouse, a job, and community and church responsibilities would have much of a chance to experience. In my life, and probably in your life, serenity is viewed as a luxury, not as essential to the life of your body, mind, and soul. Serenity is essential to every living creature, and if we don't experience serenity in some form we will experience *dis-ease* on some level. Serenity practices have always been known to be good for the soul, but there is growing evidence that it is good for the body as well.

With studies we now know that we connect with some miraculous source of healing when you experience times of serenity. Your blood pressure goes down, your immune system gets a boost, and you slow down the aging process. Scientific research clearly reveals that your body replenishes and heals as you practice serenity. In the silence, your thermostat resets and you settle into the real rhythm of your mind, body, and soul. Your inner voice, your inner self knows what you need to heal and prosper, but you just don't know how to listen. It really isn't your fault. Most of our houses of worship don't teach us this, our educational system's health classes don't teach us this, and we don't learn it in our families, so where would we go to learn these essential life giving practices?

Your Choices into Serenity

The wonderful result of the exploding field of mind-body medicine is that many sources are developing where we can learn this emerging information.

MEDITATION AND THE RELAXATION RESPONSE

Ten million American adults now say they practice some form of meditation regularly.[2] This is twice as many as a decade ago. Professionals, homemakers, farmers, prisoners, physicians, teachers, children, religious and nonreligious people are all flocking to learn the practice of meditation. You no longer have to go to an ashram or monastery to study with a monk or a guru to learn meditation practices. You can learn at hospitals, libraries, prisons, wellness centers, spas, airports, and in the privacy of your home. Serenity practices, especially meditation, are being recommended by more physicians and often by other members of the medical community.

Meditation has been taken from the realms of "fringe" or "new age" to mainstream as the science of serenity becomes demystified. The mind goes through ingenious changes during the practice of meditation.

The term *meditation* is also referred to as the "relaxation response." This term was coined by Dr. Herbert Benson of Harvard in his seminal studies on stress in 1967. Dr. Benson measured the heart rate, blood pressure, skin temperature and rectal temperature of 36 meditaters. He discovered that those individuals practicing meditation used 17 percent less oxygen, lowered their heart rates by three beats a minute and increased their theta brain waves, the relaxing ones that appear right before sleep.[3]

Emerging scientific studies show that the relaxation response (meditation) has proven benefits in a variety of diseases:

- *Stress:* Herbert Benson, M.D., Harvard, measured blood pressure, heart rate, and norepinephrine levels of patients during stress and then after a 20-minute practice of the relaxation response. After 28 days, the group showed significantly lower heart rate, lower blood pressure, and higher norepinephrine levels.[4]

- *Hypertension:* Under J. Stuart Lesserman, M.D., Harvard, patients with hypertension for at least 10 years went through 10 weeks of the relaxation response. Diastolic and systolic blood pressure decreased and patients maintained their lower blood pressure throughout later follow-ups.[5]

- *Insomnia:* G. Jacobs, Ph.D., Harvard, had 100 patients with insomnia practice the relaxation response for 10 weeks. One hundred percent of patients reported some type of improvement in sleep, and 91 percent stopped or decreased their sleep medication use.[6]

- *Infertility:* Alice Domar, Ph.D., Harvard, worked with women with infertility for over three and one-half years who were severely depressed. They practiced 10 weeks of the relaxation response, which resulted in significant decrease in depression and anxiety. One third of the women, who averaged three and one-half years of infertility, became pregnant.[7]

- *Chronic Pain:* Margaret Caudill, M.D., Harvard, had 109 patients suffering with chronic pain for 6.5 years practice the relaxation response for 10 weeks. It resulted in improved symptoms and a 36 percent reduction in HMO visits in a one-year follow-up, and it increased to a 50 percent reduction by the second year.[8]

▶ *Longevity:* Research by Robert H. Schneider, M.D., Maharishi University Institute for Natural Medicine and Prevention, showed two studies of meditation groups, who had normal to high blood pressure, were 23 percent less likely to die than people who did not use meditation. The meditation groups studied had a 30 percent decrease in the rate of deaths due to heart disease and stroke, and a 50 percent reduced rate of cancer deaths.[9]

Meditation, or the relaxation response, has demonstrated effects on the immune function and the brain and reveals the biological consequences of this mind-body intervention. Dr. Richard Davidson, Ph.D., of the University of Wisconsin and his colleagues discovered individuals who underwent eight weeks of meditation training produced more antibodies to a flu vaccine and showed signs of increased electrical activity in areas of the brain related to positive emotions than the individuals who did not meditate. Employees at a biotechnology company participated in this study with half receiving weekly meditation training and the other half not receiving training.[10]

The *Journal of Memory and Cognition* reported college students meditating displayed significant improvements in memory performance over a two-week period on a perceptual and short-term memory test.[11] The International Journal of Neuroscience published findings showing meditation reverses the aging process. Individuals practicing meditation for more than five years were physiologically 12 years younger than their chronological age, as measured by reduction of blood pressure, and better near point vision and auditory discrimination. Short-term meditaters were physiologically five years younger than their chronological age. The study controlled for the effect of diet and exercise.[12]

The *Journal of Social Behavior and Personality* published a longitudinal study showing that cholesterol levels significantly decreased through meditation in patients with elevated cholesterol, compared to match controls, over an 11-month period.[13]

Addiction takes one of the greatest tolls in terms of the costs of suffering of families, the costs to our prison system, costs to our health-care system, and the cost of lost productivity of human potential. The *Journal of Alcoholism Treatment Quarterly* and the *International Journal of the Addictions* report that meditation can even decrease cigarette, alcohol, and drug abuse. An analysis of 198 independent treatment outcomes found that meditation produced a significantly larger reduction in tobacco, alcohol, and illicit drug use than either standard substance abuse treatments (including counseling, pharmacological treatments, relaxation training, and Twelve Step programs) or prevention programs (such as programs to counteract peer pressure and promote personal development). Whereas, the effects of conventional programs typically decreased sharply by three months, effects of meditation on total abstinence from tobacco, alcohol, and illicit drugs ranged from 50 percent to 89 percent over a 18- to 22-month period of study.[14]

It is impossible to dispute the overwhelming research demonstrating the health benefits of practicing meditation, but I continue to be amazed at the psychological and spiritual benefits of meditation. I learned the practice of meditation and began to try to teach it in Atlanta. As I began to talk about the incredible science of meditation and how it had been a life changing practice not only in my own life but in the life of countless others, I was shocked by the responses of intelligent people. I would get strange looks and then comments would emerge revealing misconceptions about meditation. It was so frustrating to have discovered this incredible window into health, prosperity, and happiness and yet most of the responses I received were fear and ignorance.

I obtained wonderful insight after many years of studying with spiritual and religious leaders. Meditation is a type of prayer. Most prayer is when you are talking to the Divine or the Holy. Meditation is when you are silent, surrender, trust, and listen to the Infinite and believe you will get what you need. In meditation you receive a healing gift in the magnificent silence. It is an ancient spiritual practice in all religions and spiritualities. It is just in recent times, the last 500 years since the Protestant reformation, that this reverent practice has been pushed to the margins in favor of preaching, evangelism, and any activity that creates noise and movement. It was as if there was some innate distrust of silence.

We live in a society of noise and chaos. Our world has developed a phobic reaction to the awing experience of silence. The serenity practices were the most terrifying challenges of my life. My life was filled with movement, noise, and busyness, so the choice to engage silence was truly terrifying and life changing. I want to invite you to this wondrous root to true happiness and balance.

Here are a few simple steps so you can teach yourself how to meditate and use the relaxation response.

1. *Find a quiet place:* Discover a place where you have few distractions so it will be easier to concentrate. If possible use this particular place regularly.

2. *Close your eyes:* This helps quiet the outside world and focus you inward.

3. *Choose a word:* Choose a word or short phrase that means something calming and soothing to you. Many traditions use a name for God, or words or phrases such as "love," "all is well," "keep letting go," or "ohm."

4. *Repeat the word:* Repeat the word or saying as you slowly inhale and just release and settle into a deeper peace with each exhale. Repeat this process over and over again. This rhythm will relax and connect your mind, body, and soul.

5. *Focus the mind:* When you have distracting thoughts, imagine they are clouds blowing by, balloons floating off into the sky, or leaves floating down the flowing water of a creek. Do not attach to the thought, just release it and let it float away and focus back on your word or words.

The longer you can practice meditation each time the better. If your goal is 20 minutes, that's great. Many of the individuals I work with do not have that much time so I ask them to practice "mini-meditations" of three to ten minutes whenever they can throughout the day; in the car, at the office, in the bedroom, or in the carpool line.

When I was at Harvard, Dr. Herbert Benson was teaching about meditation, and one of the students told him how frustrating it was trying to meditate, and how she felt she was really bad at it. Dr. Benson smiled and responded, "The only bad meditation is the one you don't do. Any moment you attempt to clear the mind creates the intention of healing." I say amen to that!

GUIDED IMAGERY

Guided imagery is a proven form of focused relaxation that integrates the mind and body by listening to a skilled professional introduce peaceful images and healing music into your mind. Guided imagery is a simple but powerful practice that focuses and directs your imagination. Over the past 25 years the benefits of guided imagery has been established by research findings that reveal its impact on your health, creativity, and performance. Ten minutes of guided imagery can reduce blood pressure, cholesterol, and glucose levels in the blood and boost your immunity. It has been used to alleviate depression and stress disorders and reduce the adverse effects of chemotherapy. It is easier for westerners than traditional meditation because you sit and relax while you listen to someone guide you with their voice into a very relaxing healing state.

Guided imagery evokes your senses and they respond. Olympic athletes have been using guided imagery for many years. The Olympic swimmers close their eyes and imagine themselves swimming in the water touching the finish line. Their mind believes they have already won the race and they subsequently do win. When you fall in love, you may find yourself thinking about being with the person you love. You are imagining touching and hearing the other person. Your heart begins to beat faster and you may begin to breath faster. This is a type of guided imagery. Your body immediately responds to your thoughts. This is how guided imagery works. Your mind perceives something through the senses and your body immediately responds to the stimuli in a positive way

Guided imagery can aid you in any treatment or procedure. Research demonstrates that guided imagery can help people overcome stress, anger, pain, depression, insomnia, and other problems associated with illness and surgical procedures.

Guided imagery also can:

▶ Strengthen the immune system and enhance your ability to heal

▶ Reduce your recovery time in the hospital

▶ Dramatically decrease pain and the need for pain medication

▶ Enhance sleep

▶ Increase confidence

▶ Reduce stress and depression

I have used guided imagery myself and with clients and patients for many years, now with astounding efficacy. To find places to purchase guided imagery tapes on every disease from cancer, heart disease, diabetes, stress, depression, obesity, and more, see Appendix A.

DEEP BREATHING

Life is in the breath. He who half breathes, half lives.

Ancient Proverb

Every day you take between 14,000 and 25,000 breaths. You breathe six quarts of air each minute. It is the single most critical process of our bodies and yet we very often don't give any attention to how "wrong" most of us breathe. Your breath is your first line of defense in stress and can create almost instant calm and relaxation.

We are a world of fast shallow breathers. We are on the run most of our waking day and we aren't aware of our breath. The result of this constant state of shallow short breathing is that you don't get the amount of oxygen your organs and systems of the body need to perform at their best and your body gets stressed, resulting in anxiety or depression. You feed your body other essential elements of food and water, but we really don't have reverence for the spiritual and physical nature of the breath.

The breath and the spirit are two words in English, but they are one word in other languages. Breath and vital spirit are one. Breath and spirit mean vital energy, life, and are *ruah* in Hebrew. The breath is *prana* in Hindu, *pneuma* in Latin and Greek, and *chi* in Chinese. In many cultures you cannot separate the breath from the soul.

As a chaplain years ago I learned reverence and awe for the relationship of the breath and spirit. The breath demanded my respect when I was present as we unplugged a dying newborn from the ventilator. I handed her to her mother in a rocking chair. I watched that tiny chest surrender to her last breath as we sat in the stark silence.

Being in the labor and delivery room, I witnessed the birth of a baby who was still blue after all of the innumerable, drastic attempts of the doctor to make that stillborn baby breathe failed. Sitting in the silence with the mother and the father, I stood holding that precious baby boy who could not take that sacred breath that accessed his spirit.

I sat in the intensive care unit for days with a 13-year-old boy who had tried to commit suicide and watched his young chest go up and down, but the doctors said he was brain dead and it was just a matter of time when he would stop breathing. I'll never forget sitting by his head when he took his last breath and in a split second, life was gone, tragically wasted.

These stories are valuable lessons to all of us that life is so precious and our breath is what connects us to this life. It is the first thing we do when we leave our mother's womb and it is the last experience we will have as we leave this world. You must have reverent respect for your breath. I wish we taught our children this sacred principle before we taught them to read and write. I really believe the world would be a different place if we all had greater respect for the relationship between our mind, body, and soul and our breath.

A quick note on why you should breathe through your nose if possible. There are fine hairs in your nose that act as a filter for unwanted germs and particles. The nose serves as a regulator in the sense that if you breathe in cold air through the nose by the time the air reaches your lungs it is a warmer temperature and is moist for more efficiency of the body. In contrast to our age of plastic surgery, the ancients prized large noses as a sign of power and health. Isn't it interesting that they knew a large nose was actually a larger filter for our sacred breath?

Take a Cleansing Breath

1. Inhale deeply into your belly, through the nose (if you can't, use your mouth), bringing the air deeply into the lower lobes of your lungs. As you do this your abdomen will rise. On your out breath, your abdomen will sink back into your spine.

2. Be aware of your ribs. Experience your rib cage expanding and contracting with each deep breath.

3. Inhale to the count of five, then hold for a moment and then exhale to the count of five.

Notice how clear your mind feels, how refreshed your body feels, and what strength and power you experience. Set an alarm or have reminders on your mirror, in your car, or at your desk to take cleansing breaths during your busy days and don't forget to pass it on to your children, spouse, and coworkers. It is the gift of life, literally.

PRAYER

I consider meditation a form of prayer. I believe prayer is the most intimate experience we have as human beings and that is why I am very cautiously and humbly approaching this subject briefly. Prayer is an energy, light, or mental action that is beyond time, place, and distance.

Some believe that the Divine is within us, and when we pray we are connecting our inner spark of the Divine with the outer spark of the Divine. This belief clearly grounds the holy within us; prayer is the synergy of this fusion. But most Western religions believe that God is above us, transcendent, outside of us. Therefore the prayer is going out to God, or upward to God. This type of prayer makes the Divine exterior.

Every thought and emotion is energy, light, or an electrical stimulation. Science tells us that with every emotion and thought a chemical is released into our bodies. If you are experiencing anxiety this puts your brain on alert and it triggers a series of changes in brain chemicals and hormones. Your hypothalamus and pituitary gland respond to the stress signals and tell your adrenal glands to release the stress hormone, cortisol.

Pretend it's a beautiful day and you are playing with your dog in the park, and all of a sudden your close friend walks up and gives you a big hug. Your brain becomes happy and releases endorphins and then serotonin. As you continue to laugh and feel loved, you continue to produce these nurturing hormones that create health in your body.

So if science is proving that this sequence of events happens with every thought, that there is actual electrical stimulation and energy produced, how does prayer work? The answer is we don't know, and that is what all the fascination is about. We have research that shows it works but we really don't know how. Why do some prayers work and others don't? How can you pray for someone 3,000 miles away and it has the same efficacy as if you pray for your child in the next room? Is there a difference between a group of people praying and an individual?

There are literally more questions on prayer that will never be answered, but there is a brilliant physician, Dr. Larry Dossey, who has been a pioneer in researching prayer. Dr. Dossey has written several books researching studies on prayer from his scientific perspective. In his book, *Reinventing Medicine, Beyond Mind-Body to a New Era of Healing,* Dr. Dossey refers to the work of many researchers on prayer, which he refers to as "non-local healing."[15]

Cardiologist Dr. Randolph Byrd at the San Francisco General Hospital focused his prayer study on his heart disease patients. Of the 393 patients in the study, 192 patients were assigned to at home prayer groups and the 201 other patients were not prayed for. The groups that were to pray were only given the first name of the patients and a brief description of their diagnosis and condition. Each patient had between five to seven people praying for her or him. Each person prayed for many different patients. The patients that were prayed for had the following results:

▶ Fewer patients in the prayed-for group died (thirteen compared to seventeen).

▶ Patients in the prayed-for group were five times less likely to require antibiotics (three patients to sixteen patients).

▶ None of the prayed-for group required endotracheal intubations—an airway being inserted into the throat and attached to a ventilator. Twelve in the not-prayed-for group required endotracheal intubations and ventilation.

▶ The prayed-for patients were three times less likely to develop pulmonary edema (six compared to eighteen in the non-prayed-for group).[16]

Another interesting study was done by Dr. Erlendur Haraldsson, professor of psychology, and Dr. Thorstein Thorsteinsson, a biochemist, both on the faculty of the University of Iceland. Seven individuals took part in the study: two spiritual healers, one physician who believed in and practiced prayer, and four students with no experience or interest in prayer and healing. Ten test tubes contained yeast cells and another ten were controls. The seven individuals tried to stimulate the growth of the yeast cells in the ten test tubes. They had to stand no closer than one foot away and they were not allowed to touch the test tubes. The test tubes were then stored in the same place for 24 hours, after which the growth of the yeast cells was measured by sophisticated methods used by the microbiologists. The technicians were blinded and did not know which tubes had been prayed for and which had not been prayed for.

The test tubes that were prayed over showed greater growth than the controls. Interestingly, the greater influence on the yeast cells was due to the three individuals who were actively involved in healing in their lives.

The odds were less than two in 10,000 that the yeast cells growth could have occurred by chance. This study created more questions. Does practice make one more connected to some source of energy since the three practitioners of prayer had the greater results? Are there born healers? If so, how would we identify them?[17]

Cardiologist Dr. Mitchell Krucoff, associate professor of medicine and cardiology at Duke University Medical Center, and nurse practitioner Suzanne Crater presented a study at the Harvard meeting, which became the focus of a *Time* magazine article. They conducted a project called "cardio-spiritual" program, in which they combined high-tech cardiology, intercessory prayer, music, guided imagery, and touch. The results were presented not only at Harvard but at the American Heart Association's annual meeting. The prayed-for groups outcomes were 50 to 100 percent better than those of a not-prayed-for group. This was an especially interesting outcome because of the way the project chose those who prayed for the group. The "pray-ers" were composed from a variety of religious groups: Carmelite Sisters in Baltimore, Nalanda Monastery in France, Buddhist monks in Nepal, Silent Unity, an Interdenominational Christian prayer group, Moravians, Baptists, and others.[18]

A Duke study of a group of 4,000 people over age 64 found that those who prayed regularly had significantly lower blood pressure than those who prayed intermittently. At Dartmouth Medical Center, one of the best predictors of survival among 232 heart surgery patients was the degree to which they drew comfort from prayer.[19] In studies at several medical centers, prayer has been shown to speed recovery from depression, stroke, hip surgery, rheumatoid arthritis, heart attacks, bypass surgery, and alcoholism.

In my many years of working with clients, I have been amazed by the various paths individuals choose to pray or make a connection to the Divine and others. I suggest you explore different methods of prayer and discover what resonates with you. Some individuals pray memorized prayers, others choose to sit in silence with the Divine, some sing or chant, some sit in nature, and others use prayer beads. Prayer is the most personal and intimate of all spiritual practices.

AFFIRMATIONS
Affirmations are positive statements we tell ourselves. Our mind believes what we tell it. When you tell your brain positive information, you are feeding your brain extremely valuable food that heals your mind and body.

Many of the researchers in the field of mind-body medicine use affirmations with patients. When you tell yourself something over and over again, it gets recorded in your brain; then your mind and body believe it and you become what you have been telling yourself. A positive affirmation is a self-fulfilling prophesy.

How to Create Your Own Positive Affirmations

1. Decide what area of your life you want to transform by creating a positive affirmation: work, health, success, happiness, family, love, or money.

2. Make your affirmations in the present tense: "I am" or "I have." Your subconscious mind will hear that it is in the present, not in the future.

3. If you feel you are afraid of not being loved when you are your real authentic Self, make an affirmation like "People love me when I am myself." If you feel you don't earn enough money, maybe make an affirmation such as "My income is now increasing."

JOURNALING

Journaling our thoughts and experiences is an ancient serenity practice with its origin at the beginning of humankind. We can look back into caves and view the stories of our ancestors carved into the walls as spectacular petroglyphs. These were early journals revealing how people lived and survived, what was important, and what kind of deity they worshipped. When we don't record our lives much of it is gone with the setting of the sun, never to be retrieved, relived or learned from.

So much of the ancient history that enriches our lives comes from individuals who journaled. In most major religions and spiritualities journaling has been considered a spiritual practice. Regularly connecting and reflecting on your self and the world around you leads to living an intentional life.

Research shows us there are health benefits to writing your thoughts, emotions, and experiences down on paper. Scientists are proving that individuals with illnesses benefit by journaling. Joshua M. Smyth, Ph.D., professor of psychology at North Dakota State University, showed in a recent study that 47 percent of patients with asthma and rheumatoid arthritis improved after writing about the most traumatic event in their lives. In the control group who wrote about everyday topics, 24 percent improved.[20] Dr. James Pennebaker, a psychologist at the University of Texas, has shown that when individuals regularly write about things that are upsetting them, their immune systems boom and they require less medical care.[21]

Journaling involves the entire body and slows you down. When you journal you connect your thoughts with your body and process the experience at a deep level. I believe journaling moves your emotions and thoughts from your body to the paper. Journaling also integrates the mind, body, and soul.

Beginning to Journal

1. Choose the best time of day to journal. Take five minutes in the carpool line, when you get back from lunch, or before you go to bed. If you have more time, journal more; if not, make it a disciplined practice to do it for a few minutes once a day.

2. Choose a journal that you love. You may want to keep one at work, one in your car, and one in your drawer by your bed so you can use it at a free moment in your busy life. I keep a beautiful one by my bed and a small one in my purse. You can use your laptop for the quick and easy journaling of your thoughts and feelings.

3. Write your intimate authentic feelings about the experiences in your life. Writing the words helps take pain, grief, and anger out of your body.

4. Write continuously and don't worry about your grammar, spelling, or punctuation.

5. You may feel more expressive of your feelings by drawing instead of using words.

GRATITUDE

By feeling gratitude towards life, I move towards light, wholeness, universal energy, love. I move beyond the bounds of my own life and discover that I am an expression or form of universal life, of Divine Energy.
Arnaud Desjardins

Gratitude is actually a physical energy. Research shows grateful individuals report having more energy and less physical complaints than their nongrateful counterparts. Studies tell us daily gratitude exercises resulted in higher levels of alertness, enthusiasm, determination, optimism, and energy. Modern science has proven what all the great religions and cultures have taught us for centuries: Gratitude is a powerful, physical, palpable energy that can be measured and documented. Studies have shown an openness of the heart improves physical and mental well-being, demonstrating what William Blake observed centuries ago: "Gratitude is heaven itself."

Stop for a moment, center yourself on your heart, and be grateful for something in your life right now. Breathe slowly and deeply. Be truly grateful. Notice the immediate transformation of your mind, body, and soul. You have entered a state of grace: a life-giving, healing energy stream that is available at any moment.

If you look closely at the lives of great spiritual leaders, you will see they practice the simple but profound energy of gratitude every day. Nobel Peace Prize winners build their phenomenal lives on the solid foundation of a daily practice of gratitude, and as a result, they become gifts to our world. His Holiness the Dalai Lama, Bishop Desmond Tutu, President Jimmy Carter, and Mother Teresa all drew inner strength in the face of great challenges and grew to see that these events taught them forgiveness and gratitude.

Here are some easy ways for you to bring gratitude into your day-to-day life:

▶ *Give thanks for your breath:* Your breath is your source of life, the pivotal connection between your body and soul. At your birth you moved from the water of your mother's womb to your first breath, and your breath will be the last experience you have when you leave the earth. Just as you take food and water into your body to nourish your body and soul, your breath is an essential ingredient for life. Each breath feeds every cell in your body and every vital organ. When you don't breathe deeply and fully, you starve your body of oxygen. The way you breathe and the amount of oxygen you take in is crucial to the health of your brain and body.

Three deep abdominal breaths will leave you feeling focused, cleansed and reenergized, especially when you experience this practice with reverence and gratitude for the gift of your source of life, your breath.

▶ *Appreciate your physical body:* Most of us go to work, eat, sleep and live our entire lives without thanking our body for the miraculous work it does. You should be thankful to your body because it works very hard for you; your heart beats 3.3 billion times in your lifetime, you breathe 6 quarts of air every minute, and you expel 1,000 pounds of feces a year. Recent research has proven the critical nature of the mind-body connection, demonstrating that each cell of your body has an intelligence that is in constant communication with the master intelligence in the brain. Stop for a moment, take an inner tour of your body, and express how grateful you are for all the support.

Your brain stem and your heart were the first organs formed in your mother's body. Your heart and your brain have been working since your conception, day and night, year after year. Thank your organs in your body for the gift of life, especially when your body has been assaulted by drugs, alcohol, food, sleep deprivation, diets, depression, stress, anxiety, and the environment. Begin with the top of your head and move down organ by organ. Continue this process, acknowledging and showing gratitude for every organ and system of your body.

▶ *Honor the past:* Many cultures, especially the Asian and Native American traditions, are grounded in reverence for their ancestors. These cultures are keenly aware that it is only through the sacrifice, choices, and experiences of thousands of years of ancestors that we sit here today. We are the highest expression of our gene pool because we have survived. All of the dominant genes of our past are expressed in our presence, thanks to the ancestors who came before us.

Sadly, our fragmented nation has become disconnected from a deep awareness of the part our ancestors play in our culture. Being "self-made" in our culture is hallowed, but in fact none of us are truly "self-made," and would not be here without the lives of our ancestors. Take time to give thanks to grandmothers and grandfathers and those before them for giving you life. You may want to make a special display of old family photographs and mementos to keep your ancestors close to your heart.

It is important not only to silently practice gratitude for your family, friends, and community, but also to thank them verbally for the blessings they bestow on your life. By this simple act of acknowledgement, you will create a deeper communion with others. And gratitude is contagious!

❱ *Make every day a holiday:* In every culture, holiday celebrations revolve around food and celebration of the bountiful gifts of the earth. Bring this awareness into your daily life and make "saying grace" a regular practice. We often rush through meals without a thought to the amazing abundance and web of support that brought the food to our table. This year give thanks for the food you eat, not only on holiday occasions, but with every meal.

❱ *Give thanks during hard times:* Be grateful for the kaleidoscope of experiences in your life. It may seem difficult to be grateful for loss and grief, but all sacred texts and spiritual teachers tell us there is a purpose for everything. Again, if you look to great spiritual leaders, you see they have transformed their grief into a state of grace through gratitude.

If you can see every experience—even the ones you feel anything but grateful for—as a divine plan for your spiritual journey in this life and a path for you to fulfill your true purpose, you can live a more meaningful and peaceful life.

Gratitude is one of the most transformational powers in the universe, and practicing it can start a "cascade effect" of spiritual growth. As Cicero told us, "Gratitude is not only the greatest of virtues, but the parent of all others."

WATER

Since our conception we have naturally been drawn to the relaxing healing power of water. We are formed in our mother's womb where our life is nourished and supported by water. We have made pilgrimages to water through out time: to oceans, lakes, rivers, streams, and springs. This hasn't changed throughout the course of human history.

There is a sensual and sexual freedom we experience when we encounter water. Water makes us calm and peaceful, makes us laugh and fortifies our soul. Our bodies were not only formed in water, but we, our bodies, are made of mostly water. Our bodies are 75 percent water, our brain is 85 percent water, our blood is 94 percent water and our teeth are 5 percent water.

Water is a source of great energy, power, and healing. All major religions and spiritualities use water in sacred rituals to symbolize purification, new beginnings or the sign of a promise.

The bath is one of the most ancient and revered practices we have. A recent study at the Mayo Clinic discovered that soaking in a hot bath provides many health benefits. Soaking in the hot bath increases your heart rate while lowering blood pressure. After a few minutes in warm water, your warm blood causes the blood vessels to dilate, and this lessens resistance to blood flow and lowers your blood pressure.[22]

A study of sleep disorder clinics has observed that bathing in warm water was very helpful in the treatment of sleep disorders. The warm water relaxes muscles and this helps you transition into a restful sleep.

A shower can be restful or invigorating depending on your intention. The power of the water pounding your skin can refresh a tired body. Make each shower a new and vital experience in your day. Your attitude in the morning shower can affect your entire day.

I suggest that you keep different fragrances of soaps and scrubs by your shower or bath. Certain fragrances such as lavender and chamomile will create calm and shift you from your anxiety. A fragrance such as peppermint will stimulate your senses and snap you out of a depressed flat mood. Citrus fragrances invigorate and invite you to smile and relax. Each individual's sense of smell is quite different. Go to any store and try out the various scents to see how they make you feel. Aromatherapy has helped many of the patients I have worked with. They keep many scents they love by their bath and shower area and each day choose a fragrance that will help their mood.

Don't underestimate how powerful of a tool water can be in you developing your serenity practices and rituals. Many people treat water as if it is just a common resource. There is great power in water just waiting to be discovered by you.

There are many solutions to reducing stress, and each individual responds in a different manner. Appendix B contains some quick simple tips to reducing the stress in your life.

Serenity is the lifeblood of our mind, body, and soul. When we root our lives in serenity we experience abundance, happiness, and balance in our lives. Experience the healing balm of serenity in your mind, body and soul. Peace, autonomy and health are the essence of happiness and these are the fruits of serenity. Serenity is experiencing peace and living mindfully in your life. Open your mind, body, and soul to serenity and experience balance and harmony in your life.

～ BEGIN TODAY ～

Ask Your Self   What is keeping me from practicing serenity?

Am I satisfied with my meditation or prayer practices?

Do I need to learn more stress management techniques?

Tell Your Self   I experience calm and balance in my life.

Give Your Self   Create personal space for practicing serenity in your home and office.

Commit to practicing serenity for five to ten minutes each day.

Rent or buy a video, CD, or DVD on a new serenity practice, such as guided imagery, meditation, yoga, Qigong, or tai chi.

CHAPTER 7

Exercise
Revive Your Rhythm

AS JOAN'S FEET pounded the treadmill, her thoughts ran back to her experience four hours earlier that day. She remembered rising with her client, the defendant, in the hushed courtroom, and taking a deep breath to quiet her mind, which had been reeling through the solid year she'd devoted to this one challenging case.

Joan was so intent on remaining calm that she nearly missed hearing the jury foreman read the verdict: "Guilty on all counts." Her feet slapped the treadmill to the beat of the foreman's deep voice echoing in her head: "guil-ty-on-all-counts."

Joan grew up in courtrooms, in the law library of her father's firm and in the café across from the courthouse on the square of her small town. Her mother died when she was only five, killed by a drunk driver, and she was known throughout town as her father's shadow. Everyone, including her father, naturally assumed she would inherit her father's practice after her graduation, and, as was expected, she walked off the stage with her diploma and through the mahogany doors of her father's office.

As she finished her five-mile run, in one instant, Joan realized her overwhelming exhaustion sprang not just from that one verdict, but from the litany of verdicts she had heard read in her 20 years of trying cases in that same musty courtroom. As if on cue, the treadmill slowed to a stop.

She climbed off and dragged herself through the fitness center toward the shower, feeling drained, depressed, and disconnected.

As she began to pull off her sweat-drenched clothing, she heard the sound of women laughing, and then the laughter stopped as abruptly as it had begun. Since laughter was a sound she seldom heard, especially in her gym, she became curious and walked down the hall. There, in an exercise room, a yoga class was getting underway. Joan had read about the benefits of yoga in her women's health magazines, but had never seen anyone practicing yoga before. Just then, the door opened to the class and the clerk of the court walked out and noticed Joan standing there watching the class. "Joan, why don't you come on in and join us? We're having a ball!"

Hesitantly, Joan followed the clerk back into the class and began guardedly listening to the willowy instructor lying on the mat on the floor. Within a few minutes, Joan found herself lying on the floor, stretching and breathing, soothing and softening her weary body and soul. Her mind quieted and she felt a primordial rhythm pulse through her that she had never felt before.

Little did she know that the odd sense of connectedness and peace she discovered that day would open the door to a new life she could never have imagined. Joan began to devotedly attend every class she could find. When the instructor asked Joan if she would like to attend a workshop on teaching yoga, she was at once flattered and terrified.

Three years later, Joan is still practicing law, but only part-time. Her life swings between that old musty courtroom and the sweet smell of incense in her yoga studio. Success, as defined by her law practice, is no longer her highest priority. Joan has discovered a radical new definition of happiness for her life.

Joan had inherited a life of serial monotony. But one magical day, the universe nudged her out of her mundane life of habituation and security to a new life of connection, rhythm, and energy. Joan achieved mind-body-soul alignment and changed her life by identifying the exercise that created a life force and resonated throughout her being.

For Joan, yoga opened the door to a new life filled with laughter, passion, and fulfillment. No matter what your experience or current state of health, you too can find a practice that brings you renewal. The only thing you have to do is be willing to look within—not without—for the answer.

Understanding Exercise as Alignment

When you live from the *outside in,* "exercise" is something you dread, force yourself to do, and above all, merely endure. By constantly trying to achieve society's or someone else's idea of "exercise," you lose touch with your body's innate wisdom that can guide you to the movement it needs to restore you on all levels.

Often when I speak or teach a seminar, individuals tell me that they feel tired all of the time and can't seem to find a natural way to increase their energy levels. Billions of dollars are spent each year on drinks, bars, and supplements that promise to restore the depleted energy of our over-worked society. True exercise restores balance and alignment according to natural laws that govern our universe. A balanced and aligned body enables the energy to flow efficiently through our system, and exercise is the primary way to achieve alignment. Just as a floor lamp expresses its energy as light only when it is plugged into a higher source of power, when we plug into this Source of vital energy, we fully express ourselves.

Alignment means finding your rhythm or flow. We are a body of energy that is constantly flowing. This energy flows at different frequencies in each of our individual bodies. Our energies are similar, but all somewhat unique. The key to your alignment, or exercise, is for you to discover the energy, your chi, flowing through your body. We can get this life-giving energy that will transform our own life force through exercise.

Maybe instead of perceiving exercise as something we do from the outside in, let's consider exercise as aligning ourselves with the natural force, or the chi energy or life force. In ages past we did more physical labor. In modern times we are a very immobile, labile culture. Our entire energy systems are getting plugged up, like a stopped up drain. We are losing our connection or our flow. Not to mention the world of technology and massive energy all around us we don't perceive.

How do we get into alignment with this life force energy? Each of us is different and we have different electrical systems, different body types, different experiences, different genetic makeup, and different psychological makeup. You are the only one who can know the life-giving experience of exercise when you are connected to this vital energy.

When you study with spiritual leaders they very quickly explain the disciplines or paths to a spiritual life. They don't ask you whether you "want" to do this or that discipline. If you decide to live on a specific spiritual path, you follow their guidance. I believe this is the same with exercise. If you want physical, mental, and physical health and well-being, exercise is not a choice; it is a discipline that one must embrace. I have worked with patients and clients for many years and one thing I make clear is that exercise is a discipline or a spiritual practice. The biggest mistake my patients make is to ask themselves, "Do I feel like exercising today? Do I want to do this?" These questions bring anxiety and frustration and a host of excuses. This just wastes time, energy, and subsequently your life and health.

True physical exercise, in whatever form it takes, is the practice of aligning yourself with your source of energy. If you dread, postpone, and complain about your current exercise routine, or if you have no exercise routine, it is time to discover a new practice that brings you home.

You have the capacity, through exercise and alignment, to create abundant energy within yourself. Exercise is movement that brings you into alignment with your true self.

Choose Life

Exercise is critical—literally for the length and quality of your life. It is time that you educate yourself about the importance of exercise during your entire life. With the plague of obesity, cancer, heart disease, depression, hypertension, and diabetes in our country, we can no longer avoid this essential issue in our lives. We will not be able to continue the mounting health care costs very much longer.

The shadow side of our postmodern lavish lifestyles is our lack of movement of our bodies. Most of us have long commutes in a car, train, or airplane. Many of us live in front of computers either at the office or in our homes. To add more fuel to a lifestyle that is already sedentary and out of control, the average person watches more than four hours of television each day. By the time a person is 65 years old, she or he will have watched nine years of television.[1]

The CDC and the government of the United States have made obesity and the sedentary state of the United States a number one priority. Because of their sedentary lifestyle, our children are the first generation whose life expectancy may be less than their parents' generation.

Consider how magnificently exercise benefits our health and well-being. Exercise lowers blood pressure, reduces cholesterol, and controls blood sugar. It strengthens and builds muscle tone and bones, increases energy levels, reduces body fat, and helps increase the strength of the heart. It prevents heart disease, cancer, arthritis, and a host of other serious medical conditions.

Do anything—from walking, treadmills, tread climbers, to yoga, tai chi, or Qigong—something that integrates with your lifestyle and hopefully something you love. As you align yourself with something that brings you passion and energy, you create health in both your mind and your body. Exercise gets essential nutrition into our bodies.

Exercise alleviates stress, anxiety, and depression. It strengthens the immune system, stimulating "natural killer cells" that play a vital role in fighting cancer, bacteria, and viruses.

Our bodies were meant to *move:* Lack of activity contributes to a host of physical and psychological disorders. Robert M. Butler, M.D., of Mt. Sinai Medical School in New York proclaims, "If exercise could be packaged into a pill, it would be the single most prescribed and beneficial medication in the nation."[2]

EXERCISE IS A GIFT FOR OUR MIND, BODY, AND SOUL

So if it's so good for us, why do we dislike it so much? Exercise in America has often been experienced as penance, punishment, and ordeal. We see exercise as competition, and our failure to "measure up" as defeat. A study published in the *Journal of the American Medical Association* found that one of the key reasons Americans don't exercise is the misconception that you need to do vigorous exercise to experience any benefits.[3] The more research we have on exercise the more we know that this just isn't true.

But if you choose to see yourself as vigorous and fit, instead of "not measuring up," in time your very cell structure will mirror the pictures you hold in your mind. Just as Eastern practices such as martial arts, yoga, tai chi, or Qigong are readily understood as mind/body disciplines, you can reimagine your everyday routine and experience any form of exercise as a vehicle to refresh and renew mind, body, and soul. Practice awareness as you do jumping jacks, lift weights, or pound away on your elliptical machine. Repeat a mantra or affirmation with each movement. Keep your attention in your body and on your breathing, and you will restore yourself on multiple levels.

Exercise is an essential element of the mind-body-soul balance because it literally affects all three. Sacred texts throughout the ages have spoken of our bodies as vessels or temples that need to be honored and cared for. When we exercise, we display reverence for the magnificence of our bodies.

EXERCISE IS AN ANCIENT SPIRITUAL TRADITION

Walking is a revered historical practice. When you study with most ancient spiritual traditions there is undoubtedly a walking meditation so one becomes aware of your connection with the holiness within your Self, with the Divine, and with the elements of the earth. You were created to move that magnificent body.

Native Americans, Christian monastics, Islamic Sufis, Buddhist monks, Hindu priests and Taoist monks make walking a part of their deeply grounded spiritual path.

Jesus walked from town to town healing the sick and teaching. Buddha spent his entire life walking from village to village teaching. Mahatma Gandhi walked 150 miles on the infamous Salt March that forever changed the future of India. Dr. Martin Luther King, Jr., walked the roads of Alabama and Georgia, and Susan B. Anthony spent her entire life, joined with a multitude of other women, walking for the right to the ballot box.

Experience your walk as a pilgrimage. Pilgrimages are a part of every spiritual tradition. Jews go to Jerusalem, Christians go the Holy Land, and Muslims go to Mecca. Just imagine something you want to learn or focus on before you leave on your pilgrimage each day, and when you return you have gone on your own journey and are following a deep rich tradition. On your walk notice the birds, the sky, the clouds, the trees, the sounds, the smells, and the colors. Your walk is packed with a kaleidoscope of possibilities. Choose a different route for a different experience. Create a group of people to walk with in the morning or evening or walk alone for some introspection and alone time.

Exercise to Your Rhythm

Discover the exercise that matches the rhythms of your day and the needs of your body. Be sure to breathe deeply as you move your muscles; oddly, many of us develop the habit of holding our breath as we lift a weight or swing a racket, depriving our muscles of much-needed oxygen.

Weave exercise into the fabric of your day: Make a commitment to stretch whenever you get up from your desk, to choose the outer edges of every parking lot, to spend 10 minutes before bedtime practicing yoga. Find exercise that is fun for you: dancing, backpacking, even swinging on the swing set in your neighborhood park.

Don't let injuries or illnesses make you "give up" on exercise. Everyone can do some form of movement sitting in a chair, or even lying in bed. Simply breathing deeply and tensing and relaxing muscles can be immensely restorative. Turn on some music and move your body in whatever way feels comfortable. Start slowly and build up the amount of time you devote to movement each day.

Focus on pleasure, not pain. Exercise should feel *good*. If you don't look forward to your daily exercise, it's time to reexamine your choices. Release the idea that exercise has to be extremely vigorous, take an hour or more, and make you suffer. Studies show that three 10-minute increments of exercise spread throughout your day have the same health-giving benefits as one 30-minute session.

Exercise videos are a great way to sample a new discipline before you commit to taking a class. Some videos are broken down into short 10- or 20-minute segments to give you a quick lift when you're feeling out of balance. If you try something and you aren't enjoying it, try something else. Sample the wide variety of fun routines available and find the ones that restore and renew you. There are videos that give you instructions on how to exercise or do yoga in your bed, a chair, or an airplane seat. When you find something that clicks for you, you'll know it.

Make your choice: Walk, swim, go to the gym, practice Pilates, yoga, tai chi, or Qigong. Move your body and bring a deeper, more satisfying balance to the rhythm of your days.

Exercise and the Family

Exercise can make many twists and turns throughout your busy life. When your children are small and you are busy, you may need to include your children in your softer exercise program. As they watch cartoons or play, you may be on the floor doing sit-ups or lifting weights. Or you might put on some of their favorite music from *Cinderella* or *Beauty and the Beast* and dance together. Be creative, as long as you are moving it's great.

With small children it can be wonderful to organize a walking group in your neighborhood in the morning or in the evening, as the youngsters are sleeping and your spouse is home with them. As your children grow you can expand your options.

My children still laugh at me remembering their childhood, with me dressed in my red leg warmers, red leotards, and red headband, jumping around with Richard Simmons. All three of us would cry as the heavy women would tell their heart-jerking stories about how their obesity had caused them so much suffering. Richard would put his arms around the crying women and console them. We still love Richard Simmons. He is intricately woven into our precious family memories of many years ago.

Childhood and adult obesity is directly related to our sedentary lifestyle. It is our responsibility to create new ways to keep our families moving so we stay healthy. Teach your children fun ways of exercising in your family and they will do them for the rest of their lives. When you give them the gift of exercise you bestow on them the gift of life.

Go on family walks every other day after supper. Don't forget the dog; she needs exercise too. Put up a basketball hoop and have family basketball games or take turns trying to make shots from different distances from the hoop. This gets the family moving, interacting and laughing. Putting up a badminton net in your back yard is great idea. It only takes two of you to hit the birdie back and forth and get those bodies moving. Just these few hints give you three viable exercises to do every week as a family. Your children will follow your lead. We always exercised as a family and it is still something we enjoy doing together.

It is an incredible gift when a busy couple can organize their time so they can exercise together. We know that when you have a partner you exercise with you will be more compliant and be more committed to the practice. My husband and I have always walked together since the day we married a very long time ago. We have both always had such busy lives, so our walks became a time of sharing, laughing, and catching up on the news of the day. This simple practice that we have always made a priority in our lives has enriched our long, loving relationship. When our lives were overwhelmed with children, careers, and bills, our walks became our intimate time alone where we shared our fears, hopes, and many times our tears. At times in our life when our marriage hit some difficult intersections, our practice of walking forced us to be together and talk. Remember, when you walk, your body releases healing hormones such as endorphins and serotonin, which also helps your relationship.

We now have adopted something new that replaces our daily walk. We have a treadmill and a tread climber in our basement. He gets on his treadmill and I climb on my tread climber almost every evening, then lift our weights together and finish with sit-ups. We alternate this with practicing yoga. This is a great way to age together and get support in this healthy practice. As you age, discover new ways to move your body.

Work

Corporations must take more responsibility for helping their valuable employees get their bodies moving. Health care costs include the days you are out of work, and the cost of your prescriptions and insurance affect the company's bottom line as well. Exercise is good for your business. Researchers at Indiana's Ball State University discovered businesses owned by runners who ran at least four times a week had average sales two to three times higher than companies whose owners didn't run regularly.[4] Exercise of any kind produces endorphins, which increase creativity, optimism, and well-being. Wouldn't it be wonderful that in light of our research on exercise and productivity corporations would really begin to take work-life balance as a priority in their companies? If you work for a company that is not supporting work-life balance efforts there is plenty of science you can take to the table to show that care of the staff directly affects the bottom line of the company. Volunteer to be on the committee to create this health initiative.

Cancer

The science has weighed in on the affect of exercise on cancer. Women who moderately exercised 1.5 hours per week had a 50 percent reduction in cancer risk. There are lower rates of colon cancer in individuals who exercise regularly.

Researchers examining 74,000 women enrolled in the Women's Health Initiative study recently found that exercise reduced the risk of breast cancer regardless of age. Women who exercise regularly have lower rates of breast cancer.[5]

Michelle Holmes, M.D., Ph.D., assistant professor at Harvard Medical School, just reported a study in the *Journal of the American Medical Association* on the benefits of exercise on breast cancer. Walking three hours a week at an average pace of 2 to 2.9 miles per hour cuts the risk of dying from breast cancer in half. Even a little exercise—one to three hours a week—cut the risk of breast cancer death by 20 percent.[6]

These studies are very encouraging, not only for women with breast cancer but for everyone with or without cancer. We are continually being told by all studies we must exercise to live a long and healthy life.

Walking Can Literally Save Your Life

The *Journal of the American Medical Association* found that walking 30 minutes a day reduces the chances of premature death almost as much as running 30 to 40 miles a week. Death rates from all causes, including heart disease and cancer, are much lower in people walking 30 minutes a day than those who are inactive. Individuals walking 30 minutes a day have one-third fewer deaths from all causes, including heart disease, and stroke that those who were sedentary. Walking 30 minutes a day lowers the risk of stroke, diabetes, arthritis, high blood pressure, and osteoporosis.[7]

Aging

Exercise is an essential element in healthful aging. Research reveals exercise not only makes us live longer but we live independently and healthier as we age. Everything is positively affected by exercise as we age: memory, heart, blood pressure, blood sugar, immune function, healthy skin, and the healthier functioning of every major organ and system of the body.

As you exercise you create endorphins; you exercise the muscles and also send blood and oxygen to your vital organs, especially to your brain. Exercise just doesn't make your muscles stronger; it slows the aging of your entire body.

Researchers at University of Illinois, Dr. Arthur Kramer and Dr. Stanley Colcombe, have found that exercise postpones the effects of aging. They have demonstrated that athletic older adults have denser brains than their inactive counterparts, suggesting that workouts protected their brains. Colcombe and Kramer believe that exercise does more than simply preserve brain tissue, it can also improve thinking. In 18 recent studies they found inactive older adults who began an exercise routine got significantly better at cognitive tests that measured skills such as planning and paying attention.[8]

At the University of Pittsburgh, researchers followed 229 women between the ages of 50 and 65 for 17 years and discovered that the women who were sedentary over the study period were 1.5 times more likely than active women to have a difficult time with daily activities, such as shopping, household chores, and climbing stairs.[9] Being active is an investment in your senior years. You don't only want to live longer, but you probably want to live longer independently.

Exercise improves long-term memory and brain function. It helps prevent the arterial aging that contributes to aging and Alzheimer's disease. A study of more than 18,000 nurses over 70 showed the women who walked at least 1.5 hours per week scored higher on tests of general thinking ability, verbal memory, and attention than did women who walked less than 40 minutes per week.[10] A study of more than 2,000 men over 70 showed that regular walking reduced the development of dementia, including Alzheimer's disease.[11]

The improved oxygen movement to the brain during exercise feeds the brain and causes better memory functioning.

Stress

Research consistently shows that individuals who exercise are more stress resistant than those who don't exercise. Exercise has a relaxing effect upon the mind and body. Exercise lowers the activity of the sympathetic nervous system, your heart rate and blood pressure. When people who regularly exercise are exposed to stress, their heart rates do not rise as much as when people who do not exercise are exposed to stress. Individuals who exercise are not only sick less than nonexercisers, but the severity of their illness is less than nonexercisers.

Regular exercise can be compared to an athlete preparing for the Olympics. The athlete exercises for strength and hardiness. A person who regularly exercises is creating strength and hardiness that produces healing chemicals in the body allowing them to diminish the effects of the stress in their lives.

Depression and Anxiety Disorders

Researchers at Duke University showed that regular exercise relieves major depression just as effectively as antidepressant medication.

Dr. James Blumenthal's research shows that 30 minutes of aerobic exercise three times a week is sufficient for reducing the symptoms of depression. In his study of 10 months, exercise was a significant predictor of depression levels. People who engaged in 50 minutes of exercise a week had a 50 percent decrease in the likelihood of being depressed.[12]

Exercise releases "happy chemicals" into the body such as endorphins and serotonin. Exercise also helps regulate dopamine production, the neurotransmitter that helps cells communicate with each other.

Insomnia

Exercise helps create deeper sleep patterns and patients fall asleep faster when they exercise. Dr. Gregg Jacobs of Harvard maintains the benefit of exercise on sleep is because exercise is a stressor on the body. The brain compensates for the extra physical stress of exercise by increasing the depth of sleep of the individual. He also says that people with insomnia are many times sedentary, which inhibits the rise and fall of the body temperature rhythm.[13]

Researchers at Stanford found moderate exercise improves the quality of sleep in adults, age 50 to 76. This study is important because older adults who make up 12 percent of the population receive 35 to 40 percent of all prescribed sleep medications.[14] This is especially important because sleeping agents in older persons may cause falls, confusion, agitation, and drowsiness.

Immune Function

Exercise causes your immune function to increase on a cellular level. With this increased immune function, you are less likely to develop cancer. Exercise increases the production of killer cells, "watch dog" cells that seek and destroy invading disease cells and cancer cells. Individuals who exercise have fewer colds and illnesses in general than those who are sedentary.

Our Children

Today, children don't get the physical activity they need. This could be the first generation of children in history whose life expectancy is less than that of their parents. The continued plague of obesity will cut the lifespan of our children anywhere from two to five years. Many schools have dropped or reduced their physical education programs, and a recent study shows that 92 percent of elementary schools do not provide daily physical education classes.[15] Sadly, many of our communities lack recreational facilities for our children. Too many of our children spend their leisure time in sedentary activities such as playing video games, being on the computer, or watching television. Our children do not have disciplined times of the day for exercise and activity.

Our technological world is also a culprit in luring our children to sit in front of a variety of electronic gadgets whose numbers continue to grow each day. A survey of youth ages 8 to 18 shows their daily activities as follows:

▶ Watching television: 3 hours 51 minutes

▶ Using the computer: 1 hour 2 minutes

▶ Playing video games: 49 minutes

▶ Reading: 43 minutes

More than two-thirds (68 percent) of children have a television in their bedrooms. These children watch one hour and a half more TV than those without a television in their room. Thirty-one percent of children have a computer in their rooms, and they use it 45 minutes a day more than the children without a computer in their bedroom.[16] I am of the old school when it comes to any technology in a child's bedroom. I believe when children have technology in their bedrooms they will retreat to the privacy of their rooms to use it. This draws them away from the family areas of the home and into their own world. This prohibits their interaction with parents, siblings, and other family members. Parents can easily begin to lose intimacy with their children when they retreat and begin to develop their own unsupervised world. I am quite concerned about this trend because depression rates among our young people are growing at alarming rates. I believe this technological sedentary lifestyle can lead to the isolation of our children at a time in their lives when they especially need guidance, mentoring, supervision, and exercise. Every home should have a computer area or a computer room. Many families I have worked with have made a closet into the computer room or moved the computer to an extra bedroom or basement.

The family exercise section of this chapter addresses helpful hints on getting your children moving. I also encourage enrolling your children in sports programs. This not only helps with exercise but also helps them develop social and leadership skills that will be invaluable to them in life.

Other Exercise Choices

In addition to the exercises already discussed, here are three exercises that have significant health benefits.

YOGA

Yoga is an ancient practice that comes from the Sanskrit word meaning "to yoke," which means to join the mind, body, and soul or the breath. There are 40 types of yoga. Personally, I have tried several types and you will know which one is for you. Just rent different types of yoga videos and try some until you discover one that is right for you. I maintain a regular practice of yoga and really believe that I could not function at my level without this essential practice. It is worth noting that when I studied with the pioneering research centers, all of the patients in their programs were practicing yoga because of its health benefits.

The University of Texas, M.D. Anderson Cancer Center did a study on lymphoma patients who practiced Tibetan yoga for seven weeks. They found the patients went to sleep faster, slept longer, and had better overall sleep quality and used less sleep medication compared with the control group who did not do yoga.[17]

Satish Sivasankaran, M.D., conducted a study at Yale showing practicing yoga and meditation at least three times a week may reduce blood pressure, pulse rate, and the risk of heart disease. This study demonstrated that a six-week yoga and meditation program improved blood vessel function by 17 percent in patients. Also, study participants who had heart disease had close to a 70 percent improvement of endothelial function.[18]

TAI CHI AND QIGONG

Tai chi is a traditional Chinese exercise based on two basic concepts. The first concept is energy, called qi or chi. This energy flows through the body along pathways called meridians. The second concept of Chinese medicine is that when the flow of qi or chi is blocked, the body and mind are out of balance. When the body is out of balance it can become ill. Tai chi and Qigong are done to bring the body back into balance and increase your energy.

Dr. Lyvonne Carreiro, at the University of Florida reported that patients with Parkinson's disease who took tai chi classes for 12 weeks had less decline in motor function and there was an 18-fold reduction in the frequency of falls for patients who took tai chi.[19] This practice helped to improve balance, strength, and body awareness.

Qigong is an ancient Chinese practice that I personally love. Qigong also creates health by balancing the chi, or vital energy, in your body. Qigong is about discovering one's true balance. Studies at Stanford have shown that cancer patient participants are more relaxed, feel less stressed and fatigued, and experience a greater sense of well-being.[20] Kaiser Permanente, the largest HMO in the country, offers Qigong to their patients. They report they began Qigong with their chronic pain patients and had such great results they are now providing these classes for all health care plan members. Qigong, like acupuncture, uses a system of internal pathways called meridians, which run through the body. Your chi, or vital energy, can become stagnant or blocked within these pathways and Qigong makes your chi flow and restores balance in your body. When your chi is blocked or stagnant you get sluggish, slow and can experience illness. Qigong makes me feel energized, balanced, and very happy.

SWIMMING

Swimming is an easy exercise to begin at any age. It is especially good for anyone who has injuries, diseases, or conditions that prohibit them from doing regular aerobic exercise.

There are incredible benefits to swimming. As study published in the journal *Medicine and Science in Sports and Exercise* found that water exercise improved elderly participants' health. Women from the ages of 60 to 75 years old participated in swimming and water exercise for 12 weeks. The study showed these women had increased muscle strength, greater flexibility, loss of body fat, and increased agility compared to the women who did not participate.[21]

Time on Your Side

The most common question I hear about exercise is not about what to do or the benefits of exercise, but "How can I find time to exercise in my busy day?" Here are some solutions I have found to this very real problem:

▶ Put your treadmill or tread climber in a room with one of your televisions. Tape your favorite show or pop in your favorite DVD and watch it for 30 minutes while you exercise. Because my day is so busy, I "Tivo" *Oprah* or my favorite evening shows and watch them while I exercise. Then I do a few sit ups and lift weights a few repetitions.

▶ Exercise throughout the day. Take your dog for the morning walk at a fast pace. Get home and walk her again briskly for a few minutes. After starting dinner, maybe get on the floor and do some yoga or stretching.

▶ During your lunch hour briskly walk on your first half hour and pick up and eat your lunch on the second half hour. The sunlight during this time is an added benefit that science shows makes you feel better.

▶ Whenever possible take the stairs at work or at the mall. When I shop at the mall I try to walk around briskly for a few minutes before or after I shop.

▶ For parents with younger children you can discover creative ways to exercise during your day. Take the kids with you and walk the dog in the morning. You can put on an exercise tape of Tae Bo or any other fun exercises and make it a family affair by having the children exercising with you. Anytime during the day or evening throw on some of your favorite lively music and dance with your children and your spouse. This makes exercise playful and teaches your children at a young age to keep their bodies moving.

The research is totally conclusive that if you want to live a life of physical, mental, and spiritual well-being, you must exercise. If this is something you have been dreading, don't. Just like a diabetic who has to take insulin each day, or a person with any condition who has to undertake a certain regimen, you have to get your body aligned to this great healing energy of life.

I have given you just a few options about different exercises. There are too many to name these days. Pilates and many combinations of others are available. If you don't have time to attend a class, do what I do. Rent a videotape or DVD of a type of exercise you are interested in and try it. If you like it, do it at home on your schedule and you will keep it up.

The natural aging process slows down all of the systems of the body, but exercise will keep you from slowing down or aging as fast. I have literally seen individuals who have never exercised begin practicing this root and it has transformed their lives. They find that they not only have more energy, but they are optimistic, strong, look and feel better, and have a new life they never could have imagined.

Get moving any way you can, in any direction you can, at any time you can. Exercise is truly the bread of life. Our bodies were created for movement. As you begin your exercise remember you are aligning your energy with the greater energy of nature, the Source, and there is a synergistic affect that heals your mind, body, and soul. Saunter around your neighborhood, a park or around your home, just get moving!

∼ BEGIN TODAY ∼

Ask Your Self   What is stopping me from exercising regularly?

What is my resistance for doing yoga?

What am I doing daily to experience movement in my body?

Tell Your Self   I experience a great force within me when I exercise.

Give Your Self   Do 20 to 30 minutes of exercise at least three times a week.

Rent or buy DVD of new types of exercise, like Pilates, yoga, tai chi, or aerobics.

Put your treadmill in your television room, jump on for twenty minutes and watch your favorite show at the same time.

Love
Realize Your Intimacy

JERRY GRABBED HIS cell phone to call his wife Nancy and tell her his flight had been delayed because of the heavy sleet storm that had settled in at the airport. The "low battery" signal flashed brightly, mocking him, and he threw the dead phone back into his briefcase as he fell back into the small plastic airport chair, his heart racing as frustration, and anger coursed through his body.

When he looked up at the monitor and saw Delta flight 303 was delayed, he pulled his sport coat out of his bag and wrapped himself in it, surrendering to a situation he had no control over. Part of him wanted to go home, but part of him felt he would find just as much warmth in a lonely hotel room. He and Nancy had been "empty-nesters" for a year since their son Bill went off to college, but he had felt empty long before that. It wasn't that he didn't love his wife and his son; he just didn't feel a connection.

Their 20 years of marriage had been filled with Bill's ball games and after-game parties: They had created a life, with Bill positioned at the center, and a marriage that revolved around their son. Jerry couldn't remember how long this painful loneliness had haunted him. If he were honest, it had probably been most of their marriage, but the whirlwind of their son's busy life had distracted him from that chilling reality.

Jerry had always traveled extensively in his job as a consultant, but in the year since his son left for college, he found himself accumulating more and more sky miles and rewards points with each passing month. As he sat in the terminal wrapped in his coat, he felt a sharp pain under his arm from his surgery a couple of months earlier. A heart catheterization revealed four blocked arteries which required subsequent open heart surgery to bypass. They told him he would have phantom pains for a while, but his sadness echoed within his scarred chest. The doctor had suggested that he join a support group after the heart surgery, but he felt strange at the idea of exposing his pain and fears to others. The doctor's office had called him several times asking him to come to the group, but each time he told them he was doing "just fine" and was too busy to take this time for himself.

Suddenly he heard a noise that pulled him out of his reflection and looked at the young couple sitting across from him. He noticed the new set of shiny rings on their left hands and eavesdropped on their intimate whispers and giggles, quickly surmising that they were newlyweds returning from their honeymoon. He sat there staring, straining to hear their loving words and watching their long wet kisses with a sad longing.

Tears welled up in his eyes as his pent-up emotions responded to these two young lovers freely and openly sharing their love. Like a river breaking through a dam, tears, pain, fear, loneliness, terror, and despair rolled and swirled through his tired body.

He couldn't remember ever feeling the passion and intimacy the young couple so obviously shared. Had those precious feelings evaporated over time, or were they ever really there? Thoughts, questions, and emotions reeled through his head.

In that moment of stark despair, all of a sudden, Jerry stopped. The tears stopped, he stopped thinking, he stopped trembling: It even felt as if the world stopped turning. In a split second, a clarity he had never known before sunk into his body, and it emerged as one single word: *Enough.*

I've had enough, he thought. *I cannot live numb, on the run from my emotions, my pain, and my isolation one more minute.* Jerry realized the life he created in airports, airplanes, hotels, and boardrooms could not continue. He was tired to the bone. Overhead he heard the announcement of his flight's two-hour delay. The word "delayed" lingered in his ears as Jerry realized, that for entirely too long, he had delayed this pivotal awakening to his need for true intimacy.

How many of us have "delayed" intimacy in our own lives? How many of us make excuses, or create a life that moves so fast we try to keep our pain, loneliness, and isolation at bay?

What Is Intimacy?

Intimacy invites us to "into-me-see." Could this be one of the reasons that we fear intimacy so much? How many of us are willing to be vulnerable enough to let others see into our real selves? For that matter, how many of us are willing to be vulnerable enough to look into ourselves alone? It takes great courage and compassion to enter this sacred painful place for many of us. The landscape of intimacy is fraught with uncertainty and questions. But it is also filled with love, hope, partnership, sharing, communion, and endless possibilities for transformation and new life. Intimacy is an essential element for anyone to experience a life of true happiness.

True intimacy with oneself, with another, and with community promises endless opportunities for physical, mental, and spiritual growth and well-being. Our cultural myth of rugged individualism is destroying us on every level, but the truth is "isolation kills and community heals."

Love as intimacy replenishes and sustains our minds, bodies, and souls, and is created and fostered in community. It is a primal need of humans as social beings to belong to something greater than our individual selves. A transcendent healing power transforms us and graces us when we live and thrive in community.

Relationships heal and sustain us in all of their forms including families, friends, clubs, organizations, neighborhoods, towns, states, and countries. Studies have shown how isolation leads to chronic stress and disease. Relationship is the path to real intimacy and the feelings of connection that heal. It draws us together and makes us whole.

As we expand our definition of love, intimacy, and community we can begin to discover the nurturing support that is the path to true happiness in life.

Intimacy and Your Self

Intimacy is closeness, familiarity, affection, understanding, and connection—essentially with your Self and with others. Intimacy understood as connection, communion, and vulnerability with your Self is critical. Too often you are led to believe that you can only experience intimacy if you have a partner or some "other" person in your life. In fact it is difficult to know real intimacy with another person if we don't have it with ourselves first. We are created to root our Self in an intimate relationship first with our Source, the Divine, the Holy; then we build other relationships after we have developed this foundation.

It's difficult in a busy family to focus on putting your mental, physical, and spiritual well-being first, but it is the key to experiencing true happiness. My husband and I went to a marriage counselor many years ago and he told us something I will never forget. As a matter of fact I have used this wisdom in my counseling for over 15 years. Our marriage had been under enormous stress for many different reasons and we hadn't noticed, but we had both begun to put our teenage children first in our lives. Their sports, academic, and social events had risen to the top of our priorities. It wasn't something we had designed, it had evolved over time. It was easier in this difficult time of our marriage to put the children first in our lives and put our relationship on the back burner.

What I learned that day in that session was invaluable and transformed our lives and our marriage. There is a natural order to the universe and if you don't have respect and live according to this order, you will never experience true happiness and balance. The natural order of relationship is simple: First is your relationship or connection with your Source, the Divine, the Holy; second is your relationship with your spouse; third is your relationship with your children; fourth is your relationship with your work and community. If you put your children, your spouse, or your work first, it just won't work. It is essential to root yourself in your Source, Divine Energy, or any name or image you choose to use for your Creator or God. This is the order to discover true happiness, balance, and your mental, physical and spiritual well being. This order provides an abundant source of energy, love, and intimacy.

This was hard for my husband and me to hear, but it was the truth. We had so much pain and anger in our relationship, it was easier to put our children and our work before our relationship. Many individuals don't have an intimate spiritual life of connection to some force greater than themselves that provides solace, power and love. As painful as that situation was, we now had a set of priorities that we chose to respect and focusing on this turned our life around. We learned to discover a new depth to our relationship we had never known. This takes intentional focus by you to create boundaries that firmly establish this order in your life.

Intimacy is the ability to experience love, acceptance, and a sense of wonder within oneself. It is an act of great courage to intentionally want to see who you really are. Intimacy asks of you vulnerability, surrender, forgiveness, and acceptance of the essence of who you really are. When you give yourself permission to see into yourself, you descend into a deeper, more profound connection with yourself, with the Divine, and with others. Your expectations and demands of others become less because you have discovered how to care for your intimate Self first.

Intimacy is a basic human need, like food and shelter. It is sad that most of us are on an eternal search for intimacy in our lives, but we live in the illusion that it takes someone outside of ourselves for us to experience real intimacy.

It is important to develop a sense of your own Self as the foundation for intimacy. Most of us rush into relationships only to then discover what has been hidden with in us. It then becomes easy to blame the other person in the relationship for "making" these negative inner parts of yourself affect the relationship. There are very few of us who have taken the time and energy to experience intimacy with ourselves.

Selficide

A friend of mine, Dr. Patrick Malone, in his book, *The Windows of Experience,* uses a term called "selficide."[1] Dr. Malone describes *selficide* as "the leaking of your personhood. It is a living death," he asserts. Selficide is the killing of your real inner Self that was created for a purpose, and denying yourself an intentional life of true happiness. When you cut yourself off from knowing the inner you, you commit selficide. If you have imprisoned your mind, fearing to discover who you are, what you want in life, and what your purpose is, you are committing selficide.

When you commit selficide you destroy the Divine potential of your body, soul, and mind. You injure, damage, and deaden your Self and don't even realize it. You may wonder, how do I know if I am committing selficide? I would ask if you are experiencing passion, curiosity, energy, meaningful relationships, and true happiness. Are you connected to the vast universe within yourself and the one outside your Self? Do you feel alive? Are you living confidently knowing the purpose of your life is unfolding? If you answered yes to all these, congratulations, you are obviously experiencing intimacy and happiness. But if you answered no to these questions you are committing selficide. Don't feel bad; there aren't just a few of you—millions of people commit selficide each and every day.

Journey Home to Intimacy

The journey back to our intimate Self is not an event; it is a process that takes choice, intention, and commitment. If intimacy has been missing from your life for a long time, it won't return overnight. Intimacy is like a muscle that needs to be exercised and cared for on a regular basis or it will atrophy.

You may ask, how do I begin to discover intimacy with my Self? You begin with listening to your life. Begin exploring your intimate Self through your senses; smells, touch, sounds, tastes, and images. What is your favorite plant or flower? What kind of music makes you feel passionate and connected? What scents make your heart flutter or bring an instant smile to your face? What is your favorite food? What is your favorite color and where is it in your life? Is it on your walls, your clothes, the car you drive or your shoes? Begin to discover who you are and your purpose by first becoming aware of what attracts you and what repels you.

Nature is a great place to probe your intimate Self. When it rains the next time notice how you relate to the rain. Do you notice the sound, the smell and what you see in the rain? Does it make you want to run and play in it or get under a cover in a comfortable place and read a good book as you slowly fall off into a nap? There are innumerable possibilities to experience a primal sense of intimacy in nature: the silence of a fresh snow, a summer night echoing with the sound of crickets, or the midnight sky scattered with bright stars. Nature is a powerful ally on your path to intimacy.

A good book can bring you great pleasure and get you back in touch with your intimate Self. Whether it is a love story, a book on flowers, cooking, or a self-help book with great tips, a book can nudge your curiosity and nourish your intimacy.

Many of us have been wounded or just don't know how to begin this journey into intimacy. One of my favorite things to do is watch great movies. Keep the classics or the ones you especially like in your own movie library, but you can always rent them or watch pay-per-view. Some of my movies are like a long trusted friend. When I get numb or flat I will pull out my tried and true friends, like *Out of Africa, Steel Magnolias, Prince of Tides,* or *Gandhi.* A great movie will always lead you home to your real Self, where your emotions, values, and love reside.

Create rituals that make you feel loved and nurtured. Keep your favorite tea on hand and create your own tea ceremony. Use your favorite scents, candles, and music to take a sensual bath. Make sure your bedroom is peaceful and can be made dark and silent for a restorative nap. There are innumerable paths to lead you home to your intimate Self. There are many windows to the soul. Nature, water, music, art, a pet—all of these have the potential for engaging the senses and thus creating a greater intimacy with yourself and others.

While not exclusive to intimacy, if you feel that depression, anxiety, or insomnia are keeping you from intimacy or limiting you in any other way from fully experiencing your life, you may want to explore meditation, prayer, yoga, or other mindfulness exercises. If these practices do not help you with your depression, anxiety, or insomnia, you may want to consult a physician. There are remarkable medicines available on the market today that are helping people live healthier, more productive lives. You can try different methods to help yourself or ask a professional for help, but there is no reason for you to suffer.

Intimacy is not a luxury in your life; science is telling us it is essential for your mental, physical, and spiritual well being. Most of the individuals I work with feel that intimacy with oneself is a luxury and is something that they will do when they "have time." Intimacy is not a luxury, it is necessary for you to discover true happiness and balance in your and your family's life. You can learn how to experience the power of intimacy in the everyday activities of your life.

Intimacy with Another

What is stopping you from experiencing intimacy with others? It can be past difficulties in relationships and the resulting fear, anger, or depression. Are your current relationships defined by your wounds of the past? After we are wounded by a relationship with another individual or a group, we tend to withdraw and build walls so we won't get hurt by intimacy again. Or your body and soul may have become numb as a result of a past negative experience of intimacy.

Most of us in our culture are living a sleep-deprived life. Sleep deprivation or insomnia kills intimacy. When we are exhausted, it is almost impossible to muster the energy to be intimate. Sleep is an essential basic need of your body. Your body will prioritize what it must have and what it can do without if it only has a minimal amount of energy. Intimacy will fall way down on the list when your body is sleep deprived.

Stress—a modern epidemic—creates a state of almost constant worry, exhaustion, and defensiveness. Do you find yourself worrying about what you did or did not do today, what happened yesterday, and what will happen tomorrow? Stress will rob you of intimacy and happiness. When you are stressed and worried your mind is somewhere else, you are not present in the moment and surely you are not present in the relationship. Your mind, body, and soul must be fully present or there is no possibility for intimacy with others.

Our massive technology has become one of our greatest culprits in our desire for intimacy. Cell phones, e-mails, and beepers often serve to isolate and alienate us from ourselves and from others we love in our lives. Even as you talk to a significant person on your cell phone, it may give you an illusion of intimacy with that person, but remember you need real physical presence to create the energy, the fiber of intimacy.

Our world dictates that we move faster and we live in the fantasy that intimacy is something that just "happens" when we have time. True intimacy cannot be experienced as long as you are racing through your life. Intimacy demands you slow down, a move inward first, and then you naturally organically turn outward to connect with others.

Our desire to be intimate with another person is a universal human feeling that is generated by specific chemicals and networks in your brain. We are beginning to identify sound science showing that an active sex life may led to a longer life, better health, less depression, and build a better immune system. Besides all that, the act of intercourse burns about 200 calories, the same as running for 30 minutes. Your body, driven by your brain, becomes immersed in a chemical bath of dopamine and other luscious chemicals.

There are some interesting studies about sexual activity and your health. A study in Wales showed that men who had sex twice a week or more experienced half as many heart attacks after 10 years as men who had intercourse less than once a month.[2] A study of 3,500 men in Scotland found a link between frequency of sexual intercourse and greater longevity.[3]

There is a direct relationship between love and health. Love is a relationship with people and that is what makes your life rich and rewarding.

▶ According to the study of 30,000 American men by the Harvard School of Public Health, men who become widowed, separated or divorced experience a serious downturn in health. Marriage is excellent for men's health. Divorced men are more likely than their married peers to drink, develop Alzheimer's disease, or take their own lives.[4]

▶ According to a Duke University study, married people have lower incidences of cancer, heart disease, stroke, and many other ailments than people who have never married, or who are widowed, or divorced. Those with a supportive partner also, on average, recover more quickly from serious illness.[5]

▶ A University of Pittsburgh study found that married people had lower levels of biological and lifestyle cardiovascular risk factors— such as lower blood pressure levels, cholesterol levels, and body mass index—and lower levels of psychosocial cardiovascular risk factors, such as depression, anxiety, and anger.[6]

▶ The National Center for Health Statistics and the CDC show married people are less likely to drink, smoke, or be physically inactive.[7]

▶ Professor Linda Waite, University of Chicago, finds there is a direct relationship between being married or having a partner and a decrease in death rates.[8]

Love creates an optimistic and euphoric set of healing chemicals that are released into the body. These chemicals boost your immune system to fight off diseases such as cancer. These healing chemicals also help with diseases associated with inflammation such as arthritis, lupus, and other inflammatory diseases. These chemicals are beneficial to your cardiovascular system and thus prevent strokes, hypertension, and heart disease.

We have a natural drive to experience intimacy and love. Studies reveal the incredibly powerful brain circuitry we have for romantic love. We have an innate sex drive and a deep desire for a romantic partner to share our mind, body and soul with. These drives are the most primordial needs of our existence. The desire to partner with another is the essence of most songs written, poems penned, and movies produced. The most assured way of achieving this glorious natural goal of sharing a life of intimacy with another is to first discover and nurture your intimacy with your Self.

The Science of Attraction

We know that every thought, action, and food creates a chemical response in our body. There is a common phrase in our culture that most of us have heard through the years, when we say that a certain couple has "great chemistry together."

Researchers have known about odorless molecules called pheromones that float through the air and signal survival responses in animals. Survival responses of animals are seeking a mate and finding food. But scientists have been curious to know whether humans use pheromones to communicate with each other chemically. Neurogeneticists at Rockefeller University and Yale have isolated a human gene they believe is a pheromone receptor. Pheromones attach to this receptor when they are inhaled into the mucous lining of the nose.[9]

Researchers in Utah recently found a pheromone that helps reduce tension, anxiety, and other stress in women, as reported in the *Journal of Psychoneuroendocrinology*. The study's co-author, David L. Berliner, M.D., says they definitely found that humans communicate with each other with pheromones, just like animals.[10] A study at the University of Chicago revealed that pheromones in underarm sweat synchronize the menstrual cycles of women living in close proximity to each other.[11]

Just look at your pets, your cat, and your dog. When you are angry the pets will distance themselves from you, and when you are feeling happy and amorous, the pets will come very close. These animals' survival has always depended upon their keen sense of smell.

Researchers are also studying the effects of how our bodies look when we release certain chemicals when we are angry, sad, or happy. The muscles in our bodies immediately respond to the release of these chemicals associated with our thoughts and make us draw up or expand and get flexible; therefore our bodies look different according to our thoughts and emotions.

So it only makes sense that when you have kind, compassionate, grateful thoughts, you are producing a completely different set of chemical responses in your body than when you are thinking angry, hateful, fearful thoughts. Every thought either enhances and heals your body or depletes and destroys your body. We now have the technology and science that proves this. It is time to take responsibility for the health consequences of your lifestyle; what you think, what you say, and what you eat, will create disease or health in your life.

Intimacy and Friendship

It is important to cultivate the art of friendship and to understand the critical nature of friendship in our lives. It is imperative that we discover the time for friends in our lives. Those of us who manage a family, a career, and a community can experience isolation. We live on tight schedules filled with time for kids, spouses, venues at school, sports, work, commutes, and meetings. These tight schedules can lead to isolation along with the complexities of family responsibilities, commuting, job hours, telecommuting, freelancing, and home offices. Many of the professional individuals I work with enjoy their dream job of working from home; however, the shadow side of that is the isolation from community. Having friends and spending time with them may not just be a luxury, it creates health. Friends are an essential element in work-life balance. One of the greatest challenges in our busy lives is maintaining relationships with our friends, let alone making new friends. Our demanding schedules often leave little time for the seemingly "unproductive" moments spent in the company of a dear friend.

Good friends hold us through deaths, graduations, marriages, holidays, suicides, and divorces. They lift us when we sink and celebrate when we soar. We must find creative ways to nurture these powerful bonds.

Studies show that isolation decreases immune functioning and increases mortality risk; cancer survivors with supportive friends have been shown to have twice the survival rate of control groups. Close friendships are strong indicators of mental, physical, and spiritual health. So cultivating the art of friendship is not a luxury, but is essential to work-life balance and health.

Solutions for Isolation

▶ Prioritize time with friends. Give them the same importance as a business meeting or doctor's appointment.

▶ Block out time on your calendar to e-mail, call, or send a handwritten note to someone you love at least twice a week.

❯ Share a meal with a friend at least twice a month.

❯ Exercise, study, or meditate together.

❯ Coordinate a conference call with a group of old friends once a month.

❯ Expand your concept of friendship to include women and men from all age groups and all walks of life—each has unique gifts.

Commit today to exploring the restorative power of friendship.

The Healing Power of Community

Another type of intimacy is our need for community. When we live in community our lives become greater than ourselves. We discover new meaning, purpose, and promise in our lives through community. We become part of a greater more dynamic and life changing organism.

The pioneering cardiologist, Dr. Dean Ornish, in his book *Love and Survival* states:

> Increasing scientific evidence from my own research and from the studies of others that cause me to believe that love and intimacy are among the most powerful factors in health and illness, even though these ideas are largely ignored by the medical profession. I am not aware of any other factor in medicine—not diet, not smoking, not exercise, not stress, not genetics, not drugs, not surgery—that has a greater impact on our quality of life, incidence of illness, and premature death from all causes.[12]

This is quite a profound statement and it has haunting repercussions if we consider that most individuals today live hurried lives of isolation.

Here are some studies that demonstrate the healing power of community:

❯ Dr. L. F. Berkman and colleagues of the California Department of Health Services studied 7,000 men and women living in Alameda County near San Francisco. They found those who lacked social and community ties, contact with friends, relatives, marriage, church, and group membership, were 1.9 to 3.1 times more likely to die during the nine-year follow-up period. They continued the study another eight years, a total of 17 years, and found the same results. Those with the strongest social ties had dramatically lower rates of disease and premature death than those who felt isolated and alone.[13]

▶ Dr. David Spiegel at Stanford Medical School studied women with metastatic breast cancer, researching whether individuals in a group had a prolonged life compared to those not in a group. The women who had the weekly support group lived on average twice as long as did the other group of women who didn't have the support group.[14]

▶ Dr. F.I Fawzy at UCLA School of Medicine studied patients with malignant melanoma who had participated in a support group for six weeks, six years earlier. The patients who had participated in the group support sessions had a significantly better survival rate than the comparison group. Three of thirty-four patients who were in the support group died after six years, compared with ten of the thirty-four patients dying in the nonsupport group: more than three times as many deaths. As for recurrence, seven of the group-support patients experienced recurrence compared with thirteen of the nonsupport group, almost twice as many.[15]

There is no doubt that participating in some type of group is good for your health and longevity. It shouldn't surprise us. All great spiritual and religious teachers and all sacred scriptures from all religions tell us that the path to the holy is discovered in one's intimate relationship with the Divine and through community. Science is now showing us that the "feel good" chemicals in our bodies are released when we participate in relationship with others. Your immune system is boosted by these healing chemicals the body releases when you participate in a group.

Every research institution where I studied mind-body medicine had their patients in some type of group support. It doesn't matter whether it is heart disease, cancer, obesity, insomnia, AIDS, or any other disease, attending a group is on your prescription. Since we know it is an effective tool in disease management, it just makes sense that it is a good part of disease prevention and wellness.

I have witnessed the dramatic transformation of all the individuals in the cardiac rehab group I facilitated for many years. The education and tools the participants learned in the group gave them the confidence, knowledge, and power to make healthier choices in their lives.

The vulnerability, fears, and pain they shared in the group healed wounds and gave them immense hope for their future. The enormous love that was present in each group gave the participants courage and support to begin to live new lives of mental, physical and spiritual well being. The group drew each person, including me, out of our isolation that had grown out of our physical diseases, emotional pain, or shameful events in our lives. If you ask anyone in our cardiac group what they think about their experience of the group they will undoubtedly say, "We are a family."

You can discover a community in the most unexpected places. I moved to this small rural community years ago and began to go to a local hair salon to get my hair done. These angels who stand on their feet all day long to care for the many different shapes, colors, textures and styles of hair encapsulate what love and community are all about. I sit during each visit and observe the cadre of individual lives that weave in and out of the salon. There is the little old lady who shuffles in with her walker; the high school girl excited about her new look for the senior prom; and the woman who sits down with the worn wedding band mark still on her left hand, surviving one day at a time after her bitter divorce. This is the place where divorces, losses of children and loved ones, weddings, funerals, graduations, affairs, and diseases are shared. Every shame and pain in life is humbly unleashed in this holy sanctuary of perm solutions, gel and hair rollers, only to be redeemed by simple nods, hugs, nudges, tears, or laughter. This is a sacred temple of radical acceptance, advice, and unconditional love where before you leave you are anointed with hair spray, spritzer, and a kiss. They give their final benediction and in their soft and assured voices say, "I love you, see you next time sugar." As I get into my car and fasten my seat belt I close my eyes for a moment, smile, and am overwhelmed with gratitude for these high priestesses of the tresses whose daily existence exudes that of the saints; compassion, generosity and love. This is real community.

Community is one of the roots to true happiness. As you engage in community you experience intimacy with your Self. If you are not already in some group in your neighborhood, at work, as part of your hobby, or at your place of worship, there are an infinite number of ways to locate a group. Libraries hold meetings and classes on a variety of interests. Garden clubs hold regular meetings if you love horticulture. Local environmental groups clean up rivers, streets, and are involved in caring for the earth. If you love playing cards and haven't played in a while, check out the senior center or community center in your area. Book clubs and study clubs are hot now. Go online to your city or check with the library to locate book or study clubs. Animal lovers can volunteer at the local shelter and help groom, feed or adopt out pets to desperately needed homes. If you love working with kids, check out the mentoring and tutoring programs at local schools. Follow where your passion leads you and you can't help but discover your life infused with intimacy.

Animals Create Health

Animals can be a source of intimacy for you. Many of the individuals I have worked with over the years have transformed their lives by simply getting a pet. It teaches individuals with wounds from intimacy how to trust again and how to experience a connection with something alive. An animal also allows you to actually touch, smell, hear, and smell something outside of your Self and thus stimulate your sensory Self. Most pets are naturally intimate and as you observe and interact with your animal you will grow into intimacy. They will also teach you to laugh, play, nap, and be silent, all excellent conditions for intimacy.

There is strong scientific evidence revealing the benefits of owning a pet, such as reduction of blood pressure and inducing a relaxation response in our bodies.

Pets are like having a silent best friend with you at all times. Research indicates that because pets provide people with faithful companionship, they may also provide their owners with a measure of psychological stability and, thus, a measure of protection from heart disease. People with pets make fewer visits to a doctor, are less stressed, and pets help people fight depression and loneliness.

There are even studies that show evidence of the positive effects of having pets in the workplace. A study from the State University of New York at Buffalo found those exposed to stressful situations had lower heart rates and blood pressure when their pet was nearby. Their heart rates and blood pressure proved lower than another group in the study which had a spouse or friend nearby encouraging the individual.[16] For over 25 years scientific research has shown the benefits of pet ownership including helping ward off depression, boosting immunity, and encouraging weight loss. The American Pet Products Manufacturers Association surveyed businesses and found 73 percent of the companies surveyed said pets create a more productive work environment, 27 percent reported a decrease in employee absenteeism, 96 percent said pets created positive work relations, 58 percent of employees stayed late with pets in the office, and 100 percent of the companies surveyed said they would continue to have pets in the workplace.[17] Job stress costs our corporations $300 billon annually. If we can lower job stress through pets in the workplace, we can lower this figure. We also know that people who are less stressed at work are more productive and creative.

Having a pet at work is good for employees. Pet Sitters International reports that bringing pets to work makes for happier employees and enhanced job performance. We know that pets contribute to good health in a number of ways, so pets at work means healthier workers.

There are innumerable paths to love and I hope you choose many. When you choose to root your life in love, endless potential and vast opportunities will flow into your life. Your life of happiness is rooted in your ability to embrace intimacy in all its diverse forms.

~ Begin Today ~

Ask Your Self Am I intimate with myself and in what ways?

Do I have friends? If not, why not?

Am I participating in some group I enjoy?

Tell Your Self I am perfect, whole, and complete.

Give Your Self Keep a journal to chronicle your path to greater intimacy.

Make a strong commitment to unstructured time with your loved ones.

Visit a new type of community: book club, study group, meditation group, yoga class, or online group. Discover a volunteer organization where you can volunteer once a month.

CHAPTER 9

Food

Replenish Your Self

I THOUGHT I had seen almost every kind of patient for spiritual direction, but Susan was my first insomniac. Frantic and despairing, she'd sought medical help as she went from doctor to doctor for nearly a year without finding relief, spending a small fortune on drugs and home remedies, the healing balm of sleep still eluding her.

Sleep, of course, is a primary source of human nourishment. Science has shown that the effects of sleep deprivation on our bodies and minds can be rapid and severe. I knew that if Susan didn't get help, she would soon have problems even more serious than anxiety, inability to focus, and fatigue.

Susan told me that her work forced her to spend most of her day sitting in front of a computer screen, which she disliked intensely. She spent most of her day in a daze, staring at the computer screen, exhausted from her chronic state of sleep deprivation. Her daily office routine put her on edge and so, in a failed attempt to find relief, she drank several glasses of wine each night. She also tended to eat on the run, while driving, watching television, or walking around her home. This had caused her to gain ten pounds over the last six months.

After endless tossing and turning Susan would resort to reading. She figured reading would eventually make her nod off. Her favorite author

Stephen King thrilled her, but the excitement and horror of the novels kept her captivated into the night. Susan's intentions were good but this type of reading actually stimulated her further. Some nights she would watch movies on television, but they were often violent or tragic, and after she turned off the movie she couldn't turn off her mind.

Susan was not aware of the anxiety she was creating within her body and her soul by her "unmindful consumption." By "unmindful consumption," I mean eating, reading, watching, and taking in a variety of toxins that were disrupting Susan's mental, physical, and spiritual well-being.

Susan and I spent an enormous amount of time examining her lifestyle. She was not aware of her habits and the consequences of her lifestyle. Susan was shocked as she gained new insight into her destructive lifestyle and understood how she was living a deteriorating life of habituation and mindlessness. Susan became aware that her choices were depleting her well-being and keeping her out of balance. Susan began to make new and better choices that nourished her in healthy ways. Within a short time, Susan's insomnia was gone and she was experiencing a new sense of balance and energy.

Nourish Your Mouth

Food in our culture is understood as organic material that goes into our mouths to sustain our bodies. Through my training, I have learned that other cultures and mind-body medicine have an expanded definition of food as nourishment. Nourishment is far beyond the limited context of diet and includes anything we consume into our bodies, minds or souls.

Nourishment is all sustenance taken in through our senses into our bodies—your mouth, ears, eyes, nose, and sense of touch—and it affects your physical and mental health and subsequent happiness.

Years ago when I was in the world of finance, something of value was called an asset. Webster's *Dictionary* defines an *asset* as a resource, valuable, wealth, riches, means, or a fortune. Your body is your greatest asset. Your body, your asset, is born into our world and accrues value or appreciates until fully grown in your late teens or early twenties. Your body reaches a turning point and begins to slowly depreciate after this point. Since our longevity charts tell us you will live to almost 80 years old, this is a lot of time on a depreciation schedule. The choices you make in creating your lifestyle include what you put into your body that will either accelerate or slow down your life depreciation schedule. Only you can make the choices necessary for your greatest resource to experience a life of happiness, health, and prosperity.

We have been on the run from our kitchens in years past, but there has been a revolution occurring in recent years. There is a radical desire to return to our kitchens. We are remodeling kitchens in hopes of their again becoming the heart and soul of the family space. The kitchen has become the new living room, with innovative appliances, entertainment nooks, and soft chairs inviting family and friends to gather around the table. Mealtime rituals can be the glue of our families and our society. Our lives are historically structured around our three feasts a day.

OUR CHILDREN

Most of us parents would never think of participating in life threatening behavior with our children, such as leaving them home alone or locking them in the car while we went shopping. But with childhood obesity growing and creating life threatening conditions that will plague our children's lives, we are endangering the lives of our children. We must begin to focus on this epidemic. Gerald S. Berenson, M.D., of Tulane University studied 14,000 children and young adults, making it the longest and most detailed study of children in the world. Dr. Berenson says half of these kids will die of heart disease if they continue their current lifestyle. Autopsies of children who died in accidents found that fatty streaks in their aorta began developing by age 3, and the damage showed up in the coronary arteries by age 10.[1]

The determinants of long-term health, food preferences, and eating behavior, are decided in childhood. We establish our eating patterns in childhood, and they are very difficult to change in adulthood. Richard Strauss, M.D., director of the Childhood Weight Control Program at the Robert Wood Johnson Medical School in New Brunswick, New Jersey, is concerned about the latest statistics that show one in five kids are overweight and one in eight children are obese. Our overweight children have become an urgent national health problem. Dr. Strauss believes that not getting together as a family at dinnertime has helped create this epidemic.[2]

The good news is that there is now a national campaign targeting childhood obesity, and that help is on the way. There are many things you can do now:

▶ *Eat a family meal together.* There are several large studies reported in the *Journal of Adolescent Health* that substantiate the fact that the children who sat down to evening meals with their parents ate more fruits, vegetables, and dairy foods and were less likely to skip breakfast. When parents are present at the dinner table the meal is likely to be more healthful and the children are more likely to eat it.[3]

▶ *Turn off the television, the computer, and the phone.* According to a study in the *Journal of Nutrition Education and Behavior,* families who watch television during dinner eat fewer fruits and vegetables and eat more high fat foods.[4] A Boston University study showed that children who watched three hours or more of television per day had 30 percent more body fat than similar kids who watched less than 1.75 hours per day.[5]

▶ *Control what foods are in your home.* Control the food but don't control the child. According to a studying the *American Journal of Clinical Nutrition,* five-year-olds whose mothers controlled their food intake showed significant increases in overeating by age 7 and had additional increases in eating by age 9.[6] Allow children to monitor their level of consumption while you monitor what they are consuming.

▶ *Like Mother, like Daughter, like Father, like Son.* The greatest influence upon a child's eating habits is the example set by the parents. Your children are mirrors of your behavior, so eat intentionally and choose wisely. You are literally creating their future.

WHAT HAPPENED TO OUR SUPPER?

Most of us have lived our lives in drive through lanes at restaurants and collecting to-go boxes, as we shuttle one child to soccer and another to music lessons. Many of us eat on the run and eat so fast we can't even remember what we ate in our previous meal. This behavior has resulted in a plague of obesity for us and our children. The cost of obesity in this country is $75 billion annually.[7] Obesity has a direct effect on almost all diseases, especially heart disease, hypertension, type 2 diabetes, cancer, and arthritis. According to a recent study of eating patterns, only 49 percent of the families studied ate dinner together seven nights a week, and 74 percent ate together five nights a week.[8]

Many experts have opinions on why we stopped eating dinner together. Dr. Beth Ann Sheldon, University of Texas at Arlington, believes that more women working outside the home makes family dinner difficult. Dr. Sheldon also believes more children today participate in outside activities after school, making it more difficult to coordinate dinner. Northwestern University sociology professor Allan Schnaiberg attributes the waning of the family dinner to more adolescents working today, as this interferes with going home for dinner with the family. Dr. Schnaiberg also believes the technology in our kitchens has disrupted our interpersonal relationships during dinner. His studies show that while one person is using the microwave, another is loading the dishwasher, and someone else is getting something out of the freezer to defrost.[9]

It is important for us to realize that there are two essential parts to eating dinner together. One part is the food, and the second crucial part of the meal is the sociological and psychological support we so essentially need.

NECESSARY FOODS FOR YOU

I could write a treatise on diet, but I am just going to touch on some things I believe are important for everyone to know. First and foremost, 90 to 95 percent of people who lose weight with diet gain most or all of the weight back within three to five years. Oftentimes, more body fat or weight is gained back due to yo-yo dieting. Here are several reasons diets may fail, and there most surely are more:[10]

❥ Most diets restrict caloric intake so much that metabolism slows down, thus hindering the weight loss process.

❥ Dieting may result in depression, which is counterproductive to losing weight.

❥ Most diets do not encourage lifestyle changes. To have permanent weight loss, you must make permanent changes in food choices, eating habits, and physical activity.

❥ With very low calorie diets, weight loss is usually lean body weight as opposed to fat weight.

❥ Exercise is not part of the program.

I am a big believer in "everything in moderation." Real, healthy weight loss can only occur through balanced eating and a sensible exercise program.

Whether we like it or not, the jury is in about the relationship between the amount of fat we consume and diseases such as heart disease, strokes, and certain cancers. Research has given us evidence that eating a diet that is low in fat can help prevent arterial aging, prevent strokes, and stop plaque buildup. Recent studies are showing low fat diets may have a direct effect on preventing the recurrence of certain cancers. All of this new research on the staggering implications of the amount of fat we consume is very important. The recommendation of how much fat should be in your diet varies according to different diets. I advise everyone to talk to their physicians and to get more information about fat and your diet from credible sources.

Simple lifestyle changes can reduce the risk of tumor recurrence in breast cancer survivors. A study of more than 2,400 women with early breast cancer who followed a low fat diet were 25 percent less likely to have their cancer return in five years than the women who continued to eat their typical diets. The goal was to reduce dietary fat intake to 20 percent or less of the total daily calories. Women in the study who followed the low fat diet went from 51 grams per day of fat to about 33 grams of fat per day, or from 29 percent to 21 percent of their total daily calories. This study was recently presented at the annual meeting of the American Society of Clinical Oncology. Fats in our diet have been linked to the most common cancers, including breast, colon, and prostate cancers.[11]

The American Heart Association stated that unhealthy habits account for 82 percent of heart disease in women.[12] Our lifestyle interventions are essential for our mental and physical health and well-being. Doctors believe that as much as 70 percent of all chronic disease in this country— such as hypertension, heart disease, diabetes, and cancer—can be warded off with diet and lifestyle changes.[13]

Let's focus on the foods that can prevent disease, slow down aging, and create good health in your life. There is good science telling us there are certain foods you simply must put in your diet regularly. Food is medicine. Food regulates your moods, your brain, and your health. Food is our fuel. We are what we eat. These foods promote health, help heal diseases, and retard the aging process:

▶ Eat fish. A study in the *Journal of the American Medical Association* showed that women who consume 8 oz. of fish a week cut their risk of suffering a stroke in half.[14]

❱ Eat fish rich in Omega-3 fatty acids like mackerel, lake trout, herring, sardines, albacore tuna, and salmon. This may help protect brain cells from the diseases of aging, like Alzheimer's, and may block the production of inflammatory substances linked to autoimmune diseases like rheumatoid arthritis. Omega-3s make platelets in the blood less sticky and decrease the risk of clotting.[15]

❱ Broccoli is a great source of beta-carotene, fiber, and vitamin C. A number of studies have linked regular consumption of cruciferous vegetables like broccoli to a reduced risk of breast, stomach, and colon cancers.[16]

❱ Blueberries contain more antioxidants than any other fruit or vegetable. The powerful compounds in blueberries belong to the flavonoid family. These combat free radical damage linked to heart disease and cancer. Studies show blueberries may boost your brainpower also. Blueberries, like cranberries, also fight off urinary tract infections.

❱ Strawberries promote heart and circulatory health by reducing artery damaging inflammation, according to a study by Gene Spiller, Ph.D., of the Sphera Foundation in Los Altos, California.[17]

❱ Green tea is loaded with polyphenols, a phytochemical with 100 times the antioxidant power of vitamin C. Dr. Stephen Hsu, a Medical College of Georgia researcher, discovered green tea polyphenols help eliminate free radicals, which can damage DNA and lead to cancer. He further proved that green tea induced p57; a protein that helps regulate cell growth.[18]

❱ Black tea may help protect against various forms of cancer, cardiovascular disease, Alzheimer's, Parkinson's disease, and rheumatoid arthritis, according to Dr. Jack Bukowski and other researchers at the Brigham and Women's Hospital in Boston. They found that drinking 20 oz. of tea every day for two weeks doubled or tripled the immune system's output of an infection fighting substance called interferon gamma.[19]

❱ Tomatoes cooked in soups, sauces, or ketchups reduce the risk of prostate cancer and other cancers of the digestive tract. Tomatoes contain a powerful antioxidant called lycopene. A Harvard University study found that middle-aged women, who consumed high levels of lycopene for an average of five years, were 30 percent less likely to develop heart disease than women who got far less of the antioxidant.[20]

❭ Cinnamon taken daily reduced total cholesterol, bad cholesterol, and triglycerides anywhere from 13 to 30 percent in study done by Richard Anderson, Ph.D. of the U.S. Department of Agriculture. This is comparable with statin drugs. Cinnamon seems to help the body use insulin more efficiently. Cinnamon also cuts blood sugar levels by 20 to 30 percent.[21]

❭ Beans are close to the perfect food. They are chock full of protein, vitamins, calcium, fiber, and more. Red beans have more antioxidants per serving than any other fruit or vegetable.

❭ Sauerkraut appears to unlock strong anticarcinogenic elements, according to a study in the Journal of *Agricultural and Food Chemistry.* Dr. Eeva-Liisa Ryhanen of MTT Agrifood Research Finland showed that fermented cabbage—sauerkraut—could be healthier than raw or cooked cabbage, especially for fighting cancer.[22]

❭ Vitamin B6 is found in sweet potatoes, bananas, mangoes, tuna, sunflower seeds, salmon, turkey, chicken, rice, and barley. Researchers found that vitamin B6 helps the body to manufacture chemicals, such as serotonin. Serotonin is a healing hormone that is essential for coping with anxiety.

It is such an exciting time to be alive. We now have good science that educates us on a variety of foods, so we can make informed choices that determine the quality of our lives.

In most cases children in a household will comply with a healthy diet when you can give them a reason why certain foods are especially good for them. Most of us don't have time to purchase the latest diet books and learn to cook all over again. So the basic rule of thumb is simple: eat deeply colored vegetables and fruits, grains, and protein sources. Add anything else you love but make sure your family gets the essentials.

You might want to play a game at the dinner table once a week to find out what family members know about the nutritional values of the meal. This will help you educate yourself and your family about nutrition and making healthy choices in food.

Nourish Your Nose

Scents are the food for your sense of smell. If you have to be convinced about the immense influence of smell on your well-being, let me ask you a question. Do you remember walking in on Thanksgiving and your mouth watering as you caught a whiff of the imminent feast? Do you remember the smell of fresh-baked cookies? Do you remember how your mouth watered, your heart rate increased, and your mood changed almost instantly? This is aromatherapy.

Aromatherapy has been around for more than 6,000 years. It has become big business these days. Daily you will see intermittent television commercials advertising a variety of smells you can plug into your electrical sockets, or scented candles you can place throughout your home.

Smelling something that comforts you, calms you, or makes you happy is at your fingertips these days. There are many scents that have been used for hundreds of years for many conditions.

Cultural and Historical Significance of Aromatherapy

We know aromatherapy has been used by humans since the beginning of time. Ancient cultures used aromatherapy for medicinal healing, for worship rituals, and for personal use. The ancients knew aromas had a great effect upon the body, mind, and soul. In worship, aromatherapy, through time evolving into incense and scented sacred oils, has been used since the beginning of the worship of the Divine. The royalty of ancient cultures always believed certain aromas signified power and authority.

I have used aromatherapy with my clients and patients for many years. I use lavender combinations with my patients with cancer and other critical diseases. I also use lavender for my people with grief, anxiety, and depression disorders. Lavender is an ancient herb with calming properties that works incredibly for stress, anxiety, and depression. Lavender is known for its ability to comfort. Lavender seeds were used in classrooms in 19th century France to calm boisterous children. French pharmacies sold lavender for generations as a sleep aid. Nagano College of Nursing in Japan monitored the electrocardiograms, blood flow, and respiratory rates of nursing students after they enjoyed a footbath with lavender oil, and they found significant changes in autonomic activity, which increased relaxation. I use citrus aromas—such as orange, tangerine, or lemon—for my patients and clients with depression, chronic fatigue syndrome, and anxiety. Vanilla is another aroma I have had a great experience with. Peppermint gives you a mental boost and can increase circulation and revitalize your mind and make you feel energized. Lime and citrus are invigorating. I have found that aromatherapy is a perfect adjunct therapy for physical, psychological, and spiritual conditions.

There are many aromatherapy books on the market, but I prefer a more nose-on approach. I suggest that a person go to any store where they normally shop. Wal-Mart, Target, Bath and Body Works, and even grocery stores and pharmacies all have a variety of aromatherapy products. Start by literally smelling the products, close your eyes, and be aware of how your mind, body, and soul experience that particular aroma. Ask yourself how this aroma makes you feel. Purchase the smallest quantity possible to experiment with each fragrance. You may want to begin with some body cream, a candle, incense, or an essential oil. I personally suggest that a person choose one aroma that calms and centers you, and another aroma that perks your senses and makes you feel alive. Aromatherapy is a very individual thing. Your nose will tell you what works for you.

Nourish Your Ears

We are bombarded with noise in our busy world today. Research shows us that certain high-pitch noises in cities create stress in the population.

Sound is also proven to be beneficial to our health. Aural nourishment through the form of music has proven to be helpful in many studies by reducing anxiety, relieving the symptoms of depression, and lowering blood pressure. Dr. Rosalia Staricoff of London's Chelsea and Westminster Hospital also found patients receiving chemotherapy while listening to live music had 32 percent lower anxiety levels and 31 percent lower depression levels than those who did not listen to music.[23]

It's time to nourish your ears with music. Music reduces stress by producing serotonin in our body. Listening to calming music decreases your physical responses, such as heart rate and respiration. Stimulating music increases your heart rate and respiration and causes you to feel more energetic. Music can shift you mood almost immediately. Soothing background music in companies increases productivity.

Performing music is beneficial to your health as well. A study from the University of California at Irvine found that levels of the disease-fighting protein, Immunoglobulin A, increased by 150 percent during choir rehearsals and 240 percent during performances.[24]

Nourish your ears by accumulating music that has a calming effect on you and music that invigorates you.

Nourish Your Eyes

Color can change your mood almost immediately. Take some time to surround yourself with your favorite colors. The colors that attract you can stimulate or calm you. Decide what you need at work. Do you need to be calmed at work or do you have a tendency to be slow at work and need to be stimulated?

In my experience with a variety of individuals over many years I have come to believe that color has an influence on a person's well-being. Think of how great you feel when you are wearing your favorite color and how uncomfortable you are when you are wearing a color that you dislike. A person's like or dislike of different colors is very individual and unique. When I do a history on a person I always ask about the colors they like and dislike, and where they have them located in their lives. Are these colors at your office, in your wardrobe, your car, your bedroom, or you home? If no, why not?

*　　*　　*

I was seeing a 25-year-old woman with metastatic breast cancer. She had her first lesion when she was age 21. She was not doing well, and her prognosis was horrible this time. I will never forget the look on her pale face when I asked her about her favorite color. I was sitting across from her frail body and asked, "Jenny, what is your favorite color?" She immediately got some color in her cheeks and busted out with a huge smile and immediately blurted out, "Purple, I just love purple. When I was a little girl I had a purple Care Bear and I just loved her. I have always just loved purple."

I sat there in a surprising silence because this young woman had only barely whispered for the entire 30 minutes of my interview. As she heard my question on color she became passionate and animated for the first time. "Well, Jenny, I can see you love purple. Your entire body is excited just talking about purple. So where in your life; your home, your car, your clothes, or your bedroom do you have this incredible purple?" Jenny looked down and slumped into silence for a moment and mumbled something I couldn't hear. I told her I couldn't hear her and asked her to talk louder. She whispered, "I don't have anything purple. I haven't had anything purple since I was in middle school." I asked, "What color is your bedroom?" "White," she answered. "What color is your car?" She softly said, "White." "What color clothes do you wear?" "I wear white and black clothes," she said almost shamefully.

I was intrigued and confused. "What do you think about when you think of purple Jenny?" She smiled and said, "I think of life, and happy and spiritual." I was aware that I had to go and our session was over. Her condition was so perilous that her parents were living with her to care for her. I asked Jenny if I could call her mother and talk to her. With her permission I called her mother and found out they had little money and were living from hand to mouth. Jenny's mother could sew so I asked her to go to a store that sold cloth and buy yards of purple material. I wanted her to put purple fabric on the windows and bed of Jenny's bedroom. I wanted Jenny to eat off purple place mats and to wear a simple purple dress. Whether she lived or not, I wanted this young woman to be drenched in purple before she died.

I saw Jenny a couple more times and then I never saw her again. A couple of months later I saw in the newspaper in the obituaries that Jenny had died. I called her mother to ask her how Jenny was in those last months and how she was. After a short conversation, I asked her mother, "Well, how did Jenny enjoy her purple life before she died?" There was a pause and her mother quickly said, "There was no purple. When Jenny got home her father and I told her how stupid this whole thing about purple was. I told her that I never did like purple, and white was just fine for her." I was shocked as I retorted, "You mean she didn't get any purple at all." "No ma'am." I politely hung up and cried in my office. Oh, how I wish I would have covered her with tons of purple. I wonder if it would have made a difference. I was haunted with unanswered questions for months. What difference would purple have made in a young woman's short fragile life? Could that simple desire have been a window to healing she was seeking? I'll never know, but I surely have never looked at purple the same.

*   *   *

Surround yourself with colors you love. Life is so short and wonderful. Color is a true gift to each of us. It can give you new life to surround yourself with the colors that make you happy, energetic, and powerful.

You can begin to collect art and surround yourself with meaningful objects of color. Copies of famous prints are very affordable and can bring you great joy. I have several Picasso, Degas, and Matisse prints that I love and they were very inexpensive.

Nourish Your Touch

I believe that nourishing your sense of touch is more important than ever. Many of us work on computers all day and don't use our hand to touch many different textures and surfaces anymore. You can keep a soft shawl or throw in your office and during the day make a point to touch the fabric and relax. As you eat your food, if it is bread, an apple or a candy bar, take your time and really feel the texture of your food.

Many conventional nursing schools teach therapeutic touch and encourage its use to help comfort patients. There is a great healing power in touch and research is now showing how critical touch is to our physical, mental, and spiritual well-being. Medicine and psychology are now confirming what many of us have believed: there is great healing power in touch. Many studies and experiments reveal that the simple act of touching another person results in physical benefits, such as dropping blood pressure, lowering heart rates, and increasing the recovery time of patients from illnesses.

Dr. James Lynch, professor at Baltimore's University of Maryland School of Medicine, has conducted extensive research on the impact of touch upon the body. Dr. Lynch says, "Physical contact has very dramatic effects upon psychological health. It lowers blood pressure and relaxes you."[25] Other experts agree. Research by Dr. Stephen Thayer, professor of psychology at the City University of New York, shows patients who have physical contact tend to have less anxiety and tension in their everyday lives.[26]

The fields of science and psychology are telling us something we innately know. Touching is good for you. I am a big hugger and love to be hugged. Some individuals have issues with being touched. I suggest these individuals at least get a pet they can touch and who touches them. Touching creates comfort and soothes us.

My daughter is a physician, and as part of her training she was rotating through the AIDS clinic seeing patients. At that time she was a medical student just beginning to see patients, and so she was very anxious and sensitive about interviewing patients to get their history and doing physical exams. She had just finished her work up of an AIDS patient and she felt that she had done a good job. Being pleased with herself she walked back to the nurses' station and was writing notes when one of the nurses ran up to her and asked her if she had just seen the patient in room 11. She said yes. The nurse said she could hear him sobbing and crying all the way down the hall. The nurse told her to go back and see what was going on with her patient.

My daughter walked back into the room and there sat the young gentleman on the edge of the examining table with tears running down his face. In a panic my daughter asked, "What happened? Did I hurt you? Did I say something wrong? What is going on?" There was a moment of silence as she handed him a tissue and then he said, "Thank you, Doctor. I am so grateful. Everyone sees these sores on my emaciated body and they stay away from me. No one has touched me in over a year. I had forgotten what it felt like to be touched by another human being. You were so gentle and kind and your touch was so compassionate. I can now die with dignity remembering how it feels to be touched and respected. The entire time you looked into my eyes with great respect. You touched me with such care and reverence. Thank you for this gift, Doctor. I will never forget you."

When my daughter told me this story I burst into tears and I loved her more than I can ever tell you. The power of touch is miraculous and can be a greater gift than we can probably imagine.

Mindful consumption is essential when you desire to live a life of health, happiness, and balance. The nourishment we choose to take into our bodies affects our mental, physical, and spiritual well being. Many things we choose to feed ourselves through our senses create toxins that impair our growth and health. It is vital that you become aware of how you are nourishing your body so you know how to choose life giving foods that give you life.

~ Begin Today ~

Ask Your Self   In what ways am I nourishing my mind?

What kind of healthy food choices am I making?

Are the television shows I am watching nourishing me?

Tell Your Self   I nourish my Self in loving ways.

Give Your Self Once a week, on television, DVD, or videotape, watch a program that has an educational component that interests you.

Commit to reading a book at least 10 minutes a day.

Create meals intentionally using more fruits and vegetables for your health and to aid healthy aging.

PART III: CELEBRATE YOUR NEW GROWTH

Discover Energy

THE GLIMMER OF the sun breaking over the ocean waves brought him out of his hypnotic like state. He couldn't remember what day it was or how long he had been sitting on the beach. He had to have been sitting there all night long because the sun was now rising and he had walked down and sat in the sand after the eleven o'clock evening news. That's how it had been lately for David, days of numbness, confusion, and disorientation. Ever since he sat in his doctor's office on Monday and heard the words, "We'll put you on the list for a heart transplant, but the list is long and your chances of getting a heart are small."

Everyone always said that David had more energy than anyone living. After just celebrating his 55th birthday, he seemed the picture of health. A self-proclaimed workaholic, David was always up at 4:30 A.M., to the gym by 5 A.M., showered and in the office by 6:30 A.M. This was his unbroken routine for over 30 years. He was always the first in the office and the last to leave. He set the bar for his employees and enjoyed the lauds of his competitors, always extolling that David was "self made" and how hard he worked. This routine reaped the rewards of great wealth, power, and status.

David didn't understand how someone as energetic as he was could possibly have a heart that was dying. He was always an exercise enthusiast. He had planned on slowing down when he felt he had "enough" money, but there never seemed to be enough money. He planned on slowing down and spending some time with his children as they were growing up, but before he knew it they were grown. He planned on spending some more time with his wife that he loved when he believed that he had saved enough money in his retirement, but there was never enough. They had drifted apart and seemed to grow accustomed to the silence between them. That's why David was so shocked when he received the divorce papers at his office last year.

He always felt like he had lots of energy and thought he was healthy, and he stayed active, working out every day, playing golf, tennis, and basketball twice a week. David has all the things that success promises except he will not live long enough to experience happiness and balance. I received a phone call from David just the other day with the news he was just diagnosed with cancer.

I wish I could say that there was only one David that had walked through the doors of my office, but I have seen too many women and men just like David throughout the years. Real energy does not occur by exhausting our mind, body, and soul and pushing our precious resources past their limits. It's sad; David's greatest asset was depreciated. David was unaware that what he thought was energy was really manic behavior disguised as workaholism. So many of us mistake the energy that drives our lives by anxiety, fear, and depression as real or pure energy. We begin to feed off this "false" energy.

What Is Energy?

Various cultures refer to energy in a variety of descriptions. Energy is described in Western culture as vigor, life, spirit, passion, power, and electromagnetism. The Hindus call vital energy *prana*. The Hebrew name for "vital energy" is *ruah*. The Chinese define energy as life force, or *chi*.

Prana is physical, mental, and spiritual energy in Hinduism. It is believed that *prana* is the fundamental energy and the source of all knowledge. By practicing yoga, *prana* continuously flows inside us, creating vitality in our bodies. Too little *prana* in the body can be expressed as a feeling of being stuck. You would have a lack of motivation, lack drive, and be depressed. When you lack *prana*, or vital energy, you may become ill. This philosophy believes that your state of mind is directly linked to the amount of *prana* within us. The more balanced and peaceful a person is, the more prana is inside your body. The more imbalanced or stressed you are, the more diluted the prana, or vital energy, is within your body. Prana is power, and the more you develop your breathing practices the more power you will experience.

Chi, in Eastern medicine, is the vital energy that flows though each organ and system of the body. All of these organs and systems are connected by this vital energy so if an organ is sick you must look at the entire body to find the cause of illness. This *chi,* or energy, is found at a molecular level. Western medicine would call this vital energy "electromagnetism," which holds the atoms in orbit around each other in your body. Chinese medicine works on the construct that when your body is sick, your chi, or energy, is out of balance and the flow of vital energy must be restored to a healthy flow. The way I describe this to my clients and patients is to imagine your body as a home that is wired with electrical wiring. Your body's electrical system is just like your home: Sometimes there is a short in the circuit or a loose wire. You call your electrician to get the flow of electricity going again. In Chinese medicine you can go to an acupuncture practitioner or practice tai chi or Qigong for the same effect.

Energy

Energy is one of the fundamental elements of the universe. Energy from the sun gives us light. Energy is stored in plants and released into your body when eaten, giving you energy. When we eat, the energy stored in our body from food gives us energy to work, sleep, and live. We are connected to energy in many forms. In the West we compartmentalize energy into different entities or processes. We do not construct the vision of our bodies, nature, and our lives as an interconnected realm of energy constantly flowing from one source to another. Many of us do not view our bodies as an intricate wondrous electrical system where every cell, every organ, and every system are a constant flow of energy.

Energy flow provides the ability for our cells to talk to each other and tell each other what they need. When our energy levels are healthy and strong, our cells help each other heal, rest, and work. As the energy levels in our bodies drop, the cells, organs, and systems do not communicate with great efficiency and vitality because they are tired and preserving their own energy.

False Energy

Many of us mistake false energy from real energy in our own lives. False energy is born in fear, shame, guilt, or anger. Many of us have constructed our lives to be successful or furiously working to keep our energy fast moving forward and upward so we don't ever have to experience these painful feelings again. These feelings probably overwhelmed us at some point in our lives, and so we made a pledge never to let those emotions into our lives again, no matter what. Many of us have bought into a lie that tells us when we have money, power, status, or "success" we either never deal with fear, shame, anger, or guilt again or our station in life will allow us to elude this source of suffering. My husband grew up with a saying in his family that I think is really appropriate: "It will either get you in the wash or the rinse."

False energy can arise when you live your life "busy" because you really want to be accepted, acknowledged, loved, or rewarded. This is a sad way to live and it is exhausting. Believe me, I know about this very well, as I spent many years on the run from my childhood ghosts. Almost every one who ever knew me would say I had more energy than anyone they had ever met. I didn't understand until later in my own life that I was being relentlessly driven by fear, anger, shame, and grief, which manifested itself as an energetic personality, always moving, planning, and successful. My psyche was the driving force racing so these demons wouldn't catch up to me.

It wasn't until I entered the field of mind-body medicine and began to examine my life and relationships did I discover the real difference. What I discovered in each discipline—whether it was psychology, medicine, or spirituality—was that when false energy is the driver in your life, you are destroyed at a cellular level in your body, mind, and soul.

This discovery was made by me when I started to live around and experience individuals with real energy. These individuals had an incredible power that was the result of having real energy instead of the false energy I was so familiar with. These people were living very intentional lives they were constantly creating by their powerful choices each day. They had stopped their lives, examined what they believed the purpose of their lives to be, and established the priorities around this intention.

The way to begin excavating your own life is in developing your *awareness*. Awareness begins by focusing on your life from the inside out. Here are some clues to discovering what kind of energy lives with you.

False energy is when you feel compelled to keep working, thinking, and doing. There is almost a sense of being out of control because this energy is a driving force within you. You can actually, like David, become a victim of your life. Eventually, false energy relentlessly drives you. Someone you are eating lunch with one day may say, "Hey, can you put down one of those cell phones so we can talk?" or "Since when have you carried a cell phone, a BlackBerry, and a pager?" You may pass these comments off in the moment, but later reflect and honestly say you can't remember how the madness started. Do any of your associates, friends, or family members suggest that you seem distracted and not present in the conversation?

Workaholism is the accepted addiction of our time. It is the socially accepted method of escaping from your Self, your family, and your life. Manic behavior and delaying happiness until we have a time to be really happy and experience balance is not the behavior of a successful person. This false energy accelerates over time and will consume your mind, body, and soul.

Do you juggle so many things simultaneously, or multitask, until your memory starts to get numb and you begin to ask yourself what is wrong with you? This false energy exhausts you, devours you. It is seductive because it actually makes you feel alive and that you are accomplishing many tasks in your life. The sad truth with false energy is that your life literally is passing you by because you are not present for it. Many of our lives become nothing more than hollow habituation where we eventually feel overwhelmed and empty. This is the lie that many of us live. I not only lived it, but a multitude of the people I worked with throughout my life were living this way too.

This is not an indictment or judgment, because you can't understand something until you become aware of it. The fact is, though, once you become aware of living a life of false energy you have a choice. The great blessing is once you make a choice to live a life with real energy, you will find true happiness and balance are right around the corner.

Real energy comes from deep within our soul. It has a rhythm and flow that emanates from your authentic self. Real energy is not constant, manic, or controlling. Real energy ebbs and flows with your daily challenges. Real energy will ebb and flow in various situations of life: your health, your family, your community, and your work. The different seasons of the year affect your real energy as do the seasons of your life.

Real energy is born in your awareness. It is nurtured in reflection and magnified when you choose to live an intentional life. As your life changes and new priorities and goals emerge, your real energy will grow exponentially and evolve into an awing source of power and rooting.

I want to be clear that many great things can and are accomplished by false energy. Corporations are built, countries are grown, and families are born with false energy. The sadness is that the deep connection and experience that comes with real energy is absent. It is a driving energy that whirls by instead of the source being an inner energy of peace, happiness, and balance. You can check to see if your family, friends, coworkers are being transformed also or being left behind.

Begin to be aware of your life. Do you have healthy relationships with others? Are you producing work that is authentically "you" that you love? Take a look around you, at your spouse, partner, children, your work, and your company. But most of all ask yourself whether you are experiencing happiness and when, if ever, you have a sense of balance.

Searching for Energy in the Wrong Places

Most of the people living with false energy these days, when asked how they feel, will respond, "I'm exhausted" and "I don't have time." We live in a world of overwhelmed, overworked people whose greatest wish is to find a secret formula for energy.

Who would have ever believed that the "energy" business would be a multibillion dollar business today? We spend billions of dollars on our desire for energy. We have an industry of energy drinks, energy bars, high energy foods, new exercises, and new exercise machines that guarantee to give us more energy. At PetSmart recently, they even had a special on "doggie" energy bars. We have become a culture obsessed with the desire for more energy.

Energy Bandits — Energy Thieves — Energy Busters

My work allows me to listen to the cares and concerns of so many people around the globe, and the number one physical complaint I hear on a daily basis is, "I wish I had more energy." Why are most of us walking around with the daily boring mantra announcing we are tired and need more energy?

FOOD

Are you eating food with less nutritional value and more empty calories? When we eat food with lots of sugar or eat carbohydrates, we get a rush of energy. This energy is short-lived, and since your body is tired after this stimulation, you can actually sink into an exhausted state after your "sugar" or "carbohydrate high."

STRESS

Chronic stress releases chemicals into our bodies that speed up the body processes and stimulate your organs to work at a rapid speed. Your body eventually becomes exhausted. Stress drains any type of energy you may have.

DEPRESSION AND ANXIETY

As anyone in a state of depression or anxiety knows, these conditions will suck the life energy right out of you. The constant state of agitation keeps your body struggling to survive, let alone give you real energy. Individuals with these conditions will over-function out in the world, with false energy, just to survive. There are great medicines available now that can ease so much suffering. These drugs help deal with anxiety and depression so your natural energy can flow through. Some of the new drugs have very low side effects and I have seen individuals' lives dramatically changed in a very short time. Depression and anxiety are serious conditions that literally take lives. I want the reader to know that I advocate medication as an adjunct to my advice in the book. I don't want anyone stopping their meds or feeling guilty because they don't feel real energy no matter what they do. This will just sink them into shame and a deeper depression. I want the reader to know for some of us, medicine is essential to experience "real energy."

EMOTIONS

Anger, fear, shame, jealousy, and grief can rob you of your real vital energy. These emotions are so powerful they can be the force behind false energy.

TECHNOLOGY

We can become the victims of our technology. Many of us are so conditioned to immediately answer our cell phones when they ring we don't even consider it a choice anymore. We respond just as Ivan Pavlov's dogs did in the experiments this famous Russian researcher did on conditioned reflex. Pavlov set a metronome, and then he would give the dogs food. Eventually the dogs became so conditioned to the food accompanying the sound, that they salivated even when the scientist set the metronome without giving food. The dogs had been conditioned to emit a physical response to the metronome.

Every time the cell phone rings there is a stimulus, which immediately activates a response to pick up the phone. The ring activates a set of neuropathways that keep getting reinforced. I am concerned that there can be an addiction pattern, because many of us make no conscious choice to pick up our phone. There is not thought between the ring and our immediate response.

HABITUATION

Habits are the patterns of your behavior. Habits are dangerous because they can make your life a series of mindless actions. Many people go through their entire lives living a life of habituation. They get up at the same time, jump in the shower with their mind racing, eat the same breakfast day after day, drive the same roads to work, and do the same tasks at the office each day. The neuropathways of the brain get reinforced over and over again, day after day, year after year, decade after decade. Our life can become a collection of mindless, almost thoughtless habits.

I hope you have seen the movie *Groundhog Day*, where actor Bill Murray plays Phil, an arrogant weather forecaster who gets trapped in a time warp that has him reliving the same day over and over. He gets up every day repeating his same behavior and gets the same results. He gets very frustrated until finally one day he changes his behavior. Phil's life totally changes when he changes. It is difficult to discover true happiness when we are living each day as if it were *Groundhog Day*. For many of us it feels like stepping on the same treadmill each day, with it preprogrammed to the same speed and an exact length of time, therefore yielding the exact same results each day. Albert Einstein said it best: "Insanity is doing the same thing over and over again and expecting different results." The principle of cause and effect ties into the problem of habituation. So many of the individuals I have counseled over the years have lived lives entrenched in habituation and their precious lives have passed them by.

Habituation can deaden your innate gift of awareness. You can become deaf to the voice on your inner GPS and you can't feel your inner spark.

Habituation can become an anesthetic that numbs you to the power of your choices and causes you to become the victim of your life.

You can become habituated or paralyzed in the midst of the chaos or shallowness of your lives. As you become the victim of your life, you begin to live as if you expect some outside force to come along and create happiness in your lives. No one else can bring you true happiness; not a government, a church, a spouse, a partner, or children. When you choose to create an intentional life of happiness, no event or person can get in your way.

Types of Energy

Every thought, every feeling, every emotion is energy. It creates an energy wave. It has momentum. None has ever seen a thought, feeling or emotion, but no one will deny their power and reality.

TIME IS ENERGY

Time is energy. Stop for a moment and take a deep breath. Be mindful and be present in this moment. Can you feel the power of being present in this moment in time? Time is a moving energy that propels life and creation forward. This is an incredibly powerful energy. When you practice living in the present and being mindful, your personal vital energy intersects with the energy of time and there is synergy.

Time is an interesting element that we are redefining and exploring on every level. We now talk about time in nanoseconds. (A nanosecond is one billionth of a second.) This is a concept that is hard for any human to comprehend.

For all of us living in this era it can truly be said that time is our most valuable gift. Every moment that passes is gone never to return.

Working with individuals who struggle with cancer, heart disease, and AIDS, and with many hospice patients, I have been gifted with a great respect for the sacredness of each moment in time. I am grateful for this lesson.

When I was in graduate studies at Emory we learned about two different names for and understandings of time. One is *chronos* and the other is *kairos*. *Chronos* is human's experience and measurement of time. *Chronos* is ordinary and chronological time. It is the time we live by on our clocks. This is the linear time that measures what time we eat, when we go to work, when we are born, and when we die. *Kairos* is an ancient

Greek word with a different concept of time. *Kairos* means the fullness of time. It means that now is an opportune or right time. This is a time filled with meaning and choice. *Kairos* means "holy" or "Divine" time, pregnant with new possibilities, renewal, and decisive action.

This concept was life-changing to me. What *kairos* means to me is time expands or contracts in direct relation to my own expansion, contraction, and connection to my self.

When we race through our days we miss the vital energy available because we spend time playing video games, surfing the Web, commuting, watching mindless television. Then there are the hard working, exhausted, overwhelmed parents and children racing through their lives like a train running down the tracks out of control, with the brakes burned out. Many of us know that the speed of the train called life is not sustainable, but we still choose to pull down the shade over the window so we don't see how fast the scenery is speeding by on our way to our deaths. It may sound gloomy, but too many of us are living this way.

People today almost act as if time is their enemy and not their guide and companion. As you develop reverence for your time, you will learn to have reverence and love for this gift of time. It is precious, fleeting, and every moment is full of potential until you take your last breath.

INTENTION IS ENERGY

Every thought and every emotion is energy. Every thought leads your mind, body, and soul in a direction. Every intention is energy. Imagine you have always wanted to take a cooking class and you say, "I am going to take a cooking class." You have just made the intention of taking a cooking class. The moment you claimed your intention to take this cooking class, you made this a priority in your life. You put words into your intention and announced it to your family and coworkers.

You get busy and a week later your spouse asks you what kind of cooking class you are taking and when. You admit that you had gotten busy and put it on the back burner. At work the next day a coworker tells you he saw an advertisement for cooking classes being held at the local college and he cut out the ad and hands it to you. You smile and excitedly rush to your desk and look at the date, cost, and location of the class. You choose to move other responsibilities out of the way so you can take this class you have wanted to take for years. By thinking through this exercise do you understand how powerful your intentions are and how they affect others?

If you are living your life without intentions, you may not be moving toward your full potential in your life. Intention is a powerful energy that creates an abundant intentional life of true happiness.

You are the governor or manager of your time, your life is your time on earth.

1. *Create the intentions of your life.* Live an intentional life. What is the intention of your life? Take time for reflection and ask your self what you love, what you are passionate about and what are your intentions.

2. *Prioritize.* Now that you have written what your intentions are in your life, identify and prioritize what it will take for you to realize your intentions. Sit with your family so you can all work together to help each other realize and live an intentional authentic life.

3. *Don't procrastinate.* It doesn't matter how small of an amount of your energy you put toward your intentional life, every day just focusing your thoughts is enough to keep you headed in that direction.

4. *Learn to say no.* It is time for you to focus on the purpose of your life, so you will have to make decisions on what you will have to delete from your life. Time is the most valuable jewel you have, so guard it and protect it. Healthy boundaries will be invaluable to you in giving you energy and helping you attain true happiness.

5. *Don't be distracted by others and the world.* Here is where the four roots are essential. When you ground yourself in the four roots, you will continually have more energy, power, and courage to move toward your intentional life.

CREATIVITY IS ENERGY

Do you remember when you refinished that antique chest, painted those roses in your favorite vase on a small canvas, cooked that new recipe you found in a magazine, or surprised someone you love with a shocking gift? All of your projects are using creative energy. Can you stop and remember the pure joyful energy you experience when you generate creative energy?

One of the greatest sources of creative energy is love. It still amazes me that we fall in love with someone and in that moment our entire life transforms into a never ending odyssey, a continuing exercise in creative energy. It begins with hopes and dreams, creating a home, creating children, and creating a dynamic life together. Love is an endless source of creative energy.

Every one is creative. Creativity can be defined with words like original, imaginative, expressive, inventive, freedom, trust, risk taking, humor, playfulness, and openness. Our creative energy may be in finance, gardening, marketing, public relations, or cooking. We each have unique gifts.

There can be obstacles to our creative energy. Chronic negative stress can be a powerful block to creativity. Fear of criticism can paralyze creative energy. Self-criticism will stop creative energy in its tracks. Individuals who have habitual personalities can have difficulty accessing creative energy.

There are many practices that help your creative energy flow. Don't be overtired from work. Try to be relaxed. Be positive and encourage yourself and others. Learn stress reduction techniques. These practices relax you and create wonderful creative energy. There is no right or wrong way to be creative. Be open and don't criticize your self.

Just as a Mozart, Einstein, Jane Austen, Martha Stewart, Benjamin Franklin, or Mary Cassatt developed their ingenious creative energy over their lifetimes, so can you. You have the potential to become a finely-tuned violin, propelling divine music and creative energy into the world.

Money Is Energy

Money is energy. Money creates movement and makes things happen. You work and earn your money. Your hardworking energy created the money you have in your hand. This money is energy because it allows you to buy goods, save it, or give it away.

Imagine going into a corner store and buying a candy bar and a drink. You walk up to the counter and the clerk asks you for money. You can pay with the energy of the money or you can pay with the energy of your working at the store. Energy is always moving, changing forms, creating new forms of life and many opportunities.

This money sends energy into the world and changes the world depending upon how you decide to spend this energy. If we sincerely perceived our money as a source of energy, I believe we would be more respectful and aware when and where we spend it.

Words Are Energy

Words are powerful sources of energy. Words are potential energy as they sit slumbering on the pages of books, newspapers, magazines, essays, research papers, or dissertations waiting to be discovered and ignited. Do you remember listening to a great speech or sermon, when the words challenged you to think in a new way or take some passionate action that changed your life? Two simple words have changed the lives of innumerable couples around the world, "I do." Those two simple words created thirty years of happiness, two children, and a wonderful life for me.

Look into someone's eyes you love and say, "I love you." The powerful energy of those words will possibly create a response from the other person, whether it is a verbal response, a kiss, or a hug. The ability of humans to put their feelings into words is a great responsibility and gift.

A word can make you smile, cry, laugh, or be happy, sad, angry, or frightened. Words can inspire and motivate us to noble actions or lead us into a movement of destruction and darkness. Words can heal or harm. Energetic words from the mouth of Adolf Hitler and Sojourner Truth changed the course of human history.

As we speak words we transform the energy of our thoughts and emotions into a powerful reality. Speaking and writing words are acts of incarnation. Words are thoughts and emotions made flesh.

Creating and Balancing Energy

There are a number of ways to both create and balance real, pure energy within your body.

YOGA

Yoga gives you breathing practices that harness the power of *prana,* or vital energy. You focus on your breath in yoga to move this vital force through your body. A variety of poses in yoga help facilitate the movement of this vital energy through your body to cells, organs, and body systems to create balance and health. It is believed that if this vital energy is blocked, illness can result. Research indicates that yoga helps alleviate headaches, arthritis, and a host of other conditions and diseases.

Many of the individuals I work with insist they do not have time for yoga in their busy lives. I ask them to just try this practice for a couple of weeks and they will discover a new sense of strength, energy, confidence, and balance. Between my children, husband, and my work there was never enough time for a yoga class. I saw a yoga teacher on a morning show and bought her yoga tape. I would put the tape in when I had 10 minutes after the kids were in bed and them eventually I memorized the poses. That was 18 years ago. I can honestly tell you I could not live my intense busy life without yoga. Anytime the wheels come off during the day or evening, I can just lie on the floor, do a few poses, take a few deep breaths, and an incredible amount of energy emerges. I stand up focused, energetic, and balanced. Go to a video store or online and discover a teacher you like, purchase a tape, and get ready for some new dynamic centered energy.

ACUPUNCTURE

Acupuncture is a system of medicine that works with your chi, or vital energy. Illness is an imbalance or lack of chi. Acupuncture treatment seeks to balance your imbalanced sick body and restores you to a state of health. Your energy flows through your body along energy pathways called meridians. Skilled professionals place needles along these pathways to stimulate flow and balance. Acupuncture has been used with great efficacy in many medical conditions including migraine headaches, chronic pain, infertility, depression, and allergies.

I go to a Chinese medicine doctor on a regular basis and receive acupuncture treatments because I believe it keeps me in balance. My regular acupuncture visits let me know as soon as my pulses and other measurements are out of balance. I have also referred many individuals for acupuncture with excellent results for a variety of diseases and conditions. Chinese medicine and acupuncture are wonderful options for many conditions and as an adjunct to other treatments for catastrophic diseases.

QIGONG AND TAI CHI

Qigong and tai chi are exercises described as moving meditations. Both of these focus on continual fluidic movement of your body. The different movements move and balance the chi or vital energy throughout the body and create more energy in your body. A study at the Cousins Center of Psychoneuroimmunology at UCLA reported a shingles study on individuals age 60 and over. The researchers had two groups of men and women, one group practiced tai chi in a 15-week program. The other half did no tai chi. In the tai chi group they saw a 59 percent increase in the immune cells, a boost in immunity enough to prevent shingles.[1] Steven L. Wolf, Ph.D., professor of rehabilitation medicine at Emory University, reported that elderly people who practice tai chi have a 48 percent lower risk of falls. He also reported other benefits, such as improved strength, endurance, balance, and cardiovascular health.[2]

Sources of Real Energy: The Four Roots

The four roots create real energy, happiness, and health in your life. Nourishing these roots will provide you with a constant source of real energy. Discovering the four roots of real energy connects you to your Self and to your Source.

SERENITY IS ENERGY

Serenity practices or stress reduction methods move energy through your body. Science shows us these practices shift, slow down, and change the flow of energy in your body. This is why it is essential to incorporate serenity practices into your daily life. Serenity turns the voltage of your body's electrical system down and allows this incredible vital energy to slowly move through your body healing and rejuvenating you. Your energy transforms into a slower, more powerful and intentional energy when you practice serenity.

EXERCISE IS ENERGY

Exercise is a wonderful way to move the energy through your body. In a different and almost opposite manner from serenity, exercise increases the vital energy in your body, brings nutrients, and exerts pressure on bodily systems and organs to make them stronger.

The individuals who entered the cardiopulmonary rehabilitation and wellness program where I worked had very little stamina, were sedentary, apprehensive and many were depressed. In just a matter of weeks after they began exercising they developed strength, confidence, mental sharpness, optimism and humor. Patients who had never exercised before were discovering a new source of dynamic energy they had never known. It was wonderful to observe these dramatic changes in my patients. It seemed to take years off their lives almost immediately. They also began to get exercise partners and exercise groups together, which made it fun and they again experienced intimacy in friendship and community.

LOVE IS ENERGY

Every thought that enters your mind contains energy. This powerful energy created by your thoughts immediately releases chemicals in your brain and this triggers other chemicals in your body. So every thought is energy itself and releases additional energy into your body.

When you experience love there is an immediate shift and a new energy flow of your body. Relationships transform the energy in your mind, body, and soul.

FOOD IS ENERGY

All food is energy. Every piece of broccoli or salmon you put in your mouth immediately releases energy into your body. Some foods have more energy than others. Food is the fuel for your body. This is why it is so important for you to know about what foods you are using to fuel the vital energy that gives you life.

You Are a Fountain of Untapped Energy

You were not created to live an exhausted and hollow life. Know that there is immense energy within you and in our natural world that is just waiting for you to tap into it. At every stage and situation in your life, pure vital energy is supporting your life and waiting to assist you. You just have to know how to tap into it and now you do.

~ BEGIN TODAY ~

Ask Your Self   Am I experiencing "real" or "false" energy?

In what ways do I find energy in my daily life?

What new ways have I learned to create energy?

Tell Your Self   Abundant energy flows through me perfectly.

Give Your Self   Visit a Chinese Medicine doctor.

Read a book or use a resource in time management.

Learn a few Qigong or tai chi movements to energize.

CHAPTER 11

Know Power

IT HAD BEEN a very busy day at work. My pastoral care appointments had been back to back, I had seen one person after another all day and I was mentally and physically exhausted. I was relieved to look over at my clock on the wall to read 5:00. My assistant buzzed me as I was packing my brief case and said Tom Jacobs was on the phone. Tom was one of my prominent parishioners who had become a good friend over the years. I told her to take a message and I would call him back the next day. Susan buzzed me back and said, "Tom said it was important, he was leaving his office and would be here in ten minutes, he wants you to wait for him."

I sat back down in my chair, remembering that my daughter had a basketball game that started at 6 P.M. and I didn't want to be late. I called my husband and talked for a few minutes when my door swung open and there stood Tom.

Tom was about 55 years old, came from humble beginnings, and had become an incredibly wealthy, successful man. He sat down with his perfectly coordinated suit, tie, and Gucci loafers. I asked him how he was and there was no answer. Tom just sat and sat and sat. After about five minutes, tears started streaming down his face. He pulled out his handkerchief and wiped off his face. "Kathleen, I have cancer. I haven't told anyone yet. I am worried what my wife and my children will do. I have a big company and many clients, they all depend on me. I don't want to tell anyone, because the minute I do, my life will change and be out of control. I have kept this in for a week, since I found out, and I just don't know what to do. I have always been a good provider and taken care of my family, I don't want to be dependent on them, or them to have to take care of me. This cancer is really advanced and I just don't want anyone taking care of me and seeing me sick." He was silent for a moment and then he said, "If my clients find out I am dying, they will move their business to another money manager. If my staff finds out they will start looking for another job. I don't want people at church and at the country club looking at me, and feeling sorry for me if they found out I am dying. Don't you understand? I just can't let anyone know that I'm sick."

I wish I could tell you that I only heard this story once, but I have listened to many men and women repeat similar stories over many years.

Even if there was some truth to the fears Tom revealed about his life, what a horrible trap to be living in. This is truly living from the "outside-in," not living from the "inside-out." There is so much isolation in this story that it has broken my heart many times over. Tom's experience of power is one of controller, sustainer, provider but mostly a life of isolation, lack of intimacy, and being out of balance. The good news in Tom's case was he learned how to experience a new kind of power in his life— "power with" and "power in"—instead of "power over," which had created his sense of control and isolation. In learning a new sense of power Tom opened himself to the amazing experience of love, intimacy and happiness before he left this earth.

Power is a word we use in our vocabulary on a daily basis but interestingly enough we have different definitions of power because our experience with power has been so different. The issue of power is a critical construct of our lives and is the essence of how we experience our lives and others.

My Experiment with Power

Years ago when I did my dissertation there was a portion of it dedicated to the issue of power. In my dissertation project I was taking privileged private high school students on a two-week immersion to the inner city, where they would interact with marginalized individuals with minimal economic, intellectual, or political power. The inner city groups of individuals that the privileged youth would encounter never experienced or had access to the power these high school students had. I wanted to know how this group of teens, age 16 to 18, experienced power and their definition of power. I had 12 teens and asked the question, "Who is a person who represents power in your life and why?"

This group of young people clearly defined power as control, unilateral, hierarchal, and patriarchal. Interestingly, one third of these young people defined the person of power in their life as their father, who was the disciplinary person in the household. He represented power to them, with responses such as, "My father is my person of power, because he uses a belt to discipline us and he has the power in our home," and "My father spanks us, makes the money and works hard, he represents power to me," and "My father is the person of power because of his temper, he runs our house," and "My father is CEO of a company and he is important." Only one person in twelve said that the mother was the person of power because she was so loving. Four of the young people stated they had no person that represented power in their lives. Two responded that both parents represented power to them.

This survey in my dissertation shocked me. When I was their age, my persons of power were my grandmothers, Joan of Arc, the Virgin Mary, St. Francis of Assisi, Jesus, and Ms. Hostetler, a teacher at school. My father was a very aggressive, successful man who dealt out the punishment in our home and brought home the bacon, but I viewed him as a bully, not as a powerful person. My view of power was inextricably tied to good at a young age. As a young person, my definition of real power was not "power over" but "power with." It was later in life, as I integrated into the world that I understood two very different kinds of power: power as "power over" and "power with."

Understanding Power

Dr. Bernard Loomer of the University of Chicago Divinity School has developed two concepts of power: unilateral and relational power. His definition of *unilateral power* is the capacity to influence, guide, adjust, manipulate, shape, control, or to form the human or natural environment in order to advance one's own purposes. This type of power focuses on the individual's or groups' personal goals and not on relationships or mutuality. Dr. Loomer makes a compelling assertion about unilateral power as he states:

As long as one's size and sense of worth are measured by the strength and capacity to influence others, as long as power is associated with a sense of initiative and aggressiveness, and passivity is indicative of weakness or a corresponding lack of power, then the natural and inevitable inequities among individuals and groups become the means whereby estrangements in life become wider and deeper. The rich become richer and the poor become poorer. The strong become stronger and the weak become weaker and more dependent.[1]

We see this play out especially in the abuse of power in struggling countries around the world. So many countries in our world will go through a dramatic political revolution in the name of democracy. After the struggle an ominous leader emerges and immediately there arise two classes. The two classes are the powerful group that takes over the natural resources, the military, and the political power of the country, and the powerless who disparagingly fall into hopeless poverty, starvation, and eventual death. The initial goal of the democracy was to create a new nation of relational power or power with, but they had experienced power as power over and unilateral so they replicated this oppressive power.

The goal of unilateral power is to move to maximum self-sufficiency. Dr. Loomer believes that in unilateral power, the Self is to become as self-dependent as possible. Dependency upon others and passivity are viewed as weakness.

The second concept of power is *relational power.* According to Dr. Loomer:

The aim of relational power is not to control the other either directly or indirectly by trying to guide and control the relationship. The greatest possible good cannot emerge under conditions of control. The aim is to provide those conditions of giving and receiving of influences such that there is the enlargement of the freedom of all the members to both give and receive.[2]

Relational power has the ability to both influence others and to be influenced by others. There is a balance of giving and receiving. It is truly a sign of power to receive the influence of another as it is to influence the other. Dr. Loomer has two interesting notions of power.

I define *power* as strength, energy, or force in a system that can either enhance or diminish another system. Power is an essential foundation for understanding your Self and the world. It can not be underestimated. Your definition and experience of power will define your life and your journey to happiness, balance, and well being.

Let's talk about the innumerable power systems you have probably experienced in your life. It began as you were in your mother's womb, and she literally had the power over your life and death. As children we experience the power of our family members: mother, father, siblings, grandparents, aunts, and uncles. Our places of worship and our various religions create images of power in sacred scriptures, rituals, the leaders of these institutions, and the Divine beings we worship and/or love. Our educational systems create intricate power systems of teachers, principals, schools, and the material in textbooks. Our jobs teach us about many types of power, bad and good.

The natural world holds incredible lessons in power. Notice yourself and the people around you when you are at Niagara Falls or the Grand Canyon, or watching a sunrise at the ocean or a sunset in the mountains. Watch a foal nurse from her mother, a great hawk circle over your head screeching, or a group of dolphins weave in and out of the water with great elegance and joy. The power of our sexuality is incredible and primal. These are all very different experiences of power, but it is all power.

Power as control subordinates another by dominating the other. Power as control is inherently oppressive. When one person controls another, we destroy some part of that person. The person with "power over" enhances their power when as they diminish another's power. "Power over" incorporates a righteous habit of trying to shape and control the human and natural world in accordance with your own purpose, needs, and goals. When you exercise unilateral power (power over) it is difficult for you to give yourself in openness to someone else and possibly be transformed by the other person. "Power over" or unilateral power is focused on the self-interest of an individual or group. Power as "control over" cannot create a system of balance, because balance is defined as forces in both directions being equal. When one individual has "power over" another individual, they are not equal forces.

The alternative to the unilateral approach or "power over" is relational power, or "power with"—power as life giving and receiving. This is power experienced as balance because both forces in each direction are equal. All persons have the potential to grow proportionally in this experience of relational power or "power with." In relational power, the person does not grow in power at the expense of another person's diminishment. Unlike power as control, relational power is generative and creates happiness and balance to both individuals. "Power with" or relational power creates mutual benefit.

Understanding the nature of power is essential as you journey into your life of balance and true happiness. Your experiences of power shape your entire life and every facet of your life. It is the essence of how we live out our lives in the world.

The Power of Choice

Each choice you make leads you *toward* or *away from* your authentic life of power and true happiness. Every choice *opens* a door into infinite possibilities. Every choice *creates* something new and different in your life. Every choice *invites* infinite opportunities. Every choice is a *fountain* of energy. Every choice is a *step* closer to an intentional life of mental, physical and spiritual well being. Every choice *transforms* obstacles into opportunities. Every choice is a *building block* for your life. Each choice is a *reflection* of who you are. Each choice is a new *direction* in your life.

When you make a choice, your authentic power moves you to action; away from worry, fear, confusion and chaos. If life is a classroom, then each choice is a particular lesson in life. Your choices create power, peace, prosperity, healing, and happiness in your life. You choose what you eat, drive, read, and what music you listen to. You can also choose your emotions and attitudes: anger, fear, and worry. Stop, take a deep breath, and make a new choice. There is power in knowing you have a choice. Nelson Mandela had no choice as they locked him into that prison cell and turned the key and took away 27 emotions in that cell. His prison became his classroom. Nelson Mandela chose the ultimate power of forgiveness, compassion and reconciliation. The greatest gift to give your children is to teach them the power of their choices.

Most of us have had little if any training in how to make choices in our lives, always assuming that this essential practice of life comes naturally. For those of you who struggle with making choices you can learn more in Appendix C.

Women, Men, and Power

This section deals with the touchy subject of how women and men experience power differently. We live in a world where women are born with a very different experience of power, which creates their worldview of power. Let's face it, we still live in a world where women are forced to have genital mutilation surgery; female babies are aborted, killed, or left to die because they have little worth; and feminists who speak out on women's and children's rights in many countries around the world have been killed or receive death threats and contracts on their lives.

Besides that, have you yet seen a woman president of the United States? When I was a little girl, I wanted to be the first woman president of the United States. When my English teacher asked me why I would want a job like that the answer just rolled off my tongue: "Ms. Hostetler, if I were president, I would help all the women like my mom who cry and are sad and afraid. I would build homes for moms and their kids so they would be safe and happy with their moms."

When women marry, cultural expectations say they take the male's name, and the census papers still say "who is *THE* head of household?" I have never checked into a hotel with my husband in 30 years where the person behind the registration counter stops for a minute and asks me my name. Instead, they assume and say, "Here is your key, Mrs. Hixon." It is the same when I use my American Express to check in, they look at my husband and say, "Here is your key, Mr. Hall."

How about if at the holidays we took a tour of all the homes in the world and saw who was sitting at the head of the table? Personally I like round tables; it takes care of this problem, but they just don't fit well in most rooms like a rectangular table does.

So let's face it, the issues of power are huge, and it will take many moons for the great change I would dream of seeing, but it is slowly changing. The sight of women voting in Iraq and Afghanistan made me cry and scream out, "Thank You, God." When I see little girls who really know they can do anything they choose to do in this world my heart races with pure joy and I grin from ear to ear.

When I see parents raising their little boys to respect and revere little girls and women, I want to go up and kiss the parents on the cheek and say "thank you" for contributing such a gift to the human race and our planet.

Race and Power

It doesn't take long when you live in nature to fully understand that the natural plan of the universe is diversity. Diversity and difference is to be revered and awed. Isn't it interesting that we humans extol the virtues of nature in the great variety, colors, and species of birds, horses, dogs, trees and flowers? But when it comes to the diversity of the human race we get blinded. Most of us retreat into some kind of judgment, fear, shame, and anger mode when we talk about race.

Race has everything to do with power in our world. We live in a world where white has been overshadowed by great numbers of brown, yellow, black, and a kaleidoscope of other participants of our earth. There is probably no way we can ever be color-blind, and I wouldn't want to be color-blind. I revel in the incredible diversity of humans in this world and I wish we all did.

I believe that every school and corporation should have a course on race and power. This way everyone could have a deeper understanding of the "other." But this is such a touchy subject that we pretend the elephant is not in the room or we side step it at all costs. We grow up in a world where we assume we know how it feels to be African-American, Black, Hispanic, Native American, Caucasian, Asian, or Middle Eastern. One of the greatest gifts in my life was working with a group called the Urban Training Organization of Atlanta. I was a "do-gooder." This means I wanted to go into areas of inner city poverty and show them how to live a "good life." I thought I had the power to go into these historic areas and tell these people how I thought they could live better. There wasn't a thought in my mind about their "self-determination" and listening to what their vision of their neighborhood was. I sat on the board of directors of this organization and it taught me many humble lessons about power and race.

Like other "do-gooders," many of us are good people wanting to do good, but when we are prescriptive because we come from a place of power without believing that poor, marginalized individuals and groups can have real power, we are abusing our power. This becomes power over instead of power with. A good friend has only one quote on his business cards he hands out, "More curiosity, less judgment." I believe this should be our mantra concerning race in our fragile world.

Children and Power

We don't even go a week without reading about a child in some foster care system around the country who has been lost, abused, or killed in the system. This is not an indictment on our overworked and overwhelmed foster care system. I have worked with many of the most loving, compassionate, fierce social workers, who constantly defend and protect the rights of children. It is our responsibility to protect our children—and I mean every child on this planet. This is not other people's problems, it is our problem. Children are being sold as slaves and trafficked in the sex trade around the world. We have more international laws to protect our animals than we do our children. As long as we treat children as chattel, or property, we are destined to abuse them. We must treat each child with great respect and realize the innate power and respect each child deserves. Our children are not our property, they come through us.

Power in the Family

Most of our children will emulate the power structure they experience in their primary family, and it is our responsibility to teach our children about power. Their early experiences of power will define their lives. Many families go through life and never become aware of how power has been used or abused in the family system.

When parents are overpowering, it robs from the children the gift of developing their own power by learning through their choices. On the other hand, when parents relinquish too much power in the family to their children, the family can become fractured.

Personally I liked our weekly family meetings, where all of these issues were discussed and everyone's opinions were heard and respected. Creating a time for the family to listen to each other is very powerful. This teaches each member of the family that they are valued and have power. Make sure your children take turns facilitating the family meetings. You are giving them the gift of experiencing their power and being respected within the family. This helps create self-esteem and power within each child as you prepare them to enter the world. Create your own rituals within your family that allow wounds to be opened, secrets to be revealed, and power to be shared by all.

Personal Power

Experiencing your personal power must begin with a certain order I discussed in a previous chapter. I am going to repeat "The Natural Order" for relationships in your life. It is essential to experiencing real power and realizing a life of happiness to know there is a natural order for power. Real happiness and balance require that your relationships must be in a disciplined order. This order creates well being and is supported in all three disciplines; medicine, psychology and spirituality. First, you must ground your relationship or connection with your Source, Higher Power, God, Nature or whatever you name your experience with the Holy. It is no accident that when we connect with the Holy, we become "Whole." Second is your relationship with your spouse; third is your relationship with your children; and fourth is your relationship with your work and community. This time honored sequence is the key to your real power.

Authentic power comes from within your Self. Your power rests in your roots. Therefore you must nurture and love your Self first. We may not be putting ourselves first because we either never experienced or were not taught self-care in our original family. Most of our parents did not practice self-care. Most of the parents I listen to, no matter what their age, describe their life as serial martyrdom. Many feel they sacrificed their life for their children, their spouse, their aging parents, or the job they had to keep to feed the family.

I remember drinking a cup of coffee with a friend of mine who is a psychiatrist, and I was talking about how my mother and her friends were martyrs to their children and to their husbands. This friend of mine smiled leaned forward and said, "In all my years of practicing psychiatry I've never known a martyr who wasn't mad as hell." I'll never forget the day I heard him say that. It sounded so sacrilegious to me but I couldn't help but laugh out loud. I told him that being raised Catholic, martyrs to me were holy individuals who gave their life for the church. As a child I used to pray that God would choose me to become a martyr so I could prove how brave I was. His comment made me explore the concept of people living out their entire lives as martyrs, putting themselves last.

Personal power means self-care. When you care for your mental, physical, and spiritual well-being first, then you become a healthier person who cares for others in a healthier way at home and at work. As you practice self-care you will become more confident and exude more real power and happiness. You will come from a strongly rooted center of balance instead of a wobbly, weak, off-balance footing. Your children will emulate your self-care and sense of power and they naturally become stronger individuals.

Live every day grounding your life in nourishing your four roots of true happiness. Each day make it your priority to commit to one practice in each of the four roots. When your days are especially rushed, practice serenity for just five minutes, and later in the day stretch for five minutes, and later make sure you eat enough healthy protein, and make sure you tell someone you love them. See, that wasn't so hard on your busy day. If you commit to nourishing your roots *every day of your life,* even if you only have a few moments, then you will experience real power in your life. On the days when you have a few more minutes, you can choose to spend a few minutes more on one of the four roots.

Flexibility

The key to authentic power is flexibility. There is no way to predict every event or person that will enter your life on any given day. Individuals who develop an inner energy of flexibility will always stay in balance. Physics tells us that rigid materials that are not flexible will break under a given amount of pressure. Flexible substances bend, move, and take a new shape when stressed with an outside pressure. This elementary law of physics applies to us humans also. Remember the part about flexible substances being able to take on a new shape under pressure from stress. Many times stress will unleash potential power you never knew existed. When you are flexible you experience a confidence knowing you will bend, maybe transform to something new, but you will not break.

Places of Power

We express our power in a variety of ways according to specific situations. Let's explore some of the places we experience our own power and the power of others.

HOME

This is the place where we first experience and learn to experience power as a diminishing of another or enhancing another. This is the most essential and most difficult place to claim your authentic power. Many individuals choose to express their power in negative choices that create negative consequences. Very few of us have the skills to know how to handle the fragile and longstanding relationships in a family. I suggest that you go to a counselor or therapist for support, ideas, and help with your plan. This is a professional person outside the family who will be a great source of wisdom, consolation, support, and choices.

WORK

Work is all about power issues: the good, the bad and the ugly. I was shocked when they called me to do an interview on the stressful effects of an employee bullying another employee. I had no idea there was as much of this behavior going on as there is. I thought with all the laws we have now this was a thing of the past. It turns out this is a horrible problem in the workplace, and it is also hard to prove and get others to take action on. Bullying is a growing problem in our society in our homes, schools and at work. Bullying is when a person with no power intimidates, threatens, and physically or emotionally damages another human being. This is an abuse of power and must be stopped wherever its malicious head appears. If you cower to a bully you are doing profound damage to your mind, body and soul. I have seen the victims of bullies do everything from having a nervous breakdown to committing suicide. This is a very serious situation and must be treated with serious action.

COMMUNITY

Power outside the family and work takes many forms. Every one of us who sit on boards or volunteer in the public arena knows first-hand about the use and abuse of power. In these situations that are usually out of your control you can at least maintain your personal power and attempt to influence others with your example of ethical power. In the public forum we exude into the community the essence of our own power. Never underestimate how infectious and inspiring relational power can be. Be a beacon in your community for what real power can look like.

NATURE

The subject of power and nature can be a provocative subject. Many today believe that in Genesis, God said that humans have "dominion over" nature and animals. Dominion is such a negative word as we discuss ethical issues concerning power. Volumes of individuals have reinterpreted the word "dominion," and many scholars state that in fact the word does not mean dominion. It reads instead that God said that humans have "responsibility for" nature and animals.

Responsibility is a very different notion from dominion. As a parent, I am responsible for my children but I do not have dominion over them. This one simple word has created more injustice, damage, slaughter, and unethical behavior on this sacred earth than we can ever comprehend.

Who do we think we are to strip this fragile earth and her environment of her dignity? We have no reverence for the natural world. Chief Seattle said it flawlessly when he spoke out in response to the acquisition of his tribe's lands by white settlers, "Contaminate your bed and you will one night suffocate in your own waste."

We can learn much from the reverence and awe the Native Americans and other cultures have for nature. Nature is their teacher, parent, creator, sustainer, and Divine gift from the Great Spirit. The Great Spirit swells in all living things so every living thing is revered.

One of the problems I experience living on a ranch in the mountains is that too many people still shoot and poison animals. It is heart-breaking to witness the disrespect so many have for animals because they hold no value to them. There were so many abused and homeless animals when we moved here that I started rescuing dogs and cats. We have done it for years, and every soul that migrates through this ranch has given me a gift and taught me many lessons.

We are responsible for these magnificent animals, the polar ice caps, the rain forests, the raping of the earth, and the poisoning of our water and air. Just as we teach our children that they must fix what they break, or they must apologize when they hurt someone, or they must make amends when they do something wrong, so we must take responsibility and do the right thing. Mother Nature is sore, she is bruised and she is hurt. Let's teach our children that we don't run from responsibility. We injured and disrespected her and now it is time to restore her power and authority.

Chronic Fear Is Toxic to Power

Fear is an epidemic in our society. We fear getting old, getting sick, dying, failure, success, rejection, beginning a relationship, ending a relationship, decisions and loss of control. These are just a few of a list that could continue around the earth several times. Our fear has grown to even greater proportions since 9–11. Fear is a deadly poison that will destroy your roots. Chronic fear haunts our lives and follows us like a shadow day in and day out. These are long-standing fears that are persistent and deep rooted: fear of success, fear of failure, fear of death, fear of public speaking, fear of groups, fear of losing your job, fear of being alone, fear of terrorism, fear of not being loved, fear of the dark, fear of being a victim of crime, the list can go on forever.

Chronic fear keeps us trapped living an insufficient life by its toxicity. We can never fulfill our purpose and live a life of power as long as we are riddled by our fears. Chronic fear has a direct affect upon you in three ways:

1. *Your Mind:* Fear keeps your mind in a state of worry and anxiety, overloading the brain and causing your memory to become dull. You can become defensive, aggressive, and angry. You can feel trapped and imprisoned by your own mind.

2. *Your Body:* Fear causes your brain to release epinephrine and sometimes even cortisol along with many other chemicals. Chronic fear can result in high blood pressure, cardiovascular disease, immune diseases, migraine headaches, and a host of other ailments.

3. *Your Soul:* You were created to experience freedom of your spirit and your own power. Chronic fear strips you of your energy and thus your source of power. When you are chronically fearful you become paralyzed and live in bondage to your fears. This creates a life of spiritual anguish and pain. All great spiritual and religious texts speak to how fear deteriorates the soul over time.

I really believe that life is a classroom, and not a prison. Begin to trust yourself and the purpose for your life. If you believe that everything happens as an opportunity for your growth it is easier to have real confidence in your life. Instead of living in fear, confusion and insecurity, choose to live courageously knowing that your purpose is unfolding with every breath, every experience and every task.

Moving from Fear to Power

These are the steps to begin to live a life without fear:

1. *Wake Up:* Allowing fear to grow each moment within you is making you weak and powerless. This weakness only grows like a cancer and you can eventually become a victim. Becoming aware of your fears is your first step in acknowledging where you are now. The instant you do this you move into your power.

2. *Choose:* The next step after awareness of your fear is realizing you have a clear choice. First write down the top five things that you fear. Be completely honest. Look at your list. Choose one fear that you want to begin to work with. You may want to begin with the least difficult fear. This way you begin with baby steps so you can build your confidence in the beginning. Put the other four away in a drawer or folder. Just deal with the one fear you have picked.

3. *Take Action:* Action is critical. Action is the antidote to fear. Fear hides in your shadow and hangs over your life like a cloud. Action pushes this insidious force out into the open so you can deal with it. Take the same piece of paper that you wrote the fear down on and in another color of pen write down the action you can choose to take to release this fear. Repeat writing down this action ten times in the same color pen. Now look at what you have written down as your key to freedom and power. Pretend that your fear has a voice and this action you have written is your fear calling out to you. Your fear is asking you to free it from your mind, body and soul. Action is the key to the prison of fear that has kept you from living an intentional life of happiness.

4. *Commit:* This is a crucial step. If you truly want to live the life of power and happiness you were meant to live, you must commit to the process of unleashing your fears. When you commit to this process you will experience immense energy, a new found sense of your own power and a renewed state of mental, spiritual and physical well being.

Tools for the Journey

You need support on your journey through the wasteland of chronic fears. Keep yourself surrounded with inspirational and motivational tools. Keep inspirational CDs and tapes in your car for your commute. You might want to rent or buy a motivational DVD by an inspirational author or teacher. Take a class that you have always wanted to take. Yoga, meditation, centering prayer, tai chi or Qigong are great ways to clear the body and mind of chronic fears and open them to new ways of thinking and being in the world. Find some favorite quotes that speak to you and write them on note cards, or find plaques for your mirrors, refrigerators, and computer screens to remind you of your new found freedom. Discover television shows or television personalities that inspire you to claim your personal power.

Social support is incredibly powerful. Go online in your community and discover what kinds of social support are available in your area. There are many different types of support groups at libraries, hospitals, places of worship, community centers and even online support groups. One of the reasons chronic fear haunts us relentlessly is because we become shamed by our fear, thinking we are inadequate and weak and we hide our fears. It is a powerful healing experience when we openly tell someone else what we fear. Once the words are released from our lips, we have begun our journey to real power and happiness.

You are innately powerful. The more you exude your natural power you will grow in strength and courage. The word courage comes from its Latin root cor, which means heart or center. When you come from your heart with great courage it will propel you into a life of real power. Real power originates from your pure heart and disseminates into the world to help guide, teach and heal your self and others.

~ BEGIN TODAY ~

Ask Your Self   What types of power have I experienced?

How can I practice relational power in my life more?

What words of power transformed my life?

Tell Your Self   I respect others as I would like them to respect me.

Give Your Self   Obtain a biography of a person of power you admire.

Buy yourself an inspirational CD from someone of power you respect.

Enter into some group where you can experiment with your power.

CHAPTER 12

Live an Intentional Life

THERE ARE PROBABLY more self-help and business books on the market written on "how to succeed" than on any other subject, so this is not a new phenomenon. Rather, it is as old as human existence. From the first moment we humans conceived of selling something, a motivational speaker fell out of a nearby coconut tree to help sell it better.

As a child, I lay in bed every night listening to the sound of my father's tape recorder murmuring in the kitchen until all hours of the night. My father was a salesman and believed that the philosophy of Glen Turner, the guru of "Dare to Be Great," was his sure-fire key to success. Turner ran a motivational company in the 1960s and sold packages of tapes to help salespeople create success.

When my father sold Hall's Dairy to a dairy conglomerate, he began working for the new enterprise, and a product developer came up with the idea of selling milk in a bag. Now, we lived in rural Ohio among the Amish, and I thought it was a lame idea, but my father was devoted to those tapes, and every morning he would look into my eyes at breakfast and, as I held my contempt and laughter at bay, announced, "Kathleen, wipe that smile off your face. Today is your day to dare to be great. You're going to work with me to learn how to succeed."

My mother would dress me in my Sunday best and off I would go to "Dare to Be Great" in the dairy aisle of local grocery stores. I remember standing next to the milk cooler, freezing, asking every passing customer, "Would you like to try milk in a bag?" In retrospect, forty years later, I can't even imagine what these farmers must have thought. The dairy business was huge in our area, and a lot of my potential customers had cows whose bags they milked every day. The last thing they wanted to see was more milk in a bag.

I was very persistent, but had very few takers. At 5 P.M., my father would pick me up from the grocery store, and as soon as I closed the car door, he would ask, "How does it feel to dare to be great?" My lips were purple from being in front of the coolers in the aisle all day, but I would look straight into his eyes and say with a sigh, "Great, Dad. I am daring to be great."

The tape recorder continued to lull me to sleep every night, and in time Glen Turner's voice gave way to Dale Carnegie's "How to Win Friends and Influence People" or the latest pronouncements from Norman Vincent Peale.

My childhood is flooded with memories of my father's various "Dare to Be Great" escapades. My favorite job of his was when he worked for the Keebler® Cookie Company. Every time a new type of cookie was developed, once again dressed in my Sunday best, I would live in the cookie aisles of the grocery stores handing out samples of emerging cookies. This was a warmer aisle than the milk aisle, and the farmers in our community were more attracted to cookies than they were to milk in a bag. At 5 P.M., my father would pick me up, look me in the eyes, and ask, "Kathleen, how does it feel to dare to be great?" I truly liked the cookie job, so I would emphatically answer, "Great, Dad. Really great!"

That environment molded my understanding of the power of intention and the power of choice in living. I literally grew up with Glen Turner's mantra in my head: "Kathleen, dare to be great."

So it's no wonder that I was so driven from such an early age. From hawking milk and cookies, I moved on to weaving and selling pot holders, then to buying a beauty parlor chair and setting it up in our garage to style all the neighborhood women's hair, then on to various other entrepreneurial escapades through my adolescence and young adult years. I would sit down on a regular basis to assess my intentions and revise my plans on achieving my intentions. I needed money for clothes, school, and personal items, and so I always devised plans for what I had to do to get what I needed.

The traditional definition of success was born and bred into us Halls. It was encoded into our DNA. Before I was 10, the critical nature of status, houses, cars, and clothes had been firmly imprinted in my mind. You'll notice my father's definition of success was a list of material goods. There was nothing in my family's definition of success that included a concept of balance or true happiness.

Many of us believe that we are really living. But the truth is, very few of us are actually living. We go from one appointment to another, from one meal to another, from one responsibility to another, from one cell phone call to another, from one community event to another. Many of us sit on the edge of our beds at night after a long day at work, pull the shoes off our sore feet, and wonder what our lives are all about. Many of the individuals I work with ask themselves on a regular basis, "Is this really living?"

Martha Stewart started her company with the bold claim that she could teach people how to really live by naming her corporation "Living." Millions of American women looked to Martha Stewart as an avatar of living successfully. We purchased her products, read her magazines, watched her television shows, and prepared her recipes. All of us were chasing a new definition for living that Martha promised us. But in the end, we learned that her sheets, magazines, television shows, and recipes couldn't make us feel alive. Once again we found ourselves caught in the trap of seeking outside ourselves for the gift of living, waiting for some guru outside of ourselves to deliver us from our despair.

It is time to begin living. As individuals and families, we are at the breaking point from the incredible imbalance in our lives. Just say the word "living" over and over again a few times. Living is a powerful, energetic, dynamic word. Really living is when you feel the energy, movement and rhythm of life coursing through your body, soul, and mind.

Risk Living

Living is when you turn toward risk and experience it as an invitation to your potential instead of moving away from risk which you previously felt as loss, fear, and possible failure. The true benefits of really living are courage, perseverance, intention, energy, and power. These virtues naturally emerge when you look in the mirror each day and say, "I am really living."

In our culture we have confused really living with existence. Most of us have been taught to go, go, go. You are continually rewarded for your action; "doing," "to do lists," "being productive," and "multitasking." I was always ready to answer in a second when I was asked, "What did you do today?" I was so proud of my crossed-off to-do list. My list always had twice as many tasks to do as anybody else's list. So of course I felt superior, more productive, and more efficient with the most tasks completed. I lived—or should I say existed—for many years evaluating my worth by my accomplished to-do lists.

When we race like rats in a cage we soon are a part of the chaos and disorientation. As we get exhausted, we begin to not listen to our inner voice and before we know it we are lost without a map. Sadly enough, this is the model we live by or should I say exist by.

One of the most constant comments I get from clients, patients, on the call in radio shows, and in e-mails is, "I want to care for myself but I have to be productive," or "I don't have enough time for myself."

Don't you have enough time to stop and listen to the directions of your life? Can you choose to pick up the map of your life and see where you are now, what road you are on, and what direction or turn you need to make so you don't miss your life? Remember when you were a child on vacation with your family in the car. You stopped every so often to read the map to make sure you were headed in the right direction. Isn't it interesting that we take off onto the journey of our own lives and we have an AAA card there waiting to help us in case we get lost or have an accident, but we keep it locked in the glove compartment of our lives never to be used? We all have a GPS system and we just keep it turned off as we meander around the same block in the same neighborhood over and over again until we run out of gas.

A Model for Living

Individuals who experience true happiness and balance in their lives live their lives by a model that I learned in my research at Emory, named the "reflection-action model." This is a discipline used by individuals who know how to live in balance. This is the way great leaders I have studied and worked with live their incredibly rich lives. When you live a reactive life you learn to react to what life throws at you and are constantly living your life in a reactive mode. You lose your authentic power when you are not expressing who you are and you begin feeling like your life is being manipulated by circumstances or someone else. When you choose to live an intentional life, you live a proactive life and your actions are rooted in your reflection, awareness, and choices.

Each day of our lives most of us are in constant movement and action. Our actions are important because each action increases our capacity to take risks and learn from our experiences. Parker Palmer, a theologian from Georgetown University, suggests that your actions are not about winning or losing, but are about learning. Authentic power comes when you express yourself in the world through action. Your actions become the incarnation of your thoughts and reflections. Palmer believes that the reflection or contemplation process is a critical element, because as you are reflecting you are actually changing your consciousness and subsequently you have more impact and power in the world. He also maintains that when you reflect and contemplate, a different kind of action will result.[1] Your reflection time becomes a place of discovery, creativity, and authenticity.

When you use this reflection-action model, you begin by considering a problem or situation you want to work with. Then you reflect on what the options are for a solution to this problem. After you have reflected on the situation, you will choose some course of action. After some time of action, you return to the reflection process. Many times the reflection or contemplation you engage in is the most critical element because during your reflection phase you are assessing how effective your previous action was. You evaluate how appropriate your action was and what you can do better next time. Ask yourself, if you did not get the results you wanted, what else can you do. Use resources of people, the Internet, libraries, to inform your next action. You continue this process until you embark on a conclusion to your problem or decision.

As I mentioned before, great spiritual leaders have used the reflection-action model and changed the course of human history. This is how a tiny man named Mahatma Gandhi changed history by liberating India, a country of billions of people, from the colonial power of the British. Mahatma Gandhi chose to live an intentional life that was totally focused on justice, and for him that meant liberating India from the British. Gandhi would march for a certain principle, then he would either be put in jail or return to the ashram and meet with others to decide how effective the march was and they would plan on how to make their intentions more effective the next time. Each action was a learning process and each reflection was creating a more effective method to reach their goal. The intentional actions were always rooted in intentional reflection. The list is endless of spiritual leaders who lived their intentional lives using the "reflection-action" model: Buddha, Jesus, Mohammed, Moses, Martin Luther King, Jr., Mother Teresa, Susan B. Anthony, and innumerable others.

All great military leaders use the "reflection-action" model. They plan the battle, they execute their planned actions, and then they return with a casualty count, evaluate their position, and confer with other leaders and field personnel to reflect before taking the next action.

Great companies use the "reflection-action" model each quarter. They make projections for each quarter and at the end of the quarter look at their earnings. They may choose to take a different action in their business and then return at the end of each quarter to reflect on the efficiency and accuracy of their actions. These reflections will then influence their next actions. The price of the stock and the stock market will value the effectiveness of the company's reflection-action model.

Begin Living

Really living is about creating a life that never lets you get far from your authentic Self. Don't allow any situation, event, or person to distance you from your authentic, genuine, original Self. The further you allow yourself to get caught in the current of others' lives, the further downstream you are from your own home camp. Have you ever tried to walk or swim upstream? It's tough to get back home once you have been swept away downstream. This is the great lesson I've learned. When you wake up and become aware that you aren't home, you don't have to exhaust yourself to swim against the current. You have many choices. Stop, pull over to the side, and sit on the bank. Do you choose to go back to your home camp upstream? Do you want to create a new life where you are now, or do you want to jump back into the stream and see where it takes you? If you decide to head back upstream you don't have to struggle against the currents. Just get out of the water and walk by the stream on your way back home. Going home never has to be as difficult as it may seem. That's why you need to pull over, reflect, and assess where you are, what your options are, and then make your choice.

The reason I use this metaphor is that after dealing with individuals that have come to me through the years with everything from cancer to heart disease to job loss to a spouse or child's death, I have realized that so many of these individuals have been swept away from living their life. They are overwhelmed and confused. My job has been to help them become aware that they have choices, and their choices don't necessarily have to be dramatic and painful. When the individuals I see do not have a rooted system to ground them, I teach them about the four roots of true happiness.

Living Means Nourishing Your Roots

The four roots of happiness have been tried and tested. I know because I have rooted my life in these roots. There has been much sorrow and loss in addition to great joy in my life. Many times I know the only way I have survived the painful situations in my life is by living my life grounded in the four roots. Engaging in regular practices of *serenity* has transformed my life. When anger, fear, or pain settled in and stopped me from living, I would surrender and sit in meditation. I have done it for so many years I trust this practice and it has rooted me firmly. Meditation is like taking a clear glass of water and dropping an Alka-Seltzer into the water. The water was clear before the Alka-Seltzer was dropped in, and now it is fuzzy and cloudy. You are the glass of pure clear water and your issues or problems are the tablet of Alka-Seltzer. As you continue to watch the glass it becomes clear again, the tablet is dissolved. It is important to remember that the Alka-Seltzer is still present in the water, but the water, like your mind, returns to clarity.

When depression ascended upon my life and interrupted my ability to really live, I relied on the second root of *exercise*. In the midst of this miring cloud, I would lie on the floor and do a few yoga stretches or take the dogs for a walk. These very small amounts of movement kept my head above water and the endorphins and serotonin eventually led me back home to my Self.

The root that has sustained me and so many others is the root of *love* embedded in relationships. Really loving others means risking being in their presence, vulnerable, authentic, and humble. Through the many losses in my life I have never felt alone because I feel my eternal connection to others. I frequently say to others, "separation is an illusion." In reality we cannot ever be separated as long as we have thoughts and emotions. Right now think of someone you love: an aunt, grandparent, child, spouse, or friend. Do you have a smile on your face? As you think about your loved one there is energy from your thought and this powerful energy immediately brings your loved one into your heart no matter where you are. My grandmothers are not in this realm on this earth anymore, but every day of my life when I think of them, I smile and they immediately are present in my heart. Remember, "Separation is an illusion."

Food, the fourth root of true happiness gifts you with living. As I worked with patients I discovered how various foods affect our immune systems, our cardiovascular system, our brain, and the rest of our bodies. Food heals us, comforts us, fuels us, and is just pure enjoyment. You literally are what you eat. It is interesting how much more Western medicine knows about the critical nature of food and our health, but few health-care professionals educate their patients about food. I start out each day knowing how much protein is needed for the day, how many fruits, vegetables, and grains are needed, and I eat for the day accordingly. Anywhere you eat is fun because you know what kind of choices you need to make to stay healthy. Most of us are going to live to be in our eighties. So it's not whether and how long you are going to live, but are you really *living?* Knowledge is power and self care is the key for real living.

An Intentional Life of Gratitude

Living an intentional life is impossible without the lessons and actions of gratitude. Gratitude allows us to grow and magnify ourselves on our journey to true happiness. It is physiologically impossible to be grateful and experience stress at the same time. Research shows grateful individuals report having more energy and fewer physical complaints than their non-grateful counterparts. Studies tell us daily gratitude exercises resulted in higher levels of alertness, enthusiasm, determination, optimism, and energy.

Inspiring Gratitude in Your Children

▶ *Adopting a Family:* Take in a family in need at a holiday time such as Christmas. There are many resources in your community that will supply you with a family. Choose a family a month ahead of the holiday and go to their homes. Invite them to eat meals with you, either at a restaurant or in your home. Our family really gets to know the life situation and needs of our adopted families. Over the years it has been an incredible experience for my children. My children are now adults but our holiday conversations always go to the wonderful rich memories of the families that we shared for that season. Our family became a bigger family and we all became new and different people out of that wonderful experience.

▶ *Volunteering:* Altruism is one of the greatest gifts for your children, and it inspires gratitude. Have a family meeting and give the family five choices of where you can volunteer. It is powerful when the children are involved in this choice. We have always worked at homeless shelters, public housing developments, and after school programs with our daughters throughout their lives. This instills within them a greater understanding of the larger world and helps develop compassion and gratitude in your children.

▶ *The Blessing Box:* Keep a blessing box in your home as your children are growing up. The children each put a part of their allowance or any money they have into the box during the week. Have a weekly family meeting and discuss what you should do with the money at the end of the month. Your children choose where the money should go and why it is their responsibility to care for others. This develops a great sense of compassion and gratitude in your children.

▶ *Prayer:* It is essential for our children to have reverence and gratitude for food and for meals. Your children will learn to respect the ritual of mealtime and keep it special. We have always prayed before meals and bedtime. In those prayers it is great to focus not just on your family's needs but on the needs of others in our world and community. It is also wonderful to listen as your children pray. Their prayers give you a sacred window into their hearts and minds.

▶ *Vacations:* Take your children on adventures and vacations. This valuable time allows them to experience how others live in other states, cultures, and countries. It will instill gratitude for their home, family, and their life.

▶ *Taking Children to Work:* If possible take your children to work. It allows your children to see where you work, what you do, and to get to know your coworkers. Your children share a more intimate space in your life when they share your work. Your children will be more grateful when they see how hard you work and how you sacrifice to provide for them.

ACE Your Life

There are three ingredients, or components, that are the foundation for living an intentional life. They are *awareness, choice,* and *energy,* which are easy to remember as *ACE.* These components for living an intentional life are not sequential. What is important is learning to become aware of these three key elements in your life and learn how to live them.

The process begins by developing your *awareness* (A) of daily experiences. I advise each client to pay attention and "listen to your life." Pay attention to what kindles your passion and creativity. Be aware of what gives you energy and puts a smile on your face. Be cognizant of what or who drains you or distracts you. Pay attention to who or what irritates you or extinguishes your passion. Awareness is the first step to discovering the elements of your life that are contributing or distracting you from really living.

Your awareness will lead you into making intentional *choices* (C) in your life. Your life is the result of a series of the choices you have made. Now that you are aware of your choices you can no longer be a victim. Awareness leads you to the choices you are making and you take responsibility for your life. Victim mentality ends when you understand the power of choice. You may not control many of the circumstances in your life, but you can choose your attitude and intentions in response to circumstances.

Learning to pay attention and developing your awareness, then making intentional choices in your life, creates new *energy* (E) and power. As your awareness grows, you will become more aware of what you are eating, who you are living with, and where you go to work each day. You will discover an energy swelling within you as you experience authentic energy and power. You may make new and different choices, because you now know that life is your choice. You are the hero of your life, not the victim. You will radiate confidence, energy, and a new sense of your own power. Your authentic energy will lead you into living your intentional life.

Awareness, Choice, and *Energy* (ACE) is the dynamic process to help you to begin living. Each component is woven into the fabric of living an intentional life. You may be driving to work one day and become aware that you have no *energy* or passion. You may feel "out of gas." You may be reading a novel or watching a movie and experience a profound sadness within you. Suddenly you become *aware* that the life you are living feels shallow, lonely, and fearful. You may begin to wonder if you are really living or if you are living a life of quiet desperation with no energy and not truly feeling alive. There may be an accident or event in your life that wakes you up and makes you aware that your life must change, and that a *choice* must be made.

As you begin living, you begin to grow inward and downward, rooting yourself deeply into a balanced life of true happiness. You will be able to achieve a deeper understanding of the simple, the mundane, and the ordinary moments, which bring true happiness, inner balance and fulfillment.

Ritual

Rituals offer us the opportunity to create meaning in our familiar lives. We build rituals with common symbols, like the candles on a birthday cake, wedding rings in the wedding ritual, and the white garment for our newborn's christening. Rituals are the essential threads that hold together the tapestry of life from generation to generation. Rituals recognize age-old, time-honored traditions that have sustained our families and our cultures. Rituals have been protected and respected because they represent a revered intersection of time and space.

We root the lives of our Self, families, communities, and nations in ritual. Ritual creates a safe and secure place for the transitions of our lives. Ritual connects us to the past, the present, and our future. Ritual bridges one generation to the next. Ritual engages our senses: the smell and taste of celebratory foods, the sounds of the voices and music, and the colors and decorations lead us home to this ritual space. When we experience rituals, we *re-member* (connect with our body) and we are *re-minded* (we connect to our minds).

Your evening bath can be your ritual to end the day and remind you of the baths of your childhood, or you may remember bathing your own children years before. Our meals are one of our greatest rituals and become a time for laughing, sharing, feasting, and discovering. Meals mark the celebrations and holidays of our lives and celebrate the transitions. Death rituals hold families in mind, body, and soul as they go through the process of pain, grief, loss, and transition. Ritual provides strength and power to hold onto when life seems the most uncertain and confusing.

As you protect the rituals that are most holy to you and your family, don't forget to include new rituals that keep your family woven together through time. When my children were young, every Monday we would drive by the ice cream shop and the three of us had ice cream together. It became our "girl" time together where we experimented with new flavors, laughed, and did lots of people watching. Many years later we still remember that ritual with much love and laughter. One of the greatest gifts you can give your children is the gift of respect and reverence for rituals. They are the glue of our lives.

Begin Your Intentional Life

Every thought and emotion you experience creates the energy and power to fashion your intentional life. The minute you focus on the intentions of your life, there is energy propelled into the world that drives your intentions into fulfillment. Reflect on the purpose of your life and begin to list your intentions. After you list your intentions, begin to prioritize the time in your life and watch your intentional life blossom.

～ BEGIN TODAY ～

Ask Your Self   Am I living an intentional life?

What would my intentional life look like?

What is keeping me from living an intentional life?

Tell Your Self   I am living an intentional life.

Give Your Self   Make a list of priorities or goals that lead to your intentional life.

Seek out a friend or two who will support you on your journey as you learn to live your intentional life.

Perform a personal ritual that inspires you to be authentic and to live an intentional life daily.

CHAPTER 13

Achieve Balance

THE RINGING TELEPHONE that roused me from my sound sleep seemed to be coming from a dream, but when my husband nudged me and whispered, "telephone," I fumbled in the darkness for the receiver and mumbled, "Hello?" Part of me was still in a dream state, but when I recognized my good friend Marie's voice on the other end of the line, I came back to reality, and a chill ran through me. Calls at this hour rarely herald good news.

"Kathleen," Marie said, "Forgive me for calling so late." I could tell by the tone of her voice that something was terribly wrong.

"What is it?" I asked.

In between soft sobs, Marie told me of the sudden and tragic death of her childhood friend Beth in a horrible accident in Connecticut. My heart went out to her as I said, "I'm so sorry, Marie. Tell me how I can help."

"Well, Beth was one of four of a close circle of my childhood girl-friends. Her parents were killed when she was ten years old, so the three of us were like real sisters to her. We've all gone our separate ways over the years, but we've kept in close touch and will all be there to bury our precious sister the day after tomorrow."

I thought of my close friends from childhood, and tears of compassion welled up in my eyes.

"Kathleen, I've been searching for something to represent the depth of our connection to Beth. The first thing that came to mind was that amazing hand-woven shawl you have in your catalog—the one with all the colors? It reminds me of the chakras. Somehow it seems the perfect symbol of Beth's lively spirit and the love the four of us shared that stood the test of time…and now," she said with a sob, "even death."

"Just give me the address, Marie," I said. "I'll FedEx them to you right away."

A week later Marie called and told me of the funeral, how each of Beth's "sister" pallbearers wore the matching colorful shawls and felt a deep communion with each other and with their departed sister as her casket was covered with the fourth shawl.

Marie is a perfect example of an individual who lives and breathes balance and happiness. She not only lost her best friend, her devoted husband also died after a long battle with cancer. But because she has spent a lifetime cultivating her deep rootedness in her Self, instead of imploding and spiraling downward into grief and loss, she continually reaches a new balance each time the winds of chaos blow through her life.

Marie has lived a life so deeply grounded in the roots of S.E.L.F.—serenity, exercise, love, and food—that she weathers any storm in her life and experiences true happiness during moments that most wouldn't see as opportunities for deeper growth.

Marie recently visited Colombia, South America, where very few of the children have access to education. She was working on a joint development project with her partners. She had just left her beautiful hotel on her way to meet with her partners at the building site when she noticed children playing in the filth and squalor of a large dump on the side of the road. She asked the cab driver to stop the car, walked over to the children rummaging through the garbage, and asked them when they had eaten last. The filthy, thin, and ragged children bowed their heads in shame and wouldn't answer. She walked back to the cab and asked the driver to take her to her meeting. She asked the driver about the children. The driver told her that all of these children lived at the garbage dump in old wrecked cars abandoned there. He said they had no families and waited for people to dump their trash and scavenged the bags for food. The driver said it was pitiful but there is so much poverty there was nothing to be done.

That night she couldn't eat and had a restless night remembering the haunting faces of those children. She walked on her porch overlooking the lush gardens of her hotel, and she made a vow to her late husband that she wouldn't eat another bite of food until she found a way to help these children. Two days later she had a plan, and she devoted her Self to create an orphanage and an educational project so each child would not only have food, clothing, and shelter, but would also get an education.

Marie called every person she was involved with in a large business project in which many of her partners owned businesses as she did. At the conclusion of a meeting with her partners she asked everyone to stay seated for a moment. She walked over to an easel and showed them pictures of these homeless, parentless children, and then she showed them the orphanage school she had designed. She challenged each partner to donate a percentage of the profits from their project to the orphanage. Marie invited them to join her in this incredible project and she wouldn't take no for an answer. She told them it was unethical to build a prosperous business in the middle of this poverty unless they gave back, and that meant now.

Marie defines *happiness* as being connected to the vital force of life. Energy and passion regularly infuse her life because she can see every event—even a difficult one—as an opportunity for experiencing a higher level of balance and love. My dear friend Marie is my true "shero." She reminds me of that mighty oak tree that never failed me as a child. Her arms are open, flexible, and inviting, her body sustains and protects all life, and her roots are deep and strong.

What Is Balance?

Balance is also a state of adjustment between contrasting elements. When I consider the word balance, the words stability, serenity, calm, and harmony come to mind. Balance is about becoming whole. It is about choosing to live a life in wholeness, not pieces of a life that look like the pieces of a puzzle in a box. Most of the clients I see describe their lives as fractionated parts of a puzzle in a box, shaken up, and they can't figure out how to put their life together and make the pieces fit into a whole picture.

Poisons of Balance

A poison is anything that causes injury, illness, death, or destruction. These poisons are harmful influences if you desire a life of balance and true happiness.

STRESS

Stress is the poison of real balance and happiness. Many of us just accept chronic stress as a way of life. Most of us have surrendered apathetically to our chaotic lives with no kicking or screaming; we continue to believe we can achieve lives of balance from the outside. We move to a different spouse thinking this will make our life balanced and things will be different. We go on a different new diet and think our life will change. We move from job to job, from home to home, change our wardrobes, and hope our lives will be happier and balanced, but we only mire deeper into the chaos. Sadly many of us pursue plastic surgery in hopes that changing our looks will bring true happiness into our lives but little really changes. We keep putting tiny band aids on a gaping wound. Just like the wound must heal from the inside out so we must shift to the inside to discover our purpose in life and discover true happiness. Real balance originates on the inside.

INSOMNIA

Insomnia robs your body of its healing time of rest and rejuvenation. Insomnia leaves you feeling drained of energy on every level, so we spend our days trying to get false energy from any source we can: caffeine, chocolate, candy, sugar, carbohydrates, work, or a source of addictions. Are we chronically tired from our lives being a constant cycle of false energy creating our chaotic lifestyle, and then worrying, experiencing anxiety, and not being able to sleep?

PERSONAL ILLNESS

Illness keeps us off balance. Living a life out of balance could be one of the factors that lead to the illness. Embracing the lifestyle of the four roots will restore you to a new sense of balance and power in your life.

AGING PARENTS OR CHRONICALLY ILL PERSON

Our aging parents increasingly need us. This creates stress on our time, money, and our hearts. If we worry or live in frustration about our aging parents we will become sick in our own body, mind, and soul. It is critical to practice the four roots to maintain your balance because aging parents are usually a long-term situation.

One of the most stressful things in life can be caring for a chronically or terminally ill person. Many of the patients and clients I have seen through the years are caring for a child with long-term disabilities, such

as cerebral palsy or autism. Others may care for a person who has a terminal disease, which can also be long-term care. We cannot underestimate the amount of chronic stress this kind of care places on the
caregiver. The caregiver must learn to practice self-care, or their own
mental and physical health will be destroyed over time.

WORK-LIFE IMBALANCE

Work-life balance is an emerging and fast-growing field. Being out of balance has great costs to corporations and families. It is impossible to live
two different lives for long. Your home life or your work life will eventually bleed into each other. Our work has increasingly become a cause of
stress in our lives, with 62 percent of American workers saying their work-
load has increased over the last six months, and 53 percent of American
workers saying that work leaves them "overtired and overwhelmed."[1]
More corporations are getting concerned with the issues of work-life balance. If you do not have work-life balance programs in your corporation,
gather some data about the costs of being out of balance and that will get
their attention. Being out of balance can keep a company working at a low
level of productivity and creativity.

PERFECTIONISM

A perfectionist lives a rigid self-constructed life of control. The definition
of balance is flexibility and fluidity. A perfectionist lives out of fear, and
creates a life of rigidity and lives in a prescriptive manner. A perfectionist
can't trust the rhythm of life. Perfectionists experience emotional and
physical problems. Many times individuals with this nonflexible personality will have health problems, such as high blood pressure, chronic
fatigue, heart palpitations, or insomnia.

Living a balanced life requires flexibility and this is almost impossible
for perfectionists. If you suffer with this condition I hope you seek help
from a counselor. Many of the perfectionists I have worked with live sad
lives of isolation and don't have much fun in life.

BURNOUT

Burnout is when your mind and body are excessively strained and you
subsequently become physically and emotionally fatigued. Individuals
who live with constant levels of high stress and do not practice self-
care will eventually have a mental and physical response that will lead
to burnout. After a person experiences burnout they usually feel like a

failure: hopeless and powerless. This can easily lead into a state of depression and unhappiness.

Many individuals who are on the fast track in life are in danger of burnout. Persons who are too invested in their work and do not have a well-rounded lifestyle are headed for burnout. Most persons who experience burnout live as if every action in their life is about productivity.

To prevent burnout begin practicing the four roots immediately. You can heal burnout with this self-care model that is tried, tested and true. Once you live the four-root lifestyle, you will not have as high a risk to suffer from burnout again.

Sources of Balance

In every discipline—medicine, religion, philosophy, and spirituality—there is a concept of balance. We live in a universe that is in a constant state of balance. Each of us lives a lie when we believe we can remove ourselves from the natural cycles of life. How can we believe we are above or separate from natural law? As humans, we are subject to gravity, the atmosphere, earth climatic cycles, changes in our galaxy and the universe. Just as the law of gravity affects all things on earth and we all require oxygen, water and food to live, we know we must live our lives with these laws as foundational principles of our existence. One of these fundament laws of nature we must acknowledge and embrace is the principle of balance.

NATURE

Sit by the ocean and watch the waves advance and retreat over and over again. Observe the tide as it slowly ebbs and flows. The water surrenders to the sand, and the sand surrenders to the water; the sea animals and shells have surrendered to the water and are washed upon the shore. There is a mystical synergy in nature. Each leaf on the tree surrenders to the wind and trusts its power, whisper, and invisible nature. Each element trusts the other element in nature, and the art of balance is in the surrendering. In this balanced relationship of nature is synergy.

When we experience the rain we usually walk fast or bristle as the cool drops pelt on our bodies. As the wind blows we hold our arms tight around us as our bodies get rigid and defensive. We resist the gifts of nature instead of welcoming them. We live as if the elements of nature are "other" or "outside" of our human realm. If you observe children in nature they naturally surrender with wonder to a creek, rain, a windy day, or a sudden snow storm. Our children have not been socialized to detach and resist the gift of balance the natural world bestows on us.

My prescription for you is to make sure there is no lightning, and go for a walk in the rain. Put your face to the wind and wonder where that air is visiting you from. Did this wind or rain come from China, the Arctic Circle, or South Africa? To begin to reclaim our own inner balance we must reexperience nature and surrender to her lessons.

Leisure

Leisure is considered a luxury in our world. Leisure is critical for you to create a life of balance. Since the beginning of time humans have had difficulty creating a balance between work and leisure in their lives. Workaholism has almost been revered in our culture. Working more than eight hours a day has become regularly accepted. Many of us complain that we don't have energy because we are exhausted, overbooked, overworked, and overwhelmed.

Leisure is about balance, and our society's concept of time is off balance. Nature is balance, day and night, but with the advent of electricity and human-created light sources, we continue to work later into the night. As balance becomes increasingly difficult we suffer the consequences, as our bodies, minds, and souls dry up.

Leisure is an essential part of our lives. Leisure is one of the most difficult practices because we've become doers and makers, and have forgotten how to be dreamers and reflectors. Almost every part of our life is measured by our production. We have lost the art of reflection. There are two parts of leisure: rest and play.

The concept of *rest*, or Sabbath, exists in all cultures, spiritualities, and every world religion. The Sabbath is not about God needing rest, it is about teaching *us* to rest. The Talmud gives three reasons why the Sabbath is critical: It equalizes rich and poor, it gives us time to evaluate our work to see if it is good, and it gives us time to contemplate the meaning of life. The book of Genesis tells us that after the work of creation, God stopped and rested from all work. Rest was such a revered practice that God blessed the experience of rest.

Play was the basis of leisure time throughout all societies. The function of holy days and festivals was to provide all levels of people the opportunity to play and celebrate together. It was an opportunity to equalize social classes through leisure.

Leisure allows you to connect with your heart and stretch your soul. Leisure is a time honored path for experiencing balance in mind, body, and spirit.

Leisure brings meaning to life because it allows us time reflect and listen. Leisure is essential to your health and happiness. Your work will become more meaningful and have a greater purpose when you make leisure time a priority in your life.

Explore new ways to play and rest. Discover the multitude of things you can do in nature. Be creative and make it fun. You can explore your city. Many people are so busy they have lived in their city for years and haven't learned about it. From museum openings, art festivals, and free concerts to zoos, parks, and historical sites there is so much waiting for you. The Internet is a great resource for finding current activities in your neighborhood and innovative hot spots to replenish your spirit.

Take a nap! Research tells us the many health benefits of a nap. Sit under a tree. Lay in your yard and immerse yourself in the aroma of the summer grass. Visit a local park and rediscover yourself on the playground and always remember leisure is meant for a time of exploration and discovery.

FORGIVENESS

Your life may depend upon your ability to forgive. After many years of working with patients and clients with diseases, such as cancer, heart disease, hypertension, obesity, insomnia, and stress, I have realized that one essential attribute creates and nourishes our health and well being; it is the practice of forgiveness.

There are three critical reasons why we should practice forgiveness:

1. *Your MIND:* When someone makes a genuine apology, there is an almost immediate positive impact upon the mind. The person that was not forgiven has lived in your mind, and has actually taken up physical, mental, and spiritual space in the unforgiving memory you hold. Remember that a thought creates energy. You carry this negative memory around in your mind and it actually takes energy away from your mind and thus your mental health. Consequently, when you practice forgiveness your mind will signal your physical body, and it has an immediate positive impact.

2. *Your BODY:* Scientific studies show us that as soon as a person practices forgiveness their heart rate and blood pressure lowers, their sweat levels lower, and their facial muscle tension diminishes.

3. *Your SOUL:* All religions and sacred scriptures from every tradition speak to the essential practice of forgiveness. Jesus, Mohammed, saints, rabbinic teachers, mystics, Gandhi, Desmond Tutu, Nelson Mandela, and Jimmy Carter have all lived their lives on the foundational practice of forgiveness. Most believe forgiveness is the bedrock to any real connection with the Divine.

James Carson of Duke University Medical Center found that individuals with chronic back pain who have forgiven others experience lower levels of pain, anger, and depression than non-forgivers.[2] Dr. Herbert Benson of Harvard believes there is a physiological response of healing when people forgive. He believes that forgiveness is such a critical element in health that he has created an entire course at Harvard on forgiveness and health.

Find Your Balance: Anywhere

Mothers are experiencing tremendous stress these days, and many moms become isolated during their busy day, which adds to the stress. Here are some helpful hints for moms to discover balance in the midst of your busy day.

Live life to the fullest! It's important for mothers to break out of their usual routines, let loose, and be spontaneous. It's essential to a mom's overall well-being and outlook on life to let loose and take a break, and it's good for her family as well.

There are physical and mental health benefits to the mother who takes a break once in a while. We have research that tells us women's health depends on them laughing, playing, exercising, relaxing, and enjoying pleasurable fun times.

A recent *Time* magazine issue was dedicated to the "Science of Happiness." There is an interesting study that was just done on 900 women in Texas to show the five most positive activities women do that bring them happiness, which are sex, socializing, relaxing, praying or meditating, and eating (exercising was next). It is interesting that way down the list was "taking care of my children," which was below cooking and only slightly above housework.[3]

TIPS FOR MOM'S BREAK TIME

1. *Stake out your personal space:* It is powerful to claim your personal power, boundaries, and energy with your personal space. Your desk, pictures (of loved ones or of fun vacations), mementos, statuary, your childhood baseball cards, your child's clay statue—they all become guided imagery that calms your body and creates peace and centeredness.

2. *Relax with your senses:* Think of how you can enhance your senses. What colors are around you? Get something with your favorite or energetic color near you: maybe a small throw or pillow, or a cloth under your pictures; the paint of your office walls; the paintings or a great piece of colored fabric hanging on your wall; or women may keep a shawl on a chair. For smell, keep bottles of essential oils in your desk or in your office. Peppermint picks you up, lavender calms you down, and citrus can just make you feel fresh and happy. Whatever resonates with you? For taste, keep some mints or hard candies on your desk for a pick me up. For sound, use background music that is calming and can produce serotonin, the healing calming hormone. Or use a sound machine that has sounds of nature.

3. *Take "wellness breaks":* Take breaks twice a day, for at least five to ten minutes each time. We know from research the power of the mind-body connection. Every thought and emotion you experience releases chemicals into your bloodstream.

Here is a list of things you can do on your break:

▶ *Choir Loft:* Some people have either always loved to sing and others may have always wanted to sing but have a bad voice and were ashamed to sing in public. This is your big opportunity to have your own choir loft. Singing is great for your health. Singing increases your immune cells. Singing increases the oxygen in your body, it exercises your mouth, neck, chest, stomach and lung muscles, and it shifts your mental attitude to optimism. Studies show a protein used by the immune system to fight disease—Immunoglobulin A—increased 240 percent while singing, noticeably higher, indicating enhanced immunity.[4] A study at the University of Frankfurt found anti-stress hormones increased significantly while singing.[5] In other studies singers report improved lung capacity, high energy, better posture, and enhanced feelings of relaxation, mood, and confidence.

▶ *Concert Hall-Symphony:* Listening to music changes the release of chemicals into your body. Listening to music increases serotonin and other healing chemicals into your body. Calming soft music decreases physical responses, such as heart rate and respiration, induces and maintains relaxation, and shifts mood. Energetic happy music can stimulate your physical responses, such as increased heart rate or respiration that results in more energy.

▶ *Counseling Center:* This time becomes an opportunity for you to change habits and learn new practices to improve the quality of your life. You can learn to improve your mental health in the privacy of your own space, or in the privacy of your earphones attached to a CD or tape. Learn how to heal your anger, fear, phobia, depression, divorce, or parenting; choose an area you want to learn about or you want to change in your life. This could be the first step on your path to better mental health, which you can partner with a therapist or work on in your own time.

▶ *Chapel: Your Private Temple:* You can use this time for spiritual growth, a time for inspiration and motivation. Guided imagery tapes relax you and provide healing, lower blood pressure, and create greater immunity in your body. Use a meditation tape if you are not driving a car. We have consistent studies of the health benefits of meditation. Diaphragmatic breathing (deep abdominal breathing) increases oxygen to the body, clears the brain, creates healing rhythm in the body, instant calm, and as we deeply breathe, the body increases the production of serotonin. Practice breathing regularly daily. You may decided to pray. You can send light, healing, or love to others, to coworkers, or to your family. We have good science on the efficacy of prayer. Dr. Larry Dossey has been conducting and reviewing literature on prayer study for many years now.

▶ *Comedy Club (The Science of Laughter):* Researchers found that laughter has a healthy effect on blood vessel function. They discovered under ultrasound that artery diameter increased by 22 percent during laughter and decreased by 35 percent during mental stress.[6] The magnitude of change seen in the endothelium, the lining of the blood vessel, is similar to the benefit seen with aerobic activity. Laugh regularly (15 minutes a day) for your vascular system. Play tapes or CDs of comedians that you find funny and enjoy.

▶ *Products-Resources:* I have been a professor of World Religion and studied a variety of spiritualities and cultures. Almost all cultures, religions, and spiritualities use physical tools to *re-mind*, or make people *remember*. Beads are used in Christianity, Buddhism, Taoism, Islam, Hinduism, and many other religions. Used with hands, around necks, or as bracelets, these are reminders to come home to your body, mind, and soul. You can have travel mugs, breathe beads, key chains, or even a shawl to remind you to relax, get balanced, and come home to your Self.

❱ *Website:* Go to a website that relaxes you. There are many on the Internet.

❱ *Water:* Get in touch with water. Go to a fountain and touch the water, or go into the restroom and put your hands and wrists under warm water if you want to calm down, or cold water if you want to be stimulated.

❱ *Stretch:* Practice Yoga, tai chi, or Qigong.

EASY STRESS TIPS FOR BALANCE AT WORK

❱ Be proactive, not reactive.

❱ Breathe: take a couple deep cleansing breaths.

❱ Repeat an affirmation (one to five words that bring you back to yourself).

❱ Remember you have a choice, you are not the victim, and you are the hero.

❱ Listen to the person and mirror what the person has said to you: "Did I hear you say XXXX?" When you mirror what another person has said, it brings clarity to the situation. You are in control and have maintained your power and respect.

❱ Don't let other people throw up on you!

COMMUTING CAN THROW YOUR LIFE OFF BALANCE

Work is stressful, but getting to work can be more stressful than your work. Commuters can experience greater stress than fighter pilots going into battle or riot police. Researchers compared the heart rate and blood pressure of commuters with those of fighter pilots and police officers in training exercises. Stress levels of commuters were higher.

It is critical to learn how to transform your commute into a productive time instead of a destructive time for your mental and physical health. The average commute is approximately 1.5 hours a day, 7.5 hours a week, or 48 work days a year.

Stop choosing to be the victim of your commute. Choose to be the hero of your commute. Why not make this valuable time a time of growth and health by making it a classroom. Use the stress tips I have suggested for your office; learn a language, vocabulary words, or another skill; sing, listen to music, laugh, stretch, practice breathing, or pray. It's your time so treat it with great reverence as you would a rare jewel.

Creating a Home of Balance

Our need for a haven is as old as humankind itself. We have sought sanctuary in groups, public settings, and especially in the privacy of our homes. More than ever before, since 9–11 we are more closely identifying our homes as a sanctuary or haven, where we can withdraw from the stress and fears of our world. Creating special places in your life to reflect, nourish, and connect with your Self and others is essential as you begin your life of balance.

Three Tips for Making Your Home a Haven:

1. *A Family Haven:* Designated family space can be in a public area of your home. There may be a shelf or a table that is claimed as an area of communal family space. You may choose to have family pictures, an inspirational book or other scriptures, and other memorabilia that reflect the shared lives of your family. This space becomes a place where the family visits to commemorate the memories of their lives, including mementos of grandparents gone, children's basketball games, and family travels or holidays. This haven reinforces the power, values, and continuity of the family.

2. *A Personal Haven:* Personal space is created by what is meaningful in your own life. A personal haven may be in your bedroom, office, closet, or any other place that you can claim as yours. Your private space may be an altar; a shelf with a picture, meditation or prayer beads; a journal; or objects that evoke significant memories. This haven becomes a refuge for each individual in the family to find their own source of serenity and connection.

3. *A Nature Haven:* We are all profoundly connected to nature. You can create a haven or nature refuge outdoors or within your home. You may want to keep a single plant on your window sill in your kitchen or a bonsai or simple flower in a vase near your personal or family space in your home to connect you with the natural world. If you have the outdoor space you may want to create a haven in a garden that evolves over time, adding different creations each year reflecting the years of your life. Your garden haven actually becomes a living journal and a history of your life.

Balance Every Day

Whether you work inside or outside the home, the four roots of true happiness can bring your life into balance. Whether you discipline yourself and choose five minutes to spend on each root a day, or if you can create 20 minutes a day, it is essential for your life to remember your S.E.L.F. roots everyday. When you practice these roots daily you will experience really living not just existing in a life of habituation and worry. A life rooted in balance mirrors that balance whether you are at home or work. When you cultivate balance within you, your energy and power will emanate from you into this wonderful world which so sorely needs you.

~ BEGIN TODAY ~

Ask Your Self   Do I feel I am living a life of balance?

What is keeping my life from being balanced?

What plan can I create to bring more balance into my life?

Tell Your Self   I enjoy my life of balance.

Give Your Self   Schedule leisure time for play and rest.

Go for a walk in nature and enjoy the season.

Watch your favorite movie with joy.

Embody H.O.P.E.

BARBARA WALTERS was giving a speech at a meeting I was attending, and she was talking about all of the "original" individuals she had the privilege of interviewing in her life. One of her favorites was Katherine Hepburn. Barbara Walters said she sat down to interview this powerful, independent, brilliant woman, and before she could begin with the first question Ms. Hepburn blurted out, "Ms. Walters, what kind of tree do you think you are?" Ms. Walters said she sat there stunned, not ever having considered this question before. Ms. Hepburn leaned forward and continued:

> You know, I consider myself an oak. Big, strong, deeply rooted. The minute I meet someone the first thing I do is decide what kind of tree they are, Ms. Walters. It's a good thing, you know. I've known a lot of sycamore trees, big, beautiful, and just as poisonous as a rattle snake. Then there's a pine tree, tall, beautiful, majestic, but all it takes is a little storm, you know, a little wind and rain, or ice and snow, and that pine tree will just snap. You know a pine tree doesn't have good strong roots either, and a storm will just wipe it out. Yes, I've known a lot of pine trees in my time. Here today, gone tomorrow. It saves you a lot of time and trouble if you go ahead and size up a person as a tree right away, Ms. Walters. My system has never let me down.

I will never forget Barbara Walters telling that story as we all belly laughed in the audience. For those of us who admire Katherine Hepburn and her vast body of acting, I could just hear those terse words coming out of her mouth. We just felt her presence in the room that day.

Barbara Walters got quiet for a few moments and she spoke softly and the audience was mesmerized:

> Since that interview with Katherine Hepburn I have had the privilege of interviewing innumerable famous individuals; movie stars, world leaders, and CEO's of the largest corporations in the world. I would sometimes use Ms. Hepburn's litmus test to see what kind of tree I thought they might be.
>
> But at this stage of my life I have spent much time reflecting back upon these amazing individuals. I have tried to distill if there is a common theme that runs through these celebrated leaders of our world: the most rich, famous, and powerful in the world. One word consistently emerges, "hope." Each renowned person lived their lives with incredible hope. From Anwar Sadat to Julia Roberts, from Jack Welch to Gloria Steinem, each life exuded hope. They inspired and infected others with their hope.

This statement by Barbara Walters that day really sunk into my soul and I couldn't get it out of my mind. She could have chosen any virtue and it all came down to hope. I remembered being a cheerleader in high school and in college. I loved cheering and leading the school in cheers. It surprised me to realize that my job as a cheerleader was to inspire "hope." I was a purveyor of hope.

Hope can make you feel alive. Hope is real palpable energy. Hope infects you with courage, resilience and power. Hope refuses to allow you to give up. When was the last time you experienced hope? Was it when you looked into your child's eyes, watched the sunrise or when you saw someone on the evening news perform a random act of kindness? Hope is food for the journey of life.

Whether you are struggling with a disease, condition, are unemployed, stressed out, or depressed, stop and plant the seed of hope. Hope is the sign of a new beginning. Do you remember when you planted a seed and covered it with dirt and checked on it day after day with great hope and anticipation?

Through the years I have seen many individuals who were wounded, broken, or who had lost their way in life. Their mental, physical, or spiritual well-being had been crushed in some way. The only thing I could give them was hope. Hope is strength. It will make you strong. Have you ever known a person going through intensive cancer treatment with the glow of hope? Have you ever rescued an animal, plant, or person and experienced hope as you nursed them back to health? Have you lived in a country or in a situation where you longed for a new life and your only companion that held you tight was hope?

My wish for you is that you can move past any hopelessness or despair and choose to live in hope. Our current lifestyle is literally killing us. We can't go backwards to another era or pine for a life we knew yesterday. Have you ever tried to put your feet in a pair of your old shoes and you couldn't get your heel in the shoe? You had outgrown them and there was no turning back. That's where you are now. Your lifestyle just won't work the way it did before because you now know the truth.

You now know how to begin to live a life of true happiness and balance. There are no secret potions, mysterious formulas, or clandestine destinations for you to go and find out how to live the life of happiness you have desired. It is simply by learning how to live by incorporating the four roots into your lifestyle. Yes, S.E.L.F. (serenity, exercise, love, and food) can become your roots for discovering true happiness and living an intentional life of balance.

These four roots have created hope, health, and new lives for my innumerable patients and clients. These practices have been gleaned from some of the greatest research institutions in the world such as Harvard, Duke, University of Massachusetts, Preventive Medicine Institute, and many others.

As you synthesize these healing roots of S.E.L.F into your life, I wish to leave you with one final acronym, H.O.P.E., for your journey.

H is for honesty. Whatever you do be honest with yourself. I can't tell you how many individuals I have seen who wasted my time and theirs by their fear of being honest about who they were, what they wanted, or what they had done. When you are honest about your life you experience integrity. When honesty goes, your life becomes riddled with incredible stress. True serenity is born in honesty. Honesty is a virtue that is the core of true greatness. Be honest about where you are now, where you want to go and why you aren't choosing to be there.

O is for obstacle and opportunity. Life is fraught with immense opportunities for growth that we initially perceive as obstacles. You may be living your life saying you didn't get an education or money or the life you want because of this and that obstacle. This means you have experienced the obstacles in you life as blocks, barriers, obstructions, or deterrents. I challenge you to shift your thinking today. From now on no matter what happens that seems like it is an obstacle, immediately say, "Well, isn't this an interesting opportunity for my growth. I can choose what is best for me in this opportunity because I am grounded in the four roots and feel confident and strong." When you shift from perceiving your life as a series of obstacles (barriers, blocks, obstructions) to understanding your life as a stream of opportunities (a chance for advancement, an opening, a favorable condition) you will be living a life of true happiness.

P is for perseverance. Introducing anything new into your busy life is not easy, and this is why perseverance is essential as you begin to live your new lifestyle grounded in the four roots. When you choose to persevere you are living with a purpose, determination, endurance, and resolution. Anything life changing that has ever happened in this world has happened because of perseverance. Let's say you decide that the family is going to take walks three times a week for your family exercise and your two children are not happy with your decision. They begin to pout and say nasty things, hoping you will give up. You must practice persistence. Write the days and times of the walks on the refrigerator and expect everyone to meet at the garage and that is it. Make a decision and be persistent, determined, and resolute.

E is for enjoyment. Enjoy your new lifestyle grounded in the four roots. Live in joy, love, happiness, and health. When you really enjoy your life, you will begin to savor, appreciate, and cherish your fragile, fleeting life. Treasure every breath, every relationship, every sunrise and sunset of your life.

I have intentionally chosen a tree to be the symbol for this book on balance and happiness. We are each great trees of various sized, shapes, and colors in this great forest called the earth.

It doesn't matter whether you live in a city, the suburbs, or in the woods, this isn't a bad way to imagine yourself for a moment. An oak tree has deep roots and is powerful, strong, and perseveres through many storms and survives for hundreds of years because of its profound roots. A pine tree grows very tall, is rich in color and magnificent in aroma, but the pine tree has very shallow roots. In a storm, pine trees are the first to go. They crack, they uproot, and fall over because of their shallow root system. A sycamore tree is grand, has gorgeous vast leaves, provides great shade, and has deep roots. But the sycamore leaves can be poisonous, and as we are taken with a sycamore's majesty and beauty on the outside, its lethal nature is not apparent to the naked eye.

Unlike the trees, which are the products of the acorn or seed, we have choices regarding what kind of tree we become. Our lives are a vast series of choices that determine what kind of tree we will be. This book is about giving you information to help you make the choices so you can live your intentional life. I have now passed on to you, with great reverence, the training, experiences and education of many years of my life in hopes that you may live your life in balance of true happiness.

∼ BEGIN TODAY ∼

Ask Your Self   Am I honest with my Self and others about my life?

How can I turn an obstacle into an opportunity?

What do I do in life that I really enjoy?

Tell Your Self   I bring hope into the world.

Give Your Self   Read an inspirational book.

Rent the movie *Liar, Liar,* starring Jim Carrey.

Visit someone who gives you hope.

PART IV: **APPENDIXES**

APPENDIX A

Resources

DR. KATHLEEN HALL
www.drkathleenhall.com
www.thestressinstitute.com
www.alteryourlife.com

GENERAL INFORMATION
www.webmd.com WebMD

nccam.nih.gov National Center for Complementary and Alternative Medicine

www.mayoclinic.com Mayo Clinic

www.cnn.com/HEALTH/library CNN Health Information

www.nih.gov National Institutes of Health

www.healthfinder.gov National Health Information Center, U.S. Department of Health and Human Services

www.intelihealth.com InteliHealth

www.os.dhhs.gov U.S. Department of Health and Human Services

www.cdc.gov Centers for Disease Control and Prevention

www.fda.gov Food and Drug Administration

ACUPUNCTURE
www.medicalacupuncture.org American Academy of Medical Acupuncture. 213-937-5514

www.aaom.org American Association of Oriental Medicine. 610-266-1433

ANGER

The Dance of Anger: A Woman's Guide to Changing the Patterns of Intimate Relationships, by Harriet Lerner (ISBN 0-06-091565-X)

Beyond Anger: A Guide for Men: How to Free Yourself from the Grip of Anger and Get More Out of Life, by Thomas Harbin (ISBN 1-56924-621-1)

Anger, by Thich Nhat Hanh (ISBN 1-57322-937-7)

ANIMALS

www.bestfriends.org Best Friends Animal Society

www.taoofequus.com Epona Equestrian Services

www.humanequinealliance.org Human-Equine Alliances for Learning (HEAL)

www.hsus.org Humane Society of the United States

AROMATHERAPY

The Complete Book of Essential Oils and Aromatherapy, by Valerie Ann Worwood (ISBN: 0931432820)

The Illustrated Encyclopedia of Essential Oils: The Complete Guide to the Use of Oils in Aromatherapy and Herbalism, by Julia Lawless (ISBN: 1852307218)

www.naha.org The National Association for Holistic Aromatherapy (NAHA) is an educational, nonprofit organization dedicated to enhancing public awareness of the benefits of true aromatherapy.

CANCER

www.cancer.org American Cancer Society

www.cancermonthly.com Cancer Monthly

www.answersforcancer.com Cancer information site from Eli Lilly and Company

www.cancercare.org CancerCare. 800-813-HOPE (800-813-4673)

www.preventcancer.org Cancer Research Prevention Foundation. 800-227-CRFA (800-227-2732)

www.cancer.gov National Cancer Institute. 800-4CANCER (800-422-6237)

www.canceradvocacy.org National Coalition for Cancer Survivorship. 877-NCCS-YES (877-622-7937) *www.patientadvocate.org* Patient Advocate Foundation. 800-532-5274

www.plwc.org People Living with Cancer

www.thewellnesscommunity.org The Wellness Community, National Headquarters. 888-793-WELL (888-793-9355)

www.vitaloptions.org Vital Options International. 818-788-5225

BREAST CANCER

www.stopbreastcancer.org National Breast Cancer Coalition. 800-622-2838

www.sistersnetworkinc.org Sisters Network. 866-781-1808

www.komen.org/bci Susan G. Komen Breast Cancer Foundation. 800-I'M AWARE (800-462-9273)

www.y-me.org Y-Me National Breast Cancer Organization. 800-221-2141

BRAIN CANCER

www.braintumor.org National Brain Tumor Foundation. 800-934-CURE (800-934-2873)

COLON CANCER

www.ccalliance.org Colon Cancer Alliance. 877-422-2030

www.nccra.org National Colorectal Cancer Research Alliance. 800-872-3000

LEUKEMIA AND LYMPHOMA

www.leukemia-lymphoma.org The Leukemia and Lymphoma Society. 800-955-4572

www.lymphoma.org Lymphoma Research Foundation. 800-235-6848 or 800-500-9976

LUNG CANCER

www.alcase.org Alliance for Lung Cancer Advocacy, Support, and Education. 800-298-2436

www.thewellnesscommunity.org/programs/frankly/lung/lung_cancer_home.asp The Wellness Community. 888-793-WELL (888-793-9355)

www.lungcanceronline.org Lung Cancer Online

OVARIAN CANCER

www.ovarian.org National Ovarian Cancer Coalition. 888-682-7426

www.ovariancancer.org Ovarian Cancer National Alliance. 202-331-1332

PANCREAS CANCER

www.pancan.org Pancreatic Cancer Action Network. 877-2PAN-CAN (877-272-6226)

PROSTATE CANCER

www.ustoo.com US TOO! International, Inc. 800-808-7866

DEPRESSION

What to Do When Someone You Love Is Depressed, by Mitch Golant, Susan K. Golant (ISBN: 080505829X)

Breaking the Patterns of Depression, by Michael D. Yapko (ISBN: 0385483708)

www.depression.com Depression.com

www.nimh.nih.gov/publicat/depression.cfm National Institute of Mental Health

www.depressionalliance.org Depression Alliance

www.depression-screening.org National Mental Health Association

www.psych.org American Psychiatric Association. 888-35-PSYCH (888-357-7924)

www.apa.org American Psychological Association. 800-374-2721

www.mentalhealth.org Center for Mental Health Services (CMHS) Knowledge Exchange Network (KEN). 800-789-2647

www.dbsalliance.org Depression and Bipolar Support Alliance (DBSA). 800-826-3632

www.drada.org Depression and Related Affected Disorders Association. 410-955-4647

www.nami.org National Alliance for the Mentally Ill. 800-950-NAMI (800-950-6264)

www.narsad.org National Alliance for Research on Schizophrenia and Depression. 800-829-8289

www.depression.org National Foundation for Depressive Illness, Inc. 800-239-1265 *www.nimh.nih.gov* National Institute of Mental Health (NIMH). 301-443-4513

www.nmha.org National Mental Health Association. 800-969-NMHA (800-969-6642)

www.samhsa.gov Substance Abuse and Mental Health Services Administration (SAMHSA), U.S. Department of Health and Human Services. 301-443-8956

EXERCISE

Strong Women Stay Young (Revised Edition), by Miriam Nelson, Sarah Wernick (ISBN: 055338077X)

www.acefitness.org American Council on Exercise

www.fitness.gov President's Council on Fitness and Sports

FAMILIES

Healing Family Rifts, by Mark Sichel, CSW, McGraw Hill (ISBN 0-07-141242-5)

kidshealth.org Kids' Health

www.dole5aday.com Dole 5-A-Day

FEAR

Feel the Fear and Do It Anyway, by Susan Jeffers (ISBN 0-449-90292-7)

Fear and Other Uninvited Guests, by Harriet Lerner (ISBN 0-06-0081570)

FOOD & NUTRITION

Eat, Drink, and Be Healthy: The Harvard Medical School Guide to Healthy Eating, by Walter C. Willett, P. J. Skerrett (ISBN: 0743223225)

American Dietetic Association Complete Food and Nutrition Guide, by Roberta Larson Duyff, American Dietetic Association (ISBN: 0471441449)

The Essential Guide to Nutrition and the Foods We Eat: Everything You Need to Know About the Foods You Eat, by Jean A. Thompson Pennington, American Dietetic Association, (ISBN: 006273346X)

www.eatright.org American Dietetic Association

www.nal.usda.gov/fnic The Food and Nutrition Information Center (FNIC) at the National Agricultural Library (NAL) *vm.cfsan.fda.gov* U.S. Food and Drug Administration Center for Food Safety and Applied Nutrition

www.nutrition.gov National Agriculture Library, United States Department of Agriculture.

www.vrg.org Vegetarian Resource Group

HEALTH/WELLNESS/PREVENTION

Breathing: The Master Key to Self Healing, Audio CD

8 Weeks to Optimum Health, by Andrew Weil, M.D. (ISBN 0449000265)

Spontaneous Healing, by Andrew Weil, M.D. (ISBN 0804117942)

Timeless Healing, by Herbert Benson, Marg Stark (ISBN 0684831465)

Wellness Book: The Comprehensive Guide to Maintaining Health and Treating Stress-Related Illness, by Herbert Benson, Eileen M. Stuart (ISBN 0671797506)

YOU: The Owner's Manual: An Insider's Guide to the Body that Will Make You Healthier and Younger, by Michael F. Roizen, Mehmet Oz (ISBN 0060765313)

RealAge: Are You as Young as You Can Be? by Michael F. Roizen (ISBN 0060930756)

Women's Bodies, Women's Wisdom, by Christiane Northrup (ISBN 0553382098)

www.webmd.com WebMD

nccam.nih.gov National Center for Complementary and Alternative Medicine

www.mayoclinic.com Mayo Clinic

www.cnn.com/HEALTH/library CNN Health Information

www.nih.gov National Institute of Health

www.healthfinder.gov National Health Information Center, U.S. Department of Health & Human Services

www.intelihealth.com InteliHealth

www.os.dhhs.gov Department of Health and Human Services

www.cdc.gov Centers for Disease Control and Prevention

www.fda.gov Food and Drug Administration

HEART HEALTH

Dr. Dean Ornish's Program for Reversing Heart Disease: The Only System Scientifically Proven to Reverse Heart Disease Without Drugs or Surgery, by Dean Ornish, M.D. (ISBN 0804110387)

www.nhlbi.nih.gov National Heart, Lung, and Blood Institute

INFERTILITY

Conquering Infertility: Dr. Alice Domar's Mind/Body Guide to Enhancing Fertility and Coping with Infertility, by Alice D. Domar, Ph.D., Alice Lesch Kelly (ISBN 0142002011)

INSOMNIA

Say Good Night to Insomnia: The Six-Week, Drug-Free Program Developed at Harvard Medical School, by Gregg Jacobs (ISBN: 0805055487)

Power Sleep: The Revolutionary Program That Prepares Your Mind for Peak Performance, by James B. Maas (ISBN: 0060977604)

www.4woman.gov/faq/insomnia.htm National Women's Health Information Center

INSPIRATION

Women Who Run with the Wolves, by Clarissa Pinkola Estes (ISBN 0345409876)

Offerings: Buddhist Wisdom for Every Day, by Olivier Follmi, Danielle Follmi (ISBN 1584793155)

Jesus CEO: Using Ancient Wisdom for Visionary Leadership, by Laurie Beth Jones (ISBN 0786881267)

Essential Rumi, by Coleman Barks (ISBN 0062509594)

The Illuminated Prayer: The Five-Times Prayer of the Sufis, by Coleman Barks, Michael Green (ISBN 0345435451)

Voices of Ancestors, by Dhyani Ywahoo (ISBN 0877734100)

You Can Heal Your Life, by Louise L. Hay (ISBN 0937611018)

The Way We Pray: Celebrating Spirit from Around the World, by Maggie Oman Shannon (ISBN 1573245712)

The Power of Kabbalah: This Book Contains the Secrets of the Universe and the Meaning of Our Lives, by Yehuda Berg (ISBN 1571892508)

Love & Intimacy

Love and Survival: The Scientific Basis for the Healing Power of Intimacy, by Dean Ornish, M.D. (ISBN: 0060930209)

The Dance of Intimacy: A Woman's Guide to Courageous Acts of Change in Key Relationships, by Harriet Lerner (ISBN: 006091646X)

Menopause

The Wisdom of Menopause, by Christiane Northrup (ISBN 055338080X)

Obesity

www1.umn.edu/mnoc Minnesota Obesity Center

www.naaso.org North American Association for Obesity Research

www.obesity.org American Obesity Assocation

www.asbp.org American Society of Bariatric Physicians

Online Support Groups

Healthyliving.stanford.edu Self-Management at Stanford

www.mentalhelp.net/selfhelp/ Self-Help Group Sourcebook On-Line

Qigong

Qigong for Staying Young: A Simple 20-Minute Workout to Cultivate Your Vital Energy, by Shoshanna Katzman (ISBN 1583331735)

www.nqa.org National Qigong Association: Information about Qigong and a search tool to find teachers or other practitioners in your area.

Serenity

The Relaxation Response, by Herbert Benson, Miriam Z. Klipper (ISBN 0380006766)

Coming to Our Senses: Healing Ourselves and the World Through Mindfulness, by Jon Kabat-Zinn (ISBN 0786867566)

Full Catastrophe Living: Using the Wisdom of Your Body and Mind to Face Stress, Pain, and Illness, by Jon Kabat-Zinn (ISBN 0385303122)

Wherever You Go, There You Are: Mindfulness Meditation in Everyday Life, by Jon Kabat-Zinn (ISBN 1401307787)

Healing Beyond the Body: Medicine and the Infinite Reach of the Mind, by Larry Dossey (ISBN: 1570629234)

Healing Words, by Larry Dossey (ISBN: 0061043834)

Recovering the Soul: A Scientific and Spiritual Approach, by Larry Dossey (ISBN: 055334790X)

Prayer Is Good Medicine: How to Reap the Healing Benefits of Prayer, by Larry Dossey (ISBN: 0062514245)

Reinventing Medicine: Beyond Mind-Body to a New Era of Healing, by Larry Dossey (ISBN: 0062516442)

Be Careful What You Pray For...You Just Might Get It, by Larry Dossey (ISBN: 0062514342)

Meditation as Medicine, by Dharma Singh Khalsa, M.D. and Cameron Stauth (ISBN 0-7434-0064-X)

SHAME

Healing the Shame That Binds You, by John Bradshaw (ISBN 0-932194-86-9)

STRESS, GENERAL

Who Moved My Cheese? An Amazing Way to Deal with Change in Your Work and in Your Life, by Spencer Johnson (ISBN: 0399144463)

Getting Things Done: The Art of Stress-Free Productivity, by David Allen (ISBN: 0142000280)

The Anxiety & Phobia Workbook, by Edmund J. Bourne (ISBN: 157224223X)

The Relaxation & Stress Reduction Workbook, by Martha Davis, Elizabeth Robbins Eshelman, Matthew McKay (ISBN: 1572242140)

www.stress.org American Institute of Stress

www.ncptsd.va.gov National Center for PTSD

STRESS, WORKPLACE

How to Enjoy Your Life and Your Job, by Dale Carnegie (ISBN: 0671708260)

Surviving Job Stress: How to Overcome Workday Pressures, by John Boghosian Arden (ISBN: 156414609X)

Mobbing: Emotional Abuse in the American Workplace, by Noa Davenport, Ruth D. Schwartz, Gail Pursell Elliott (ISBN: 0967180309)

Office Spa: Stress Relief for the Working Week, by Darrin Zeer (ISBN: 0811833453)

Don't Sweat the Small Stuff at Work: Simple Ways to Minimize Stress and Conflict While Bringing Out the Best in Yourself and Others, by Richard Carlson (ISBN: 0786883367)

The Truth About Burnout: How Organizations Cause Personal Stress and What to Do About It, by Christina Maslach, Michael P. Leiter (ISBN: 0787908746)

Essential Managers: Reducing Stress, by Tim Hindle (ISBN: 0789424444)

TAI CHI

Step-By-Step Tai Chi, by Master Lam Kam-Chuen (ISBN: 0671892479)

The Complete Idiot's Guide to T'ai Chi & QiGong (2nd Edition), by Bill Douglas (ISBN: 0028642643)

www.taoist.org International Taoist Tai Chi Society

www.taichinetwork.org Find tai chi teachers or events

WORK-LIFE BALANCE

www.employersforwork-lifebalance.org.uk UK site offering strategies for work-life balance with resources for individuals and organizations

wlb.monster.com Work-Life Balance information from Monster.com

www.jugglezine.com E-Zine about balancing work and life from Herman Miller

YOGA

Light on Yoga: The Bible of Modern Yoga, by B. K. S. Iyengar (ISBN: 0805210318)

Yoga: The Path to Holistic Health, by B. K. S. Iyengar (ISBN: 0789471655)

www.yogajournal.com Yoga Journal

www.yogadirectory.com Yoga Directory

www.sivananda.org The International Sivananda Yoga Vedanta Centers

www.yogafinder.com Yoga Finder

Dr. Kathleen Hall's 25 Tips to a Life in Balance

1. Practice daily stress reduction (meditation, yoga, deep breathing) at least five to ten minutes twice a day (mornings and evenings).

2. Exercise at least 20 to 30 minutes three times a week. Blend or alternate aerobics with strength training, stretching, flexibility, and agility exercises.

3. Eat eight to ten servings of fruits and vegetables daily and use organic foods whenever possible.

4. Drink at least eight 8 oz. glasses of water or herbal tea (especially green tea) daily and reduce exposure to toxins in your environment.

5. Consider the following antioxidants and supplements daily to compliment a healthy diet: Check with your doctor before taking any supplements to make sure they are right for you and do not interfere with medications you are currently taking for any diseases and conditions.

   ▶ Vitamin C: 250 to 500 mg twice a day

   ▶ Natural Selenium (from yeast): 200 mcg

   ▶ Calcium: 1500 mg (includes dietary intake) with Vitamin D 400 mg and Magnesium 400 mg

   ▶ Dark Chocolate: 1.5 ounces

   ▶ Omega-3 essential fatty acids or flaxseed: 1000 mg

6. Eat at least three servings of fish weekly. Cold-water fish such as salmon, tuna, and mackerel have Omega-3 fatty acids.

7. Laugh as often as possible to release the healing chemical endorphins.

8. Have three to four servings of cooked tomato paste or sauce weekly (with monosaturated fats such as olive oil to improve absorption) for lycopene, an effective cartenoid antioxidant that may help prevent prostate and breast cancer.

9. Reestablish "childlike" qualities.

10. Sleep at least seven hours every day.

11. Do one action a day mindfully, such as being really present when eating, showering, etc.

12. Floss your teeth daily.

13. If your doctor approves, take one regular aspirin daily (if you have no bleeding problems or allergies to aspirin).

14. Stop smoking or using tobacco products.

15. Eat breakfast.

16. Pray: It is an incredible source of healing.

17. Get a pet.

18. Three times a day stop and practice deep diaphragmatic breathing—inhale healing oxygen and exhale stress.

19. Remain connected socially with family and friends.

20. Make time to read. It keeps your mind and memory active.

21. Keep a journal. This has health benefits also.

22. Celebrate your successes in life.

23. Develop an attitude of gratitude. Saying "thank you" to someone is life giving to both of you.

24. Maintain optimism and a positive outlook. Being happy is healthy.

25. Practice altruism and philanthropy: A generous soul lives a rich, abundant life.

Five Steps for Making a Decision in Your Life

1. *The Question:* Ask yourself what change you choose to make in your life now. Make sure you are clear about the change you are proposing. Frame the change as a question and write it down on paper. Spend 10 minutes twice a day asking the one question out loud and then be silent. (For an example, if the change you are considering is "I want to move to a new home," frame the question as "Is it time for us to move to a new home?")

2. *The Rational Test:* Make a "Pro" and "Con" list of the proposed change. List as many reasons for and against the change as you can think of, go over it often, and frame a tentative solution. (For example: *Pro:* Interest rates are very low, our family has outgrown our home. *Con:* Our children will have to change schools, we love our neighbors.) Notice the length of each column. Are there more Pros or Cons?

3. *Intuition:* Use intuition to imagine your decision. Literally spend time imagining doing your new job, career, or purpose, and then journal what you see. (For example: Do a guided imagery and imagine yourself moving out of the neighborhood and into the new home you are considering. Imagine life without your neighbors, or your children at a new school). How do you feel inside?

4. *An Action Plan:* This is often where we fall off the cliff. Decide what your actions need to be to enable you to become what you envision: education, financing, or possible relocation. Begin to network at this

point. Get information from professional organizations, support groups, or on the Internet. (For example: If you have decided to move, contact a real estate agent; if you have decided not to move, you may want to remodel and add another room.) Get organized and make folders as you begin to contact resources to inform your decision.

5. *Put Your Roots Down:* Once you have made your decision, you will have second thoughts and worry. Confront your fear. You can stand strong like a tree's roots withstand tornadoes, hurricanes, or flood. Use family meetings, friends, and personal time to stabilize and support your decision. Find your roots in self-care.

N O T E S

INTRODUCTION

1. American Institute of Stress. www.stress.org/job.htm

2. Ibid.

3. Institute of Management, *The Price of Success 1999,* "Ceridian Performance: Partners/Management Today and the Quality of Working Life Report" (February 2001).

CHAPTER 1: WHAT IS TRUE HAPPINESS?

1. Claudia Wallis, "The New Science of Happiness," *Time* (January 17, 2005): A2-A9.

2. Michael Lemonick, "The Biology of Joy," *Time* (January 17, 2005): A12-A17.

3. Ibid.

4. M. Miller, "Divergent Effects of Laughter and Mental Stress on Endothelial Function: Potential Impact of Entertainment," presented at the Scientific Session of the American College of Cardiology, March 6-9, 2005, Orlando, Florida. News release, University of Maryland School of Medicine.

5. Jeffrey Kluger, "The Funny Thing About Laughter," *Time* (January 17, 2005).

6. Liz Hodgkinson, *Smile Therapy* (Century Hutchinson, 2001).

CHAPTER 2: WEATHERING THE SEASONS OF THE SOUL

1. CDC, "Deaths: Preliminary Data for 2003." News release.

2. J. T. Colcombe et al., "Cardiovascular Fitness, Cortical Plasticity and Aging," *Proceedings of the National Academy of Sciences* 101, 9 (March 2, 2004): 3316-3321.

3. http://my.webmd.com/content/article/19/1728_50311.htm

4. T. B. Kim et al., "Mediterranean Diet, Lifestyle Factors, and 10-Year Mortality in Elderly European Men and Women: The HALE Project," *JAMA* 292 (September 22/29, 2004): 1433-1439.

5. Elissa S. Epel et al., "Accelerated Telomere Shortening in Response to Life Stress," *Proceedings of the National Academy of Sciences* 101 (2004): 17312-17315.

6. Becca R. Levy et al., "Longevity Increased by Positive Self-Perceptions of Aging," *Journal of Personality and Social Psychology* (August 2002): 261-270.

7. Nicholas Wilton, "Positive Outlook," *Yoga Journal* (January/February 2002): 78-83.

8. E. Giltay, "Dispositional Optimism and All-Cause and Cardiovascular Mortality in a Prospective Cohort of Elderly Dutch Men and Women," *Archives of General Psychiatry* 61 (November 2004): 1126-1135.

9. "The McArthur Foundation Study of Aging in America."

10. M. Miller, "Divergent Effects of Laughter and Mental Stress on Endothelial Function: Potential Impact of Entertainment," presented at the Scientific Session of the American College of Cardiology, March 6 to 9, 2005, Orlando, Florida. News release, University of Maryland School of Medicine.

11. Ibid.

12. Stephen G. Post "Altruism, Happiness, and Health: It's Good to Be Good" *International Journal of Behavioral Medicine* 12 (2005): 66-77.

13. http://buddhism.about.com/library/weekly/aa112902a.htm

CHAPTER 3: UNDERSTANDING THE DIRECTION OF HAPPINESS

1. *American Heritage Dictionary of the English Language,* 4th edition.

2. Sharon Begley, "Religion and the Brain," *Newsweek* (May 7, 2001): 50-57.

CHAPTER 4: FINDING YOUR PULSE

1. www.yinyanghouse.com/

2. http://nccam.nih.gov/health/acupuncture/

3. "Stress: It's Worse Than You Think." www.medicinenet.com/script/main/art.asp?articlekey=35249&pf=3

4. Ibid.

5. Ibid.

6. Ibid.

7. Amy F. T. Arnsten, Beth Murphy, and Kalpana Merchant, "The selective dopamine d4 receptor antagonist, pnu-101387g, prevents stress-induced cognitive deficits in monkeys, *Neuropsychopharmacology* 23 (2000): 405-410.

8. "Stress: It's Worse Than You Think." www.medicinenet.com

9. Ibid.

10. David Weeks, *Secrets of the Superyoung* (Berkley Publishing Group, 1999).

CHAPTER 5: S.E.L.F.: THE FOUR ROOTS

1. Len Lichtenfeld et al., 41st Annual Meeting of the American Society of Clinical Oncology, Orlando, Florida, May 13-17, 2005.

2. "A Nation at Risk: Obesity in the United States, A Statistical Sourcebook," The Robert Wood Johnson Foundation, May 2005.

3. "Health After 50," *Johns Hopkins Medical Letter* 15, 6 (August 2003).

4. "A brief history of pain." http://abcnews.go.com/Health/PaiManagement/story?id=731553&page=1

5. "Insomnia, sleep disorders." http://content.nhiondemand.com/dse/consumer/HC2.asp?objID=100232&cType=hc

6. Gregg D. Jacobs, *Say Goodnight to Insomnia* (Owl Books, 1999).

7. "Depression soaring for college students." www.detnews.com/2002/homelife/0206/05/d03-500849.htm

8. "The Science of Anxiety," *Time,* June 10, 2002.

CHAPTER 6: SERENITY: RECLAIM YOUR SOURCE

1. "Stress: It's Worse Than You Think." www.medicinenet.com/script/main/art.asp?articlekey=35249&pf=3

2. "Mind & Body/Mediation," *Time, A to Z Health Guide,* 2003, p. 81-83.

3. H. Benson, *The Relaxation Response* (New York: William Morrow, 1975).

4. H. Benson, "The Relaxation response and norepinephrine," *Integrative Psychiatry* 1 (May-June 1983): 15-19.

5. E. Stuart et al., "Nonpharmacologic treatment of hypertension: a multiple risk factor approach," *Journal of Cardiovascular Nursing* 1 (1987): 1-4.

6. G. D. Jacobs, P.A. Rosenberg, R. Friedman, et al. "Multifactor behavioral treatment of chronic sleep-onset insomnia using stimulus control and the relaxation response." *Behavior Modification* 17, 4 (1993b): 498-509.

7. A. D. Domar, P.C. Zuttermeister, M. Seibel, and H. Benson, "Psychological improvement in infertile women after behavioral treatment: a replication." *Fertility and Sterility* 58 (1992): 144-147.

8. Margaret Caudill, "Decreased clinic utilization by chronic pain patients after behavioral medicine intervention," *Pain* 45 (1991): 334-335.

9. R. H. Schneider, C.N. Alexander, and R.K. Wallace, "In search of an optimal behavioral treatment for hypertension: a review and focus on transcendental meditation," In *Personality, Elevated Blood Pressure, and Essential Hypertension,* eds. E.H. Johnson, W.D. Gentry, and S. Julius (Washington, D.C: Hemisphere, 1992).

10. Richard J. Davidson et al., "Alterations in brain and immune function produced by mindfulness meditation," *Psychosomatic Medicine,* 65 (July/August 2003): 564-570.

11. M. C. Dillbeck, "Meditation and flexibility of visual perception and verbal problem solving," *Memory and Cognition* 10, 3 (1982): 207-215.

12. R. K. Wallace, et al., "The effects of the transcendental meditation and tm-sidhi program on the aging process," *International Journal of Neuroscience* 16 (1982): 53-58.

13. C. N. Alexander, M. Rainforth, and P. Gelderloos, "Transcendental meditation, self-actualization, and psychological health: a conceptual overview and statistical meta-analysis. special issue: handbook of self-actualization." *Journal of Social Behavior and Personality* 6, 5 (1991): 189-248.

14. C. N. Alexander, P. Robinson, and M. Rainforth, "Treating and preventing alcohol, nicotine, and drug abuse through transcendental meditation: A Review and Statistical Meta-Analysis," *Alcoholism Treatment Quarterly* 11, 1-2 (1994): 13-87.

15. Larry Dossey, *Reinventing Medicine: Beyond Mind-Body to a New Era of Healing* (San Francisco: Harper, 1999).

16. Randolph C. Byrd, "Positive therapeutic effects of intercessory prayer in a coronary care unit population," *Southern Medical Journal* 81, 7 (1988): 826-29.

17. Erlendur Haraldsson and Thorstein Thorsteinsson, "Psychokinetic effects on yeast: an exploratory experiment," *Research in Parapsychology* 1972 (Metuchen, N. J.: Scarecrow Press, 1973): pp. 20-21.

18. Can prayer heal? http://my.webmd.com/content/article/11/1674_51527.htm?printing=true

19. *Parade* magazine, "Why Prayer Could Be Good Medicine," March 23, 2003.

20. Joshua M. Smyth, Arthur A. Stone, Adam Hurewitz, and Alan Kaell, "Effects of writing about stressful experiences on symptom reduction in patients with asthma or rheumatoid arthritis: a randomized trial," *Journal of the American Medical Association* 281 (April 1999): 1304-1309.

21. "How journaling keeps you healthy," www.healthierliving.org/health/journaling.html

22. Thomas G. Allison et al., "Cardiovascular responses to immersion in a hot tub in comparison with exercise in male subjects with coronary artery disease," *Mayo Clinic Proceedings* 68 (January 1993): 19-25.

CHAPTER 7: EXERCISE: REVIVE YOUR RHYTHM

1. www.csun.edu/~vceed002/health/docs/tv&health.html

2. Personal Communication.

3. S. N. Blair, H. W. Kohl III, et al., "Physical fitness and all-cause mortality: a prospective study of healthy men and women," *Journal of the American Medical Association* 262 (1989): 2395-2401.

4. "Study finds entrepreneurs who run do better in sales." www.bsu.edu/news/article/0,,12913—,00.html

5. Anne McTiernan et al., "Recreational physical activity and the risk of breast cancer in postmenopausal women: the women's health initiative cohort study," *Journal of the American Medical Association* 290 (September 2003): 1331-1336.

6. Michelle D. Holmes et al., "Physical activity and survival after breast cancer diagnosis," *Journal of the American Medical Association* 293 (May 25, 2005): 2479-2486.

7. Urho M. Kujala et al., "Relationship of leisure-time physical activity and mortality: the Finnish twin cohort," *Journal of the American Medical Association* 279 (February 1998): 440-444.

8. S. J. Colcombe and A. F. Kramer, "Fitness effects on the cognitive function of older adults: a meta-analytic study," *Psychological Science* 14 (2003): 125-130.

9. *Health,* May 2004.

10. Jennifer K. Weuve et al., "Physical activity, including walking, and cognitive function in women." *Journal of the American Medical Association* 292 (September 22/29, 2004): 1454-1461.

11. Robert D. Abbott et al., "Walking and Dementia in Physically Capable Elderly Men," *Journal of the American Medical Association* 292 (September 22/29, 2004): 1447–1453.

12. James A. Blumenthal et al., "Effects of exercise training on older patients with major depression," *Archives of Internal Medicine* 159 (October 1999): 2349-2356.

13. Gregg D. Jacobs, *Say Goodnight to Insomnia* (Owl Books, 1999).

14. A. C. King et al., "Moderate-intensity exercise and self-rated quality of sleep in older adults: a randomized controlled trial," *Journal of the American Medical Association* 277 (January 1997): 32-37.

15. "School health policy and programs study 2000," *Journal of School Health* 71, 7 (2001).

16. Kaiser Family Foundation, "Zero to Six: Electronic Media in the Lives of Infants, Toddlers and Preschoolers Information, *Program for the Study of Entertainment Media and Health.*" Publication Number 3378: October 28, 2003.

17. Lorenzo Cohen et al., "Psychological Adjustment and Sleep Quality in a Randomized Trial of the Effects of a Tibetan Yoga Intervention in Patients with Lymphoma," Sixth World Congress of Psycho-Oncology, Banff, Alberta, Canada, April 23-27, 2003.

18. Satish Sivasankaran, "The Effect of a Six-Week Yoga Training and Meditation Program on Endothelial Function," American Heart Association Scientific Sessions, New Orleans, November 7-10, 2004.

19. "Tai chi and yohimbine could help Parkinson's." www.worldhealth. net/p/275,1526.html

20. C. Crillo, "Complimentary therapies: into the mainstream," *Cure* (Survivor Issue 2002).

21. M. J. L. Alexander and J. E. Butcher, "Effects of an aquatic exercise program on physical performance of older females with arthritis," *Medicine & Science in Sports & Exercise* 33, 5 (Supplement 1:S38) May 2001.

CHAPTER 8: LOVE: REALIZE YOUR INTIMACY

1. Patrick Malone and Thomas Malone, *The Windows of Experience: Moving Beyond Recovery to Wholeness* (New York: Simon & Schuster, 1992).

2. George Davey Smith, S. Frankel, and Y. Yarnell, "Sex and death: are they related? Findings from the Caerphilly Cohort Study," *British Medical Journal* 315 (1997): 1641-1644.

3. Can Good Sex Keep You Young? http://my.webmd.com/content/article/14/1738_50976.htm?printing=true

4. Patricia Mona Eng et al., "Effects of marital transitions on changes in dietary and other health behaviours in U.S. male health professionals," *Journal of Epidemiology and Community Health* 59 (2005): 56-62.

5. "For better or worse—marriage and health." www.50plushealth.co.uk/index.cfm?articleid=1717

6. Linda C. Gallo et al., "Marital status and quality in middle-aged women: Associations with levels and trajectories of cardiovascular risk factors," *Health Psychology* 22 (2003): 435-463.

7. C. A. Schoenborn, "Marital status and health: United States, 1999–2002. Advance Data from Vital and Health Statistics; no 351." (Hyattsville, Maryland: National Center for Health Statistics, 2004).

8. Linda J. Waite, "Does marriage matter?" Presidential Address to the American Population Association of America, April 8, 1995, *Demography* 32 (1995): 483-507.

9. Ivan Rodriguez, "A putative pheromone receptor gene expressed in human olfactory mucosa," *Nature Genetics* 26 (2000): 18-19. Brief Communications.

10. Bernard I. Grosser et al., "Behavioral and electrophysiological effects of androstadienone, a human pheromone," *Psychoneuroendocrinology* 25, 3 (April 2000): 289-299.

11. Kathleen Stern and Martha K. McClintock, "Regulation of ovulation by human pheromones," *Nature* 392 (March 12, 1998): 177-179.

12. Dean Ornish, M.D., *Love and Survival* (New York: Harper Collins, 1998).

13. T. E. Seeman et al., "Social network ties and mortality among the elderly in the Alameda County Study," *American Journal of Epidemiology* 126 (1987) 714-723.

14. D. Spiegel, J. R. Bloom, and E. Gottheil, "Effects of psychosocial treatment on survival of patients with metastatic breast cancer," *Lancet* 2 (1989): 888-891.

15. F. I. Fawzy et al., "Malignant melanoma: Effects of an early structured psychiatric intervention, coping, and affective state on recurrence and survival 6 years later," *Archives of General Psychiatry* 50, 9 (September 1993): 681-689.

16. K. Allen, J. Blascovich, and W. B. Mendes, "Cardiovascular reactivity and the presence of pets, friends, and spouses: The truth about cats and dogs," *Psychosomatic Medicine* 64, 5 (September-October 2002): 727-739.

17. APPMA National pet owners survey. www.appma.org/pubs_survey.asp

CHAPTER 9: FOOD: REPLENISH YOUR SELF

1. Shengxu Li et al., "Childhood cardiovascular risk factors and carotid vascular changes in adulthood," The Bogalusa Heart Study, *Journal of the American Medical Association* 290 (2003): 2271-2276.

2. Richard S. Strauss and Harold A. Pollack, "Epidemic increase in childhood overweight, 1986-1998," *Journal of the American Medical Association* 286 (2001): 2845-2848.

3. T. M. Videon and C. K. Manning, "Influences on adolescent eating patterns: The importance of family meals," *Journal of Adolescent Health* 32, 5 (2003): 365-373.

4. Tata Parker-Pope, "How to Give Your Child a Longer Life," *Wall Street Journal*, December 9, 2003.

5. Stephanie Miller, "Who's Coming to Dinner: The Importance of Family Meals." MSUE Press Release, May 19, 2003.

6. Leann L. Birch and Jennifer O. Fisher, "Mothers' child-feeding practices influence daughters' eating and weight," *American Journal of Clinical Nutrition* 71 (May 2000): 1054-1061.

7. Eric A. Finkelstein, Ian C. Fiebelkorn, and Guijing Wang, "State-level estimates of annual medical expenditures attributable to obesity," *Obesity Research* 12 (2004): 18-24.

8. Miller, "Who's Coming to Dinner."

9. www.medill.northwestern.edu/journalism/magazine/raisingteens/feats/dinner.html

10. James Griffing, "Why diets fail." www.exrx.net/FatLoss/Why DietsFail.html. Reprinted with permission.

11. Len Lichtenfeld et al., 41st Annual Meeting of the American Society of Clinical Oncology, Orlando, Florida, May 13-17, 2005.

12. Claudia Kalb and Karen Springen, "Putting It All Together," *Newsweek* (May 10, 2004): 54-61.

13. Christine Gorman, "Repairing the Damage," *Time* (February 5, 2001): 53-58.

14. Hiroyasu Iso et al., "Intake of fish and omega-3 fatty acids and risk of stroke in women," *Journal of the American Medical Association* 285 (2001): 304-312.

15. AHA Scientific Statement: "Fish consumption, fish oil, omega-3 fatty acids and cardiovascular disease," #71-0241, *Circulation* 106 (2002): 2747-2757.

16. http://my.webmd.com/content/article/13/1671_50592.htm

17. "Strawberries are ripe for eating," *Health* (May 2003): 151.

18. *General Dentistry*, March-April 2002.

19. *Proceedings of the National Academy of Sciences* 100, 10 (May 13, 2003): 6009-6014.

20. "Your heart aches for tomatoes," *Health* (June 2004): 55.

21. Alam Khan et al., "Cinnamon improves glucose and lipids of people with type 2 diabetes," *Diabetes Care* 26 (2003): 3215-3218.

22. M. Tolonen, "Plant-derived biomolecules in fermented cabbage," *Journal of Agriculture, Food, and Chemistry* 50, 23 (2002): 6798-6803.

23. "The Environment for Care: An NHS Estates Symposium" (2004).

24. Robert Beck and Thomas Cesario, "Choral singing, performance perception, and immune system changes in salivary immunoglobulin a and cortisol," *Music Perception* 18 (Winter 2000).

25. James Lynch, *The Broken Heart: The Medical Consequences of Loneliness* (Baltimore: Johns Hopkins University Press, 1981).

26. S. Thayer, "Close encounters," *Psychology Today,* March 1988.

CHAPTER 10: DISCOVER ENERGY

1. Michael R. Irwin et al., "Effects of a behavioral intervention, tai chi chih, on varicella-zoster virus-specific immunity and health functioning in older adults," *Psychosomatic Medicine* 65 (September 2003): 824-830.

2. Steven L. Wolf et al., "Intense tai chi exercise training and fall occurrences in older, transitionally frail adults: A randomized, controlled trial," *Journal of the American Geriatric Society* 51, 12 (December 2003): 1974-1803.

CHAPTER 11: KNOW POWER

1. Bernard M. Loomer, *Two Kinds of Power* (Chicago: Criterion, University of Chicago Divinity School, 1976).

2. Ibid.

CHAPTER 12: LIVE AN INTENTIONAL LIFE

1. Parker Palmer, *The Active Life* (San Francisco: Harper, 1990).

CHAPTER 13: ACHIEVE BALANCE

1. www.kronos.com/about/nytimes1.htm

2. James Carson, "Loving-kindness meditation for chronic low back pain: results from a pilot trial," *Journal of Holistic Nursing* 23, 3 (2005): 287-304.

3. "The New Science of Happiness," *Time* (January 17, 2005): A2-A9.

4. Robert Beck and Thomas Cesario, "Choral singing, performance perception, and immune system changes in salivary immunoglobulin a and cortisol," *Music Perception,* 18 (Winter 2000).

5. Gunter Kreutz et al., "Effects of choir singing or listening on secretory Immunoglobulin A, cortisol, and emotional state," *Journal of Behavioral Medicine* 27, 6 (2004): 623-635.

6. M. Miller, "Divergent Effects of Laughter and Mental Stress on Endothelial Function: Potential Impact of Entertainment," presented at the Scientific Session of the American College of Cardiology, March 6 to 9, 2005, Orlando, Florida.

INDEX